THE INDIAN UNIVERSITY
A Critical History

Debaditya Bhattacharya

Orient BlackSwan

THE INDIAN UNIVERSITY: A CRITICAL HISTORY

ORIENT BLACKSWAN PRIVATE LIMITED

Registered Office
3-6-752 Himayatnagar, Hyderabad 500 029, Telangana, India
Email: centraloffice@orientblackswan.com

Other Offices
Bengaluru, Chennai, Guwahati, Hyderabad, Kolkata, Mumbai,
New Delhi, Noida, Patna

First published 2025

041932

ISBN 978 93 5442 636 0

Typeset in Minion Pro BT 10.5/13 *by*
K. Divya, Hyderabad 500 060

Printed at
Kensington Printing & Packaging, Noida 201 301

Published by
Orient Blackswan Private Limited
3-6-752, Himayatnagar,
Hyderabad 500 029, Telangana, India
Email: info@orientblackswan.com

To Rina and Sneha, for teaching me out of the sound of words.
And into their substance, in the everyday.

Contents

Acknowledgements

About half of this book was written while we were waging a movement to reclaim the public character of a provincial state university in lower Bengal. Hollowed out of public resources by the decadent whims of a politically installed leadership, the university administration had launched into a violent cost-recovery programme through increased student fees and precaritisation of both teaching and non-teaching labour. The initial days of our movement were laced with a degree of headiness, which – as the movement wore on and brought the worst assaults on our dignity and safety on campus – transformed into alternating moments of exhaustion and desperation. We did not give up, and there were indeed some gains that came by way of our persistence. The leadership was replaced, we returned to work, and business proceeded as usual. Within two months, it was clear that nothing really had changed in terms of the structural organs and operations of the university's everyday.

Students, who fought with us and whose unfazed resolve kept us together despite the many secret betrayals from within our teaching community, started asking in classrooms and corridors soon after: is this what we staked our lives and careers for? We did not have an answer, except the premonition that it was the beginning of a lasting disillusionment. Through the long nights of that disappointment, I kept tugging at the strings of this book – almost as simultaneous acts of catharsis and transformative hope. During those times (and before and after), and for every other academic event I was called for, I had several among my audience tell me (or at least hint by other means) that I was more an activist – and less an academic. In fact, there is a delicious euphemism for distinguishing the activist: 'you're so passionate'! Because I chose to speak about the site of the university in its current-day contortions and string it into a story of our fall from grace, most in my closest circles thought (and occasionally said) that I was too politically decibeled for seminar-conference acoustics.

I argued with myself – and my partner – that I didn't mind their aspersions. Deep inside, I did. But this bifurcation of the activist's predilections from the academic's expertise is definitely not new. What is indeed new is the fear of the former as potentially corrupting, if not simply motivated. When I sensed this fear among friends and audiences, it felt liberating. It was as if there was an acknowledgment of the charm of activistic work, in the very disdain that it was met with.

Frankly, the activistic versus the academic is a false opposition. The point is whether one comes across as ruffling feathers or moulting into them. This book is a hard long look at the historical conditions that have brought us here. It therefore uses the truth-potential of history to stage the ideological edges of critique. I call it a 'critical history' – the ruse of a truth-telling that is as partisan as the activist's vocation, as it is annotative like the historian's calling. This book therefore must owe its first and fullest debt to the students who asked: is a movement worth a future that is not any freer? I attempt an answer here, through a series of archival readings measured against the laboratory experiments of a failed revolution. I realised, in the process, that the battle really is in seeing through the terms of our unfreedom. Much of freedom's promise lies in questioning our imagination of what it means. And my students from Kazi Nazrul University (KNU) – Suman, Tridev, Subhadip, Shahzadi, Suraj, Shalini, Chandrani, Soumyanetra, Saumyashree and those others I can't name but remember still – have taught me the courage to persist in the face of unfreedom. The rest of that courage came from my contractual non-teaching colleagues at KNU – Debjit, Rajesh, Tarun, Joy, Usha-di, Somnath, Naresh, Subhadip, Piyali.

A movement that withers away its revolutionary spell generates explosive amounts of angst. For such angst to be converted into manuscript material, there has to be a compulsory rite of passage through a friend. As for every other bit of my attempt at writing –

with or without the provocation of movements – words beaded up at the loose ends of telephonic conversations with Rina. Without her, I can only write in blanks.

Conversations with Upal, Sukanya, Anwesha, Mani, Anandaroop, Swati, Madhuri, Sonali, Priyanka, Ghazala and Sandhya cemented ideas into suggestions for readings. Upal's terrific work in conserving Presidency College's history into a digital repository was absolutely crucial in allowing me access to much of the archives I have mobilised in the second chapter. From Simi, I learnt how to silently work at structures beyond the floss of big ideas. Sreenath, at Orient BlackSwan, has been a most constant source of support and understanding, while the anonymous reviewers he sent my early manuscript to have shaped much of what is in your hands. Excerpts from my chapters on twentieth-century reform in higher education will appear, in revised form, in an essay included in Volume 6 of the Bloomsbury series on *Cultural History of Higher Learning*. The editors, Hannah Forsyth and Chris Newfield, have propped me up with some very valuable comments on the text.

Joan Scott, Judith Butler and Wendy Brown are my charmed circle. One could think I am using their names to muster celebrity currency, but I leave it to them to know what they mean to everything I do.

Finally, how do you acknowledge the love (and labour) that co-writes a work over evenings of tea-time conversation, late night frustration and crack-of-dawn waking up to ideas? One probably cannot. And therefore, Sneha, yours is the debt I will leave unpaid – quite helplessly.

Debaditya Bhattacharya

16 February 2025

Introduction

What is the 'Indian' University?

Origins of an Idea

In a lecture delivered to an audience in Madras (Chennai) in early 1919, Rabindranath Tagore – the poet-pedagogue from Bengal – went as far as dubbing the *swadeshi* demand for a 'National University' as an 'unnatural desire', marred by an 'unfortunate weakness for imitation' (5). The transcript of this lecture, later published in the form of a book, might presciently serve as the opening frame for my reflections here. Taking off from Tagore, I must inaugurally ask: is there an idea of an 'Indian university', as the title of this volume conveniently assumes? What accounts for the *Indianness* of such an 'Indian university', if at all? Is it a residue of the political demand for a 'National University', surviving as an anti-colonial legacy from the heady days of the *swadeshi*, boycott and non-cooperation movements of the early twentieth century? But if it were so, isn't it always-already a creature of weak imitation, as Tagore had warned us at the very moment of its articulation?

If the idea of an 'Indian university' is congenitally contaminated by the foreignness of the idea of the 'university' itself, surely 'Indianness' cannot be conjured as a parable of national 'origins'. Leaving aside the etymological story of roots in the Latin *universitas* of medieval vintage, neither history nor geography can adjudicate the ownership claims of the Indian 'nation' over the university. The university was undoubtedly a colonial import of an idea, and no amount of control over its fortunes can convert it into a crop of our local climes. Must we then forsake the search and the sense of an 'Indian university', for purposes of our current inquiry, as a deluded quest? Far from it, I would argue. Instead, the question itself needs to be rephrased, insofar as the borrowing of the 'idea' does not belie our ownership of its 'experience'.

What is at stake therefore is not the *idea* of the university, but the material life-worlds that it embodies and connects – which cannot but be the substance of its 'Indianness'. This is a book that therefore consists in examining the contortions of a loaned 'idea' within histories and contexts that were radically different. To such extent, I contend that the university's distinctive character derives not from some philosophical norm of precedence – whether Humboldtian or Nazi[1] – but the organic materiality of the life that it inhabits, inherits and is inhibited by it. Put simply and pointedly, the 'Indian university' is an Indian experience of the university, not a pure intellectual heritage of an 'idea'. This is also exactly the gist of Tagore's argument in the lecture I referenced above – *The Centre of Indian Culture* – where the poet does not disparage the existing system of colonial education for its being foreign, but for its grafting onto a soil that does not fulfil the conditions of an organic sustenance. To implant the physical and institutional infrastructures of the 'university' – that is, 'its buildings, its furniture, its regulations, its syllabus' (Tagore 11) – without taking care to answer the needs of its 'larger body' is

---

[1] These, to my mind, are the limits to an archive of the working-out of a university 'idea'. Wilhelm von Humboldt, along with Friedrich Schleiermacher and Johann Gottlieb Fichte, thought through a philosophy of the modern university in the material instance of the University of Berlin (set up in 1809–10). For these German philosophers, the autonomy assured by a disinterested pursuit of science (*wissenschaft*) and the cultural cause of a 'common progress' (*allgemeine bildung*) were to be the twin distinctions that separated the modern university from an ecclesiastical guild-structure of the medieval *universitas*. It is this spirit of an Enlightenment ideal in the modern German university that came to be appropriated and subverted by the ideology of Nazism in the early-twentieth century. For a Nazi *use* of the university, the logic of autonomy had to be imploded; and this could only be achieved by making the philosophical anchorage of science (in *wissenschaft*) give in to a rearticulation of 'knowledge-service' (*wissensdienst*) as service to the German nation. The latter is exactly what Martin Heidegger, as Rector of the University of Freiburg im Breisgau in 1933, formulates as the 'historical mission' of the German university – 'a place of spiritual legislation . . . for the highest service to the people in its state' (12).

to not only impoverish the idea by rooting it out of its sources of nourishment, but also to make a grave error of judgment. The mechanical labours of imitation deny the force of history that accounts for the slow making of the imitated ideal; it assumes that the object of imitation was blessed with its current shape and had therefore bypassed the tedium of social reproduction. It is here that the accretive gradualism of the *social* is exorcised from the imitative exercise, and the idea becomes an end in itself.

> [The] solidly complete Universities, over which our country is brooding, are like hard-boiled eggs from which you cannot expect chickens to come out. Not only ourselves, but our European schoolmaster himself seems to have forgotten that his University has grown with the growth of the nation he belongs to, and that its material magnificence was not in its beginning and does not belong to its essential truth. . . . But as the kernel of the coconut is in the whole coconut, so the University, in the case of Europeans, is in their society, in their parliament, in their literature, in the numerous activities of their corporate life. They have their thoughts published in their books, as well as the living men who think those thoughts and criticize, compare and disseminate them. One common medium of mind connects their teachers and students in an educational relationship which is living and luminous. In short their education has its permanent vessel which is their own mind; its permanent supply which is their own living spring of culture; its permanent field for irrigation which is their own social life. (Tagore 6, 11–12)

In short, there is no university that does not materially reproduce itself in the 'living spring of culture' and 'social life' that it grows out of, and matures in conversation with. It is in its unavoidable collisions with a choreography of public life – a *publicness* that counts for 'the numerous activities of . . . corporate life' – that the European university sought a realisation of its 'idea'. Tagore cautions: abstracting the institutionality of a structure cannot reproduce its effects in an environment which is alien; and therefore a theory of 'ideas' cannot stand on a ground devoid of the historical differentiations of living publics. What transpires from this is a meaning of the 'national' university as inhering not in abstract geographical space, but in the latter's being unequally claimed and contested by living populations. Following from such a turn of argument, an Indian university is indeed possible – despite the distant ancestry of the 'idea' behind it – but only in reference to the former's relationship with distinctly divergent publics surrounding it. Might we say, stretching a little further, that there is only ever an idea of a 'public' university as the sole legitimating condition of a 'national' university – where again, the meanings of *publicness* are open to contests of power and relative visibility?

Publicness: Idea or Experience?

There's only one other point at which Tagore's lecture re-confronts the mutual inherence of a 'truly national organization' (40) of the university within an order of *publicness*. And that is with regard to what he calls 'the economic question' (39). Understandably, for Tagore, the funding of a 'truly' Indian university could not be left to the political-legislative priorities of a colonial government – and especially after a century of its channelling of public monies towards the creation of petty bureaucratic-professional offices of profit. When public resources are expropriated in the cause of imperial economic interest, and thus held in the charge of a foreign administration, a different imagination of *publicness* had to occupy the everyday means of reproduction of the university. The answer however was neither to be sought in the 'patronage of the rich' (in other words, elite private philanthropy) nor in the 'dead imposition of . . . accumulated funds' (that is, primitive accumulative desire) (Tagore 40).

Instead, for Tagore, it was in a cooperative model of economic co-existence – through small-scale experimental efforts at working towards and creating a rural 'commons' – that the Indian university's sustainability paradigm had to be ensured. By rooting itself in the productive possibilities of an immediate public – which may receive as much from the university as it is capable of giving to it – the Indian university could both remedy the historical disconnect between practices of intellectuality and systems of social production, as well as secure its own uncertain economic futures.

Sounding out his ideas for a cooperative university within months of the opening of Visva-Bharati in December 1918, Tagore went on to found an Institute of Rural Reconstruction soon after (in February 1922) in Sriniketan as the first step towards resolving the question of funding through a dogged attentiveness to the material vectors of *publicness* (Das Gupta; Elmhirst; "Sriniketan"). The 'Indian university', as a conduit for what I will call the '*will to worldness*', is not only made immanent in the rhetorical enfolding of the 'world' and the 'nation' (the *visva* [world] and the *bharati* [Indian]), but in also then staging the scene of this 'worlding' in the materialities of a provincial economic setting. The 'truly national organization' of Tagore's university-imagination lay in its being first and foremost a public university – that is, a university founded in and through a *commoning* of public resources and coordinated public stake-holding in the everyday. That, he believed, was the only route to the 'national' – so as to 'perpetually keep in real touch with the life of the future ages and not continue its existence as a parasite feeding upon the charity of the past' (40).

Prophetic as it may sound more than a hundred years hence, there are two instructive registers that Tagore's definition of an 'Indian university' leaves us with: the social-historical and the economic-productive, with both eventually converging in the life-worlds of the 'public'. At the same time, the bardic vision also warns us against the dangers of imagining the 'national' outside of its referential mooring in *publicness* – again, by etching out two alternative scenarios. The first imagines the 'national' as carved out for a special destiny of uniqueness and superiority, and therefore begins by disclaiming every trace of difference as false or foreign. Tagore calls such paranoid conscription of the 'national university' as a form of 'moral dipsomania, which is the hankering after the continual stimulation of self-flattery' (28) – and reminds us,

> [T]he doctrine of special creation is out of date, and the idea of a specially favoured race belongs to a barbaric age. We have come to understand in modern times that any special truth, or special culture, which is wholly dissociated from the universal, is not true at all. Only the prisoner condemned to a solitary cell is separate from the world.

> He who declares that India has been condemned by Providence to intellectual solitary confinement does not help to glorify her. (ibid.)

Unanchored in a sense of its publics, the 'Indian university' translates into the privatism of being God's chosen child – easily swinging between the accents of racial supremacy and missionary purpose. Or worse still, as Tagore's second scenario portends, the Indian university might proceed from these empty declamations of nationalist pride to claims for majoritarian proprietorship over 'culture':

> A National University, in our minds, has been only another name for a Hindu University. So, whenever we give any thought to the question, we think of the Hindu religion alone. Unable as we are to rise to the conception of the Great India, we try to divide it, in the case of our culture, just as we have done by our religious rites and social customs. In other words, the idea of such unity as we are capable of achieving for ourselves not only fails to rouse enthusiasm in our hearts, but gives rise to some amount of antipathy. (42)

Shunning the 'Indian university' as a special creation of God or of a Hindu God implies that we have to relentlessly embrace the meanings of 'publicness' that might otherwise attach to such a creature of history. How much of that 'publicness' have we achieved, seventy-five years into our sovereign claim to self-governance? And, among such claims, how much of it is materially borne out by the 'facts' of India's public life – and the latter's relationship with the university? It is to these questions that I will turn now, having laboured long enough on the 'Indian' contents of the university as consisting in its changing negotiations with Indian publics.

Looking for 'Facts': The Stuff of History?

My excursus into the terrain of 'facts' would call for an engagement with the sleights of statistical documentation, issuing for the most part from the arbiter of public will in the government of the day. I have carefully stayed away from dabbling in too much statistical data through the rest of this book, for reasons I will recount in a minute. But suffice it to say that I must compensate for this writerly decision of avoiding cursory survey data (except as historical archive) by plunging headlong into it here, albeit with a different purpose than treating it as self-evident truth. The representational form of the statistic carries within it a regime of associations, linking the fact and the figure. That facticity – and its truth-value – derives from its convertibility (without a remainder) into figural forms, representable as both number and image, is the statistical norm. In sum, there is no data that resists summation in a total way, where totality signifies the equivalence between radically different frames of representation. Data posits a compulsory fullness, and demonstrates an aching distrust of the fragment. This is the only condition of felicity for the discipline of statistics. But, does that hold true of the material world, of which the 'fact' claims to be a full and final aggregate?

Never. And pointing at this non-coincidence of the fact and the world (unfolding behind it) is precisely the work of history. I argue that the historian's vocation lies in accounting, without calculable gains, for the atrophy that accompanies the truth's rite of passage from fact to text. History, phrased more poignantly, is the invisible cursive writing that underlies the trick of the statistic. And therefore, its own fruition – as a discipline – lies in busting the myth-making techniques of data. That is what I set out to perform in this book, examining the fact of the 'Indian university' in the gaps that belie its statistical accounts, and through the lens of what has been titularly termed as a 'critical history'. But, for that, I must first lay out the claims-making processes that these statistical accounts cobble up. Once laid out as they are received, the claims to 'publicness' made by the 'Indian university' will be held up for two rounds of scrutiny. The first round is simple: it subjects statistic to an alternative calculative rigour in order to separate the claim from the fact. The second round is more complex, and concerns the historiographic attempt made by each of the chapters of this book. It goes on to look for explanations in the chasms that separate claims from facts. The secret of truth's atrophy *as* history might, in all likelihood, be glimpsed in the ground seceded by facts and claims. That is the space I aspire to.

Surveying the Indian University

Let me get to the first round of scrutiny first, by routine recourse to statistical numbers. The definitive source for these numbers is a 336-page report published by the Ministry of Education in January 2024, and titled as *All India Survey on Higher Education* (AISHE) 2021–22. Coming at the start of an election year, and with a decisive mandate to mould public opinion on questions of higher education, the Report was also intended to celebrate (and congratulate) the immediate impact of the *National Education Policy* (NEP) 2020. This was, in effect, the first full catalogue on the state of the 'Indian university' since the NEP 2020 was rammed in without parliamentary approval, at the peak of the pandemic.[2]

[2] A short policy history might be in order here, though much of it will be taken up for backdrop and analysis in subsequent chapters. A new National Education Policy (NEP) – proposing a thoroughgoing educational reform – had been an electoral plank for the currently-ruling Bharatiya Janata Party (BJP) since its bid for power in 2014. Soon after, in 2015, the new government under Prime Minister Narendra Modi set up a committee to deliberate on a possible NEP draft under the chairmanship of former bureaucrat T.S.R. Subramanian. A Draft Report was submitted in 2016, arguing for a wholesale neoliberal reforms-agenda and devolving into mass privatisation routines – which however did not find favour with the political leadership. In 2017, the government notified the constitution of a separate committee – this time, with space scientist K. Kasturirangan at its head – to reformulate the policy template for NEP. In December 2018, barely months before the next general elections, the Kasturirangan Committee submitted its recommendations to the then Human Resource Development (HRD) Minister. The government, unsure of how a public discourse on education might affect its impending electoral prospects, shelved the Report for nearly six months – until immediately after Modi's return to power in May 2019. What was released as a 484-page Draft Report in 2019 was finally brought in, without being tabled in Parliament and with a blanket Cabinet approval, at the peak of the first wave of Covid in July 2020. The NEP 2020, now excised into a 66-page bare skeleton of the Kasturirangan Committee report, thus

I will take up the *Policy* text for much closer commentary, across several chapters of this book – and will, for now, confine myself to a discussion around the AISHE Report. The Survey, instituted in 2011 by an erstwhile government, usually does not occasion much public concern beyond stray newspaper reportage. But, in early 2024, the mainstream popular media strung together a steady flow of encomiums about the dramatic rates of increase in enrolments among Scheduled Caste (SC), Scheduled Tribe (ST), Other Backward Class (OBC) and women students.[3] The reason for this surfeit of media enthusiasm does not require looking much further than the government's own press briefing about the 2021–22 Report – which absurdly used data from 2014–15 as the denominator for making time-series calculations.[4] This is symptomatic of the brazenness with which statistics may be manipulated, insofar as the AISHE's method for data analysis had so far regarded the immediately preceding five-year-period as base reference for all time-series computations. The sudden shift in referential frame from 2017–18 (the normative base year) to 2014–15 indicates the desire for a political dividend – in that it conjures all relative projections as the absolute achievement of successive governments under Prime Minister Narendra Modi, who came to power in May 2014.

Thus never losing sight of the electoral-political contingencies that govern the making of survey data, let us move on. The 2021–22 Report maintains that the 'Indian university' sector has registered an addition of 341 universities since 2014–15, while a comparison with the 2015 document projects the actual difference in number as 408.[5] Similarly, in the case of colleges, the arithmetic of institutional

---

took effect at a time when all of India's schools and colleges were conscripted into an indefinite closure and with no opportunity for even the pretence of a political debate.

[3] See, for example, Radhika; Iftikhar; "Higher Education Enrolment".

[4] Refer to "Press Release: Ministry of Education".

[5] Section 2.1.1 of AISHE 2014–15 pegs the total number of universities at 760, while Section 2.1.1 of AISHE 2021–22 projects a total of 1168. The documented 'addition' in institutional strength should thus have been 408.

expansion is pegged at 6,975 between 2014–15 and 2021–22, while the actual comparison of cumulative counts bears out an increase to the tune of 8,373 colleges.[6] Does this underreporting of actual numbers, in the absence of ready reference to the text of the 2014–15 Report for a lay audience, indicate something quite contrary to the surface rhetoric of 'expansion' of higher educational opportunity? If the real increase falls far short of the documented difference in numbers, might such a margin hint at a stealthy merger (or closure) of a proportion of India's higher educational institutions over the past eight years – to the tune of (408–341=) 67 universities and (8,373–6,975=) 1,398 colleges? There is no statistical answer to be found in the AISHE Reports from any of the interceding years, and it is here that the cause of a 'critical history' to the 'Indian university' must be discerned. The abyss which, as I said, separates claims from facts is the space for such history – and the reader must wait for it all the way through the six chapters of this volume.

As another demonstrative instance of how the 'public'-facedness of the 'Indian university' has evolved since 2014–15, the AISHE 2021–22 glaringly records the rate of growth of public-funded/government-aided universities at a mere 40.37 per cent as opposed to that of private unaided universities swelling at the rate of 81.2 per cent in the same time period.[7] Extrapolating from this, it is clear that private universities have boomed at more than double the speed of public ones over successive terms of the Modi regime. This one detail militates against the entirety of the current survey's statistical bracketing of the 'regime' as a harbinger of great positive

[6] Again, compare Section 2.1.2 of AISHE 2014–15 with the corresponding Section 2.1.2 of AISHE 2021–22, to arrive at the actual difference.

[7] These ratios are borne out by comparing the growth rates of different 'types' of universities/university-level institutions as well as 'management-wise' differentiation of colleges between 2014–15 and 2021–22 data. Refer to Figure 1 of Section 2.1 in both Reports, for concurrence on university-level data. For corresponding figures on college-level respondents, see Figure 3 in Section 2.1.2(a) in AISHE 2014–15 and Figure 6 in Section 2.1.2.5 in AISHE 2021–22 respectively.

change in public access to higher education. Returning our gaze to the relative spread of colleges in the country, it appears that the proportion of public-funded colleges as a share of the total college sector has fallen from 23 per cent in 2014–15 to 21.5 per cent in 2021–22. This again gives the lie to an otherwise burgeoning number of colleges in absolute terms, 78.5 per cent of which owes to private profiteering initiative.[8] District-wise college density – which is the only authoritative indicator of geographical access – has registered negligible improvement in these past eight years, with more than 19 per cent of India's districts still recording the existence of less than 10 colleges.[9] Cross-verified against official information on district mapping, around 18 of the country's currently listed district-zones function without a single college in their entire vicinity.

Proceeding to the question of enrolments, the 2021–22 data holds that the relative proportion of students entering undergraduate education in India has fallen by 0.5 per cent since 2014–15, even as the proportion of postgraduate admissions has only marginally increased from 11.3 per cent to 12.06 per cent.[10] All of these indicators, when adjusted against real increases (in absolute numbers) of youth of college-going age, might in fact underline a constriction of opportunities for higher education at both the undergraduate and postgraduate levels. In terms of vertical mobility between these two levels, there is again hardly any discernible evidence of improvement. Ph.D. enrolments, on the other hand, have effectively fallen from 2.13 lakhs (inclusive of integrated research programmes) in 2020–21 to 2.12 lakhs in

[8] Includes both private aided (13.2 per cent) and private unaided colleges (65.3 per cent), as reported in AISHE 2021–22 (Section 2.1.2.5).

[9] According to *Indiastat* data on 'state-wise number of administrative units' – as per Census 2011 and as on 30 June 2021 – the number of districts was pegged at 733. Compare this figure against data tabulated in Box 3 of Section 2.1.2.1 in AISHE 2021–22.

[10] Compare Figure 6 in Section 2.2.1 from AISHE 2014–15 with Figure 13 in Section 2.2.4 from AISHE 2021–22, for the relative proportion of undergraduate and postgraduate 'level-wise' enrolments.

2021–22.[11] I take the data from the immediately preceding year for comparison here, because it is in this intervening period that both the M.Phil. and the integrated research courses were summarily scrapped, courtesy the NEP 2020's unilateral fiat.[12] Translated into effective numbers, research enrolments in India have dwindled both in absolute numbers as well as in relative proportion to higher educational access – the latter plummeting from 0.51 per cent of total higher educational enrolments in 2020–21 to 0.49 per cent in 2021–22.

Looking at enrolment distribution on the basis of type of institutions, the AISHE 2021–22 unfurls yet another damning portrait. While the share of government universities currently stands at a little over half of the total number, they record nearly three-fourths of the aggregate enrolments in the sector. Private unaided universities, accounting for over 40 per cent of the country's sectoral spread, however register only one-fourth of the total enrolment footfall.[13] And despite such an overwhelming disparity in the relative accessibility of private universities as against those which are public-funded, we have already noted that the former's growth margin in an eight-year period has more than doubled the latter's. In the case of 'government-aided' deemed universities, not only has the institutional strength dipped from eleven to ten between 2014 and 2022, but the overall pool of enrolments in such institutions has also drastically reduced from 88,134 to 59,936.[14] This amounts to a 32 per cent fall in the intake

[11] Read the data in Section 2.2.6.3 on Ph.D-level enrolments in AISHE 2021–22, as against the corresponding numbers in Section 2.2.5 in AISHE 2020–21.

[12] Section 11.10 of NEP 2020 unilaterally announced that '[t]he M.Phil. programme shall be discontinued' (38) – which was then enshrined in the UGC (Minimum Standards and Procedures for Award of Ph.D. Degree) Regulations 2022, vide Section 14.

[13] Refer to Figure 22 in Section 2.2.8.1 of AISHE 2021–22, read in consonance with the number of institutions listed in Section 2.1.

[14] Tally the figures in Table 26 of AISHE 2014–15 against Figure 21 in Section 2.2.8 of AISHE 2021–22. For the distribution of number of such institutions, compare the charts in Section 2.1 in either Report.

of deemed universities, which consummately delivers to us the secret logic of 'government aid' for higher education.

Beyond 'Fact' or Within: Where are the Publics?

The biggest hoax of 'publicness', in the AISHE's statistical conjuration of the 'Indian university', is reserved for claims around the Gross Enrolment Ratio (GER) in higher education. As the most feted and widely cited metric for pronouncing on the policy impact of reform measures, the GER records the proportion of youth aged between 18 and 23 years (that is, within the potentially college-going cohort) in census data which has minimally reached the threshold of any higher educational institution. With little care to subsequently recalibrate these 'gross' enrolment figures against annual drop-out rates or corresponding course completion data – none of which is comprehensively collected or ever allowed into the public domain – the GER remains but an inflationist tactic, calculated to produce fictions of 'growth'. The cavalier disregard for social or structural impediments in the continuation of educational opportunities, beyond an initial count of admissions, is geared towards producing a certain public culture of statistical numeracy. The resulting insistence on reading mere 'enrolment' as the interchangeable and exhaustive index of 'access' takes us very far from substantive questions of historical justice. The latter is deliberately muddled into either an exhibitionism of empty arithmetic progression or a congratulatory statement on formal equality of opportunity.

This is exactly what followed the release of the AISHE 2021–22 data on national and caste/religious GERs. Taking a cue from the ministry's press communique, newspapers waxed eloquent about 'a significant growth in the higher education sector in India' (India Today Research Bureau). Below is an extract of a single sample, from among hordes of similar paeans that flooded channels of print media in the immediate aftermath.

> Diving into the demographic distribution of the 4.33 crore students enrolled in 2021–22, 15.3% of the total enrolment belongs to

> Scheduled Caste (SC) students, 6.3% to Scheduled Tribe (ST), and 37.8% to Other Backward Class (OBC). . . . The enrolment of SC students has seen a substantial increase, . . . marking a 25.4% rise in the last five years. Similarly, ST enrolment has increased to 27.1 lakh in 2021–22, showcasing a 41.6% increase since 2017–18. The enrolment of OBC students has also seen a rise of 27.3% to approximately 1.63 crore students in 2021–22. Notably, the Minority enrolment has surged to 30.1 lakh in 2021–22 from 21.8 lakh in 2014–15, depicting a remarkable 38% increase. . . . The Gross Enrolment Ratio (GER) in higher education for the age group 18–23 years has also increased to 28.4 in 2021–22, up from 27.3 in 2020–21 and 23.7 in 2014–15. Female GER continued to surpass male GER for the fifth consecutive year, reaching 28.5 in 2021–22. Noteworthy improvements were also observed among Scheduled Caste and Scheduled Tribe students, *emphasizing the strides in inclusivity in higher education.* SC student GER increased to 25.9 in 2021–22 from 23.1 in 2020–21, and ST student GER has risen to 21.2 in 2021–22 from 18.9 in 2020–21. (India Today Research Bureau, emphasis mine)

Working against 'population projections based on the 2011 census' (AISHE 2021–22, ii), the above data culled from the latest survey – when taken at face value – almost makes a case for the consummate felicity of affirmative action policies in terms of institutional access to higher education. If, as we are informed, Dalit students account for more than 15 per cent of total enrolments in India's college-university sector (with a GER smugly close to the national average), adivasis occupy more than 6 per cent of the sector (with a GER of more than 21) and OBC bahujan communities have come to represent nearly 38 per cent of overall enrolments, has caste-based reservation finally achieved what it sought to correct in the first place?[15] Or, better still, are we approaching a time when social justice will have become an accurately realised goal and caste-based quotas might even become

[15] A general tendency among lay readers would be to contrast these 'enrolment'/access statistics against the Union government's national-level policy for caste-based reservations as it stands now – mandating 15 per cent reservation of seats in higher educational institutions for SCs, 7.5 per cent for STs and 27 per cent for OBCs from non-creamy layers.

irrelevant or unnecessary? Alongside the subtext of such policy suggestions, our statistical competences are affronted by a woefully poor enrolment proportion among religious minorities, standing at a mere 7 per cent as against its census share of nearly 20 per cent of India's populations. The only numerical eyesore, jutting out from an otherwise even story of India's gains on knowledge capital, makes us wonder if minority publics – and of them Muslims in particular, being the largest population group – are not inherently averse to educational attainment, and therefore deserving of both popular condescension and punitive ghettoisation. A survey indicator of 'educational backwardness' is seamlessly turned into the lineaments of a moral malaise, thus justifying structures of national and communal distrust.

But, moving beyond the inductive premises of statistical reasoning, it would serve us well to probe the GER data against corresponding census figures from 2011 – which the AISHE avowedly claims as its demographic archive. When we unpack the national average enrolment ratio of 28.4 in the backdrop of its absolute measure at 43.3 million (or, 4.33 crores), it appears that India's total population in the 18–23 age bracket hovers around 152 million (AISHE 2021–22, Sections 2.2–2.3). Factoring the official census count for SC communities as comprising 16.6 per cent of India's total population, at least 25.2 million youth in the relevant age category must be assumed to be Dalits. Of them, only 6.6 million can ever breach the passage from school to college (ibid. 50). Notwithstanding the subsequent drop-outs, which may substantially alter the picture, it is therefore only one out of every four SC youth who can ever nominally access higher education. For adivasis – who the Report claims to have scaled a 65.2 per cent increase in enrolments during the Modi regime – a similar comparative exercise proves that only 2.7 out of 13.1 million can formally exercise their right to higher educational opportunity (ibid. 51). This translates into one out of every five ST youth in the country. With the OBC census figures widely varying between the Mandal Commission's estimate (1980) and the National Sample Survey Organisation's (NSSO) data (2006), one would still fathom that its current enrolment figure of 16.3 million comes from a total age-eligible youth sample ranging between 63 and 79 million.[16] Conclusively, one out of every four or five 'backward class' students ever dares to enrol in Indian higher education (ibid. 52). For minorities, alarmingly enough but perhaps not to much amazement, the corresponding figure can be pegged at one out of every ten youths (ibid. 53). What gets completely elided in the AISHE's data jugglery around the GER is the Hindu upper-caste enrolment figures, when accounted for against the relative mobility potential of SC/ST/OBC and minority populations. Deriving a mean from Mandal as well as NSSO/SECC projections, it would not be an unfair stretch to posit the quantum of caste-Hindu (*dvij* [twice-born]) communities at an average of 17.5 per cent of the total Indian census count. Translated into real numbers, this amounts to a 26.6 million-strong youth-force in the 18–23 age bracket – of which, the 2021–22 AISHE Report will insidiously ordain, a good 14.7 million are to be found in India's colleges and universities. The simpler math goes thus: *at least* one out of every two upper-caste Hindu youth finds access to Indian higher education – busting all myths about the increasing inclusivity and *publicness* of the 'Indian university'.

In terms of women's participation in higher education, the AISHE Report's euphoria is infectious – in that it announces a '32 percent increase since 2014–15' (ibid. i). However, when pored into a little deeper, it is revealed that the proportion of women students entering B.A., B.Sc. and B.Com. programmes – that is, nearly the entire ambit of undergraduate education – has actually fallen between 2020–21 and 2021–22. Similar developments plague women's enrolments within the social science, science and management streams at the postgraduate level – which have either remained stagnant or declined over the past year.

[16] This population range takes as its higher limit the Mandal Commission's OBC census projection at 52 per cent, and the 2011 Socio-Economic and Caste Census (SECC; based on NSSO's 2006 estimate) projection of 41.1 per cent as the lower limit.

The Need for a Critical History

If, as I have argued in the opening sections, the condition of possibility of the 'Indian university' lies in its historical disposition towards the claims and contests of Indian publics, the present moment in history surely does not bode well. What accounts for the impoverishment of the university's *publicness* in the present, and how do the distant and not-so-distant pasts feature within such an account? Under the shadow of 'claims' made by the most current survey of Indian higher education, and their unbridgeable distance from the materiality of 'facts', what kind of history might possibly annotate the logics that lie in between? Might we see in the contemporary 'Indian university' the cloud of a lengthening colonial prophecy, or the clear daybreak of a long and lasting legacy? The answers, dear reader, are incomplete attempts – capsuled in each of the chapters of this book.

Divided into two parts, and slashed in the middle by the event of India's political independence, the structure of the volume is intended to demonstrate that no freedom can be free from the burden of historical inheritance. I start the first chapter by invoking a part of such inheritance, belonging to the aura of the 'ancient', and yet seeking cause for repetition in India's current political conjuncture. The spectre of the great 'ancient Indian university' – mustered with vehement energy in references to Takshashila, Nalanda, Vikramshila and other such sites – is taken up for a deep historical probe here. In the process, the chapter also attempts to discern a vernacular imagination of the university's *being*, and measures the ancient charge of 'greatness' against it. How the penchant for global recognition and the impatience of nationalist glory are delicately balanced in the discourse on the 'origins' of Indian higher education is the argument at stake.

The second chapter begins by questioning an alternative 'origin' narrative for the Indian university in nineteenth-century colonial educational reform. To this effect, it posits the birth of a corporative sense of 'collegiate life' not in the centres of English-language education that translate colonial legislative will or embody elite metropolitan class interests in the example of a Hindu College.

The history of the setting up of Hindu College, and its subsequent opening to Muslim students under pressure from the Calcutta *madrassa*, is examined in the light of a caste consensus that remains as the special charge of English-language education. The relationship of the *mofussil* institutions to Presidency College, and the latter's conflicted negotiations with the University of Calcutta, again bear testimony to the deep upper-caste anxiety around rights and effects of intellectual ennoblement.

But, already by the early twentieth century, the caste-refracted right to educational opportunity had failed to translate into chances of professional advancement. The third chapter – chronicling the passage from the 1904 Indian Universities Act to the moment of political independence – takes on the question of religion with regard to fortunes of colonial higher education. With the *swadeshi* and boycott movement's channelling of disgruntled upper-caste ire against an extortionist regime of economic loot, religious identity came to define the intellectual manoeuvres of an anti-colonial resistance. Gandhi stepped in, and made opportune use of these gestures of a symbolic revival, rooted in spiritual resources – until the Meerut conspiracy case (1929–33) sealed the fate of nationalist fervour by pitting it against the irreligious communist internationalist. This chapter, taking the reader along this entire stretch of a chequered history, concludes by registering how a *seva*-ethic is eventually manufactured as the authentic marker of student subjectivity right at the cusp of India's entry into secular nationhood.

The story of India's postcolonial experiments with higher education occasions the second part of the book, again periodised somewhat unevenly into the three final chapters. To my mind, the movement of these chapters may be likened to the shifts in policy metaphors that they register – from 'welfare' to the 'market' to the 'platform'. The immediate post-independence period, stretching for nearly four decades into 1986, is my analytical frame for the fourth chapter of the volume. With the ideology of 'national welfare' as the reigning rationale, the relationship between the 'social' pact of state welfarism and the 'political' effects of caste and religion emerges as the site of the most curious evasions. I have tried taking a hard look at this relationship, extending all the way from the Radhakrishnan Commission (1948–49) to the Kothari Commission (1964–66) and the first National Policy on Education (1968). What might perhaps seem as more telling is the attempt at pitting this policy timeline against political currents in mobilising college-going youth – from Naxalbari to the student movements in Gujarat and Bihar, fuelling the post-Emergency effervescence of the Hindu right-wing.

The fact that caste and religion were left untouched by an independent India's structural reengineering of the university sector meant that these were also the twin greenfield projects for globalised finance capital. It is this turn to the wisdom of the market – as the only potential force for alleviating social exclusion – that comes to exhaust a state-sponsored discourse on higher education since the 1986 National Policy on Education. As the fifth chapter would show, the market's negotiations with the reality of discrimination had to be however routed through (and vetted by) the 'local community', a euphemism for civil society. Between 1992 and 2008, a macroeconomic history of the Indian university sector betrays its collusions with transnational capital, such that the commitment to social justice might in the final instance be financed through private initiative. The blocking of the Mandal Commission's recommendations in 1990 was crucial in playing up caste against religion, thus leaving the former's exclusions at the mercy of 'community' mobilisations against the radical outsider in the Muslim. By the time OBC reservations were finally implemented in higher educational institutions, after a twenty-eight-year lag, the global recession had found in India an 'emerging market economy' for both knowledge goods and consumer commodities. But, in less than a decade, conditions had changed and the economic justification for higher education had lost its viability.

It was time for a new and third National Education Policy (NEP) – conversations around which started soon after Narendra Modi's coming to power in 2014. With the economy plummeting and the country's electorate having reposed its faith on a variety of strongman saviourism, represented by the Prime Minister, the once-booming Indian markets were caught in the crosshairs of a 'world risk society'. It is at this point that the sixth and final chapter of this book commences, purporting to imagine the quest for a new NEP as a desperate hedging against the risks of a financialised world. What results, in the form of the 2020 policy document, sounds the age of the platform ecosystem. With the value of labour depreciating in the world's free markets, knowledge was immaterial until it could be traded as derivatives for managing the risk of an uncertain future. Such a scenario, the last chapter contends, is the closest to what we see happening today in the compulsory multidisciplinarity evangelised by the NEP 2020 – and its spawn of derivative knowledge-products finding place in university curricula, from 'Art of Being Happy' to 'Fit India'.

Covering historical ground from ancient India to the contemporary conjuncture might seem too unwieldy and expansive a project for a single volume to claim to have done with any amount of efficacy. This is precisely why I urge my reader to embark on this book, not with the expectations to be had of an orderly calendrical history. Instead, it might help to regard this work as a theoretical engagement with histories of *publicness* within the Indian university – and with a specific eye on the sub-texts that have generally eluded public attention.

Any imagination of a 'public' would do well to acknowledge that its place lies outside of the private grasp of the historian. In that same vein, the 'public' university too is beyond the neatness of historical perspective, if not as self-critique. This book might consider its work done if we, who read it through and together, might come out suspecting our 'idea' of the Indian university a little more than is usual among learned circles.

References

All India Survey on Higher Education (AISHE) 2014–15. Department of Higher Education, Ministry of Human Resource Development, 2016.

All India Survey on Higher Education (AISHE) 2020–21. Department of Higher Education, Ministry of Education, 2022.

All India Survey on Higher Education (AISHE) 2021–22. Department of Higher Education, Ministry of Education, 2023.

Das Gupta, Uma. "Rabindranath Tagore on Rural Reconstruction: The Sriniketan Experiment." *Indian Historical Review*, vol. 4, no. 2, 1978, pp. 354–78.

Elmhirst, Leonard. "Our Work at Sriniketan." *Visva-Bharati News*, January 1939 (Poet and Plowman). Visva-Bharati, 1975.

Heidegger, Martin. "The Self-Assertion of the German University." *Martin Heidegger and National Socialism*, edited and translated by Gunther Neske and Emil Kettering. Paragon House, 1990 [1933], pp. 5–13.

"Higher Education Enrolment Increased by 19 Lakh in 2021–22 From Previous Session: Govt. Survey." *The Hindu*, 26 Jan. 2024, https://www.thehindu.com/education/higher-education-enrolment-increased-by-19-lakh-in-2021-22-from-previous-session-govt-survey/article67777790.ece

Humboldt, Wilhelm von. "On the Internal and External Organisation of the Higher Scientific Institutions in Berlin." *Works (in German), Volume 4: Writings on Politics and Education*, edited by Andreas Flitner and Klaus Giel, translated by Thomas Dunlap. Wissenschaftliche Buchgesellschaft, 1982 [1810], pp. 253–65.

Iftikhar, Fareeha. "Three Key Takeaways from AISHE Report 2021–22." *Hindustan Times*, 27 Jan. 2024, https://www.hindustantimes.com/education/three-key-takeaways-from-aishe-report-202122-101706283450994.html

India Today Research Bureau. "AISHE 2021– 22: 4.33 Cr students enrolled." *India Today*, 29 Jan. 2024, https://bestcolleges.indiatoday.in/news-detail/aishe-2021-22-433-cr-students-enrolled

National Education Policy (NEP) 2020. Ministry of Human Resource Development, 2020.

"Press Release: Ministry of Education Releases All India Survey on Higher Education (AISHE) 2021–22." Press Information Bureau (PIB) Delhi, 25 Jan. 2024, https://pib.gov.in/PressReleasePage.aspx?PRID=1999713

Radhika, R. "SC, ST, OBC Student Enrolment in Higher Education Rose More than National Average in 5 Years." *The Indian Express*, 28 Jan. 2024, https://indianexpress.com/article/education/sc-st-obc-student-enrolment-in-higher-education-rose-by-18-1-in-5-years-9129752/

Report of the Backward Classes Commission (Mandal Commission Report), Volumes I–VII. Government of India, 1980.

"Sriniketan: The Institute of Rural Reconstruction." *Visva-Bharati Bulletin* 4, 1928, pp. 1–8.

"State-wise Number of Administrative Units in India (As per Census 2011 and 30.06.2021)." *Indiastat*, 30 Jun. 2021, https://www.indiastat.com/data/administrative-units/districts/data-year/2021

Tagore, Rabindranath. *The Centre of Indian Culture*. Visva-Bharati, 1951[1919].

"University Grants Commission (Minimum Standards and Procedures for Award of Ph.D. Degree) Regulations 2022." *The Gazette of India: Extraordinary* (Part III, Section 4), 7 Nov. 2022, https://www.ugc.gov.in/pdfnews/0909572_Minimum-Standards-and-Procedure-for-Award-of-PhD-Degree.pdf

Part One

Stories of a Making

ONE

The Great Ancient Indian Universities: History or Myth?

Present-ing Pasts

The *National Education Policy (NEP) 2020* hinges its vision for Indian higher education on a carefully crafted paradox. It might be worth beginning our discussion on the history of the 'Indian university' by citing this most current policy vision, in a slightly exhaustive manner:

> Moving to large multidisciplinary universities and HEI (higher educational institution) clusters is [...] the highest recommendation of this policy [NEP 2020] regarding the structure of higher education. The ancient Indian universities Takshashila, Nalanda, Vallabhi, and Vikramshila, which had thousands of students from India and the world studying in vibrant multidisciplinary environments, amply demonstrated the type of great success that large multidisciplinary research and teaching universities could bring. India urgently needs to bring back this great Indian tradition to create well-rounded and innovative individuals, and which is already transforming other countries educationally and economically. (Section 10.2)

This 'great Indian tradition' is repeatedly harped upon in subsequent sections, in order to frame the discussion on institutional restructuring as well as curricular 'reform' – and, most importantly, as the *telos* of every policy recommendation towards these ends. For example, in explaining the meaning of its most numerous insistence on 'multidisciplinarity', the policy makes an identical pitch soon after:

> India has a long tradition of holistic and multidisciplinary learning, from universities such as Takshashila and Nalanda, to the extensive literatures of India combining subjects across fields .... This notion of a 'knowledge of many arts' or what in modern times is often called

> the 'liberal arts' (i.e., a liberal notion of the arts) must be brought back to Indian education, as it is exactly the kind of education that will be required for the 21st century . . . . A holistic and multidisciplinary education, as described so beautifully in India's past, is indeed what is needed for the education of India to lead the country into the 21st century and the fourth industrial revolution. (Sections 11.1–11.4)

Notwithstanding the gross misinterpretation of 'liberal arts' as 'a liberal notion of the arts' – a problem which I will come to later – my concern here is the apparently contradictory pull that the field of Indian education is ideologically harnessed to. The desire to 'bring back' a beautiful past, as the only means of 'lead[ing] the country' into a 'fourth industrial revolution' of the future, accurately sums up the paradox that I alluded to at the start. The audience and beneficiaries of India's contemporary experiments with university reform are made to believe that a most distant past is our most opportune destination; and consequently, what is needed of policy is an imaginative time-travel into the mythical space of 'greatness'. We are told that not only did 'ancient Indian universities' – like 'Takshashila, Nalanda, Vallabhi and Vikramshila' – pre-date all universities everywhere in the world, but the 'vibrant multidisciplinary environments' enabled by them were also moments of origin as well as lessons of survival for 'other countries educationally and economically'.

But, why do I call this narrative ferment of origin and precedence a mythical space, as I just did? How is it counterposed against the claims and methods of history, as well as the conventions of historical memory? In other words, when exactly did 'Takshashila, Nalanda, Vallabhi and Vikramshila' exist as events in time and material infrastructures in physical-geographical space? I will attempt an answer to these questions at great length and with attention to archival props through this chapter, but it might suffice for our immediate purposes to suggest that these named institutions roughly occupy a temporal frame between the tenth century BC and the thirteenth century AD. So, chronologically speaking, we are referring to an institutional artefact – the 'ancient Indian university' – whose vintage consists in a detour as far back as three thousand to eight hundred years. But, how did a three-thousand-year-old institution disappear so completely that it needs to be brought back with such urgent concern for a country's imminent future? Historical annals have borne witness to the decline and effective decimation of civilisations, but institutions – once conceived and built – have survived as 'ideas' even if their material infrastructures have been destroyed. And yet, why did the Indian university bubble away both its materiality and ideational potential, insofar as we need to revive the 'idea' behind it *now*? To take a comparative case, the European *universitas* came up around the eleventh and twelfth centuries in Bologna, Oxford and Paris – and even though these medieval institutions cannot be regarded as the point of origin for the modern university (as we know it now) – they have nonetheless struggled against time and political conquest to resist disappearance as an 'idea' (Rashdall; Haskins; Durkheim; Pedersen; Wittrock).

Does it follow from the contrary fortunes of the Indian university-'idea' that Takshashila or Nalanda or Vallabhi or Vikramshila *did not* actually contain the 'idea' of the university at all? Might a punctilious reading of ancient Indian history prove that none of these had any connection with what we understand as a 'university'? Is their status as 'universities', therefore, a post-facto ascription calculated towards an ideological contest for priority? The very 'Introduction' to the NEP 2020 might gesture a probable explanation, when it proclaims on a note of self-congratulation:

> The rich heritage of ancient and eternal Indian knowledge and thought has been a guiding light for this Policy. . . . The aim of education in ancient India was not just the acquisition of knowledge as preparation for life in this world, or life beyond schooling, but for the complete realization and liberation of the self. World-class institutions of ancient India such as Takshashila, Nalanda, Vikramshila, Vallabhi, set the highest standards of multidisciplinary teaching and research and hosted scholars and students from across backgrounds and countries . . . . These rich legacies to world heritage must not only be nurtured and preserved for posterity but also researched, enhanced, and put to new uses through our education system. (4)

The postulation of an Indian tradition of knowledge and thought as 'ancient and eternal' is succinct in its aim – the 'put[ting] to new uses' of our rich heritage 'through our education system'. The use of the word 'eternal' is cardinal, inasmuch as this heritage claims exemption from historical scrutiny. What is eternal is unassailable by history or by any stretch of rational inquiry, and must therefore be above the force of questioning. The 'world-class institutions of ancient India', by distilling 'ancient and eternal Indian knowledge and thought', are also inductively beyond the pale of the historian's accounting. And, because of their metaphysical eternity, their complete disappearance is no ground for doubting their relevance and instructive significance for a time (and nation) to come. They can always be 'brought back' or 'returned to' seamlessly, in and from the present – since their transcendence of the symptoms of temporal decay makes them particularly amenable to 'new uses'. Ganesh N. Devy, a literary critic and archivist of Indian language systems, has noted that the NEP's championing of a golden age thesis contains a devious shift of focus from the *pracheen* (ancient) to the *sanatan* ('ancient and eternal' – that is, 'universal') – which, in my formulation above, corresponds to a move from history to myth.[1]

The University: 'Worldness' or Universality?

To challenge this ahistorical fetish of an 'ancient Indian university', as well as the conscription of policy fortunes of public education to such a concocted fetish, we need to do a couple of conscientious exercises in scholarship. The first consists in interrogating, and analysing, the historical conditions under which ancient Indian education thrived – and what, if any, of these conditions made such educational practice seem akin to the idea of a university. The second exercise proceeds from this re-engagement with a historical archive; it forces us to measure the reality of ancient

[1] See interview with Ganesh N. Devy, "An Amnesiac Policy", for an elaborate discussion on this point.

education against the *raison d'etre* of the university and thus confirm whether Takshashila or Nalanda (or any of the others) may at all be called a university.

The name 'university' is as important as the idea it represents and the material infrastructures it presupposes. And it will become clear in this chapter that neither the sign nor its substance can be historically separated. In order for us to probe the question of whether ancient India had anything of a 'university', we must first attempt an account of what the 'university' signifies as a sign. This is necessarily a comparative proposition, in that it will require an engagement with Indian vernacular equivalents for the 'university'. I am deliberately using a semiotic grid for my inquiry here, because that escapes the transcendentalism of definitions.

The most commonly used linguistic equivalents for the referent of the 'university', in Indian vernaculars, are *vishwavidyalaya* (shared by several scripts, including Hindi or Devanagari) and *jamia* (in Urdu, deriving from the Arabic *jami'a*). While *vishwavidyalaya* – literally a composite of the roots *vishwa* (meaning 'world'), *vidya* (meaning 'knowledge') and *aalaya* (meaning 'home') – signifies a meeting place of the knowledge(s) of the world, it has no existence in any ancient Indian literature or even in Sanskrit grammar or lexicography. Institutions for the dissemination of knowledge (*vidya*) are severally known in the *dharma-shastras* (texts of the sacred Law) as *ashramas*, *acharya-kulas*, *tols*, *mathas*, *viharas* or even *vidyalayas*. But, the sense of the *vishwa* (or the 'world') is missing from this extant referential archive on Vedic or Buddhist education. Understandably, the word *vishwavidyalaya* is a much later coinage and indicates an attempt at literally transcribing the meaning of the Latin *universitas*. *Jami'a*, on the other hand, signifies a gathering place – its official usage diverging from its original connotation of a place for religious congregation, to mean a more liberal-intellectual site for a coming together – of the distant and the distinct.

In this documentary chronicle of referential verbiage around the 'Indian' meanings of the university, two specific coordinates emerge. The first roots the idea and the practices of the 'university' in a necessary (and almost compulsory) encounter with the world – albeit in a localised 'place' marked for a physical gathering of bodies. That minds can meet only when bodies come together is a consciousness that gives the university a corporal form, while also embodying its deepest fears around pollution and touch. There will be occasion to elaborate this frighteningly self-riven character of the university-institution in this chapter and the ones that follow. However, for the time being, it is crucial to remember that without a congregationalist openness to the *world* outside – an invitation to a world without reserve – there is no university, even in the Indian sense of the term. The second implication that overlays this semiotic maze is, yet again, a form of the university's *worlding* – its relationship to the world, its *world-ness*. And here, the *vishwavidyalaya* comes even closer to its modern European cognate, in that it stresses on the worldly nature of its pursuits as opposed to the religious-monastic codes of early Indian 'places' of education. There is, at heart, a secular intent to all the different Indian inflections of the 'university'. And, this test of *being* must consequently be an immanent condition for the identification of 'university'-examples on Indian soil.

It is against these two coordinates that the rest of this chapter will measure the fittingness of the university-appellation to what the NEP 2020 calls 'world-class institutions of ancient India' (4). The irony implicit in the policy's conflation of the university's characteristic *world-ness* with a global investment-benchmarking of the 'world-class' will also be taken up for deeper examination further on. But, we first need to ask: how much of the *world* found 'place' in Takshashila? Or, was Takshashila a 'place' for the gathering of the *world*, in the first place? How were these gatherings (of bodies) organised, managed and controlled – to retain a sense of the *world*, if at all? Even though there is evidence of Nalanda and Vikramshila inviting visible traffic with different parts of the world, how worldly were the pursuits and practices of the 'places' identified as 'universities'? In other words, did these 'places' live up to the secularity of knowledges deemed worthy of the name of the 'university'? If not, why did the 'world' gather at these 'places'? And, what technologies of gathering made them susceptible to being represented under the sign of the 'university'? Finally, who were the people 'gathered' here and how did their social histories correspond with the institutional trajectories of the 'ancient Indian university'?

Takshashila: A Precursor?

Let me take the case of Takshashila first – which finds the most extensive reference as a centre for education in several of the *Jataka* tales.[2] Numerous young princes from Benaras, Kosala, Mithila, Ujjaini, Rajagriha, Madhyadesha and other kingdoms in the north were reported to have been sent off to one Takkasila [Pali for Takshashila], on attaining the age of sixteen or even earlier, in order to complete their education in the Vedas as well as to be trained out of the lineal privilege of royal birth. This period of their mental and physical disciplining, into codes of proper conduct and righteous behaviour, was also supposed to coincide with the caste mandate of *varnashrama* – whereby boys belonging to the three upper castes had to undergo *brahmacharya* (ascetic purification) before entering a worldly life (*garhasthya*). Understandably therefore, most of the questors for knowledge, travelling to Takshashila, came from largely the brahmin (priestly) and kshatriya (warrior) castes; there are records of a few enrolled vaishya (trader caste) students as well. Because the initiation ritual for a life of Vedic education involved the *upanayana* (wearing of the sacred thread), only the *dvija* (twice-born) castes were allowed into what is imagined as the 'university' of Takshashila; and there was an explicit ban on the admission of *chandala* (shudra) populations, let alone the *panchamas* (untouchable outcastes). There are even stories of shudra students enrolling for the study of the Vedas in disguise, which – when discovered – led to their immediate expulsion and severe punishments of social boycott.

[2] All references to the *Jatakas* are taken from the six-volume compilation of the tales under the editorship of E.B. Cowell, translated from Pali by various hands.

As far as the subjects of study were concerned, Takshashila specialised in three Vedas, with the specific exception of the fourth *Atharvaveda*. There are no recorded reasons for this curricular selection, except for the historically cogent assumption that the more recent composition of *Atharvaveda* and its references to practical everyday affairs might have accorded to it a lesser (and more mundane) status as compared to the others.

But, what kind of a 'university' was Takshashila and when did it achieve pre-eminence as a 'centre' for advanced education? While the *adi-kavya* (*Ramayana*) identifies Takshashila as a kingdom of great riches and material treasures, the *Mahabharata* contains a reference to the invincible King Janmejaya of Takshashila. There is no indication in either of these epics of the kingdom's intellectual aura. The *Mahavagga* however mentions the medical exploits of Jivaka Komarabhacca, who – having received his training over a number of years in the famous Takshashila – even attended on the Buddha and his *bhikshus* in their lifetime (DeGraff 1016). A detailed archaeological account of the structural remains of Taxila, as documented by John Marshall in three volumes (dating back to 1951), situates the growth and development of its planned settlements around 'the sixth century BC or thereabouts' (Volume I, xvi). But, if the reputation of the site had already attracted scholars like Jivaka to travel from Rajagriha for a practical education in medicine, it must have been in existence for a few centuries prior to the sixth. The general consensus on the period of Takshashila's evolution appears to rest on a variety of conjectures, finally converging between the tenth and seventh centuries BC. Marshall's survey attaches its educational importance to its geographical location, while also maintaining the lack of any coordinated organisation of its educational activities.

> This pre-eminence of the city as a seat of academic and practical teaching was a natural outcome of her geographical position at the north-western gateway of India and of the peculiarly cosmopolitan character of her population; for we can hardly doubt that the interchange of eastern and western ideas during the period following the Persian conquest must have done much to stimulate the spread

> of knowledge, and that this stimulus became increasingly stronger under Maurya and Greek rule in the third and second centuries BC. Whether there was any systematic organisation for the professors or their pupils we do not know. The probability is that both alike were independent of the State and that the teachers were normally independent of one another. . . . There is no reason, however, to suppose that, apart possibly from a common assembly hall, they possessed either property or endowments, or that they enjoyed the use of common lecture halls, libraries or the like. (Volume I, 43)

Marshall's contention about the complete lack of corporative character to the conduct of intellectual practice in Takshashila is adequately corroborated by the *Jataka* archive. Even though the *Jatakas* were compiled at a much later date, as a chronicling of the Buddha's social biographies prior to his enlightenment, the references to 'Takkasila' found in these tales are discrete and episodic. What they prove, beyond a shadow of doubt, is that the brahminical education of Sanskrit scripture – the possible content of Takkasila's exchanges, along with practical training in *ayurveda* (medicine) or *dhanurveda* (archery) – did not have a common built 'place' for its imparting. Nor did it possess an aggregative character in terms of the materiality of its instructional activities. Different travellers to the kingdom would seek apprenticeship with different teachers (*acharyas*) in the latter's own *ashrama*-settlements (Kane; Raja; Keay 1918, 1938; Kosambi).

Ashrama Pedagogy: Grooming under the Guru

There is very little information available on the exact pedagogy, or even the rules of intellectual fellowship, observable in Takshashila's *ashramas*. But, considering the fact that the basis of instruction lay in Vedic scripture, one might assume that Takshashila's methods of formal training could not have radically diverged from the then-current brahminical system. In fact, barring the age of entry – which, according to the *Jatakas*, was pegged a little higher – the forms of curricular organisation and principles for successful academic tutelage in Takshashila could be conceived as eminently comparable with the brahminical precedent.

In the *ashrama*-institution, every brahmin teacher, in return for a symbolic payment or a pledge for daily household labour, would agree to initiate a limited number of 'seekers' into the Vedic doctrine. There was no sense of a community between the *acharyas* or the students (*antevasins*) of different *acharyas*; and therefore, the shared mutuality of a 'gathering' that a university proposed as its inaugural condition was starkly absent. The travelling *antevasins* must have accordingly gathered around the city of Takshashila, purely out of a demographic concentration of brahmin scholars in the region. This concentration of scholarship too, as Marshall reminded us, owed to the cultural-intellectual traffic made possible by its strategic location at the north-western frontier. Also, the word '*antevasin*' – attached to the disciple or apprentice – implied habitation at the furthest limit of lived settlements; the *Taittiriya-brahmana* ordained that the student of the Vedas, living the life of a *brahmachari*, must not be able to see the roof of his own house from the place where he studies. The almost-planned residential locus of Veda-scholars in this part of Takshashila achieved a dual purpose: while being not entirely removed from human life-worlds in the interests of daily upkeep and other material necessities, the relative distance of the city called for long journeys away from students' families and birthplaces.

All said, what really needs to be taken note of is the sporadic nature of the intellectual 'centre', and the evidently unconnected locations of individual teachers and their coaching cohorts in the urban architecture of Takshashila. The obvious fallout of this was an ethic of individual genius and its unequally distributed networks of reputational currency that were instrumental in determining the size of an *acharya-kula*. In other words, both the number of students training with a guru as well as structures of demand and opportunity depended on secondary sources of fame or publicity. The course of study, comprising the three Vedas and the *Vedangas* (including *vyakarana*, *chhanda* and *nirukta*) as its mainstay, was still to be ordained by what was prescribed for the study of one's own caste and class (*svadhyayadhyayana*). As in the extant *acharya-kulas*, a similar purpose governed the dissemination of *shastras* (Vedic scripture) in Takshashila: to control and govern ('*shas*' of *anushashana*) the conduct and actions of the student subject.

In the brahminical system, there were different ages prescribed for the initiation of the three different castes into the acquisition of Vedic precepts. So, while the brahmin child could be inducted into the teacher's household through an *upanayana* ceremony at the age of eight, for the kshatriyas and the vaishyas it was respectively allowed at ages eleven and twelve. Following the wearing of the sacred girdle (*yajnopavita*), the student of the Vedas would officially embark on a routine of religious training and behavioural self-restraint – through a daily life of instruction and ritualistic morality. This would include the running of errands for the teacher's household, as well as desisting from specific desires of the flesh and fleshly upkeep. The teaching of one Veda – the *Rig Veda* – was prescribed for a period of twelve years, at the end of which the *antevasin* was bathed (*snataka*) and ordained into virtuous society before returning to his own homeland. For the brahmin scholar, it was therefore at the age of twenty that he was supposed to take up the mantle of *garhasthya* (worldly living), while for the other two castes the moment of ordination could extend up to age twenty-four. For the brahmin man wishing to continue his education beyond the study of the first Veda – with each demanding apprenticeship for a further twelve years – there was the option of retiring into a life of *naishthika brahmacharya* (permanent asceticism). The ceremony of *upasadana* (as distinct from the initiation marked by *upanayana*) was required of the latter category of non-worldly brahmins, which insisted on a renunciatory exit from the social ties of community and into the care of a specialised teacher (*upadhyaya*).

'*World-ness*' and Retreat

The reason why I recounted the ritual gradation of Vedic educational mores, replicated in the presumed 'university'-model of Takshashila, lies in the fact of its relationship with the world. It is insistently clear that the prescriptive codes of '*svadhyayadhyayana*', driving the form and substance of Vedic study, are a means of retreating from the world through the period of studentship. Contrary to an encounter with *world-ness*, the strictly religious education of Takshashila removed the curriculum and its modes of performative practice into the master's household at one 'end' of the lived world – the *antevasah*. There was no kinship with the knowledges of the world that the 'university' presumes as its ontological destiny, but merely a partaking of the knowledge (and pedagogy) that is proper to one's own caste. Structurally, this vision of education did not bring the minds (and bodies) of those desirous of learning into a single 'place' like the university, but on the contrary scattered them in ritual bondage to individual masters living separately and in no apparent connection with each other.

If there was no 'university' in Takshashila – as a perspicacious reading of historical records would warrant – what made the students of Vedic *sutras* and *samhitas* 'gather' in the town in such large numbers? Given that there were other places of brahminical education, such as Benaras, why did Takshashila gain a disproportionate share of attention in accounts of Vedic studies? Or, how did it eventually take on an aspect of a 'university' despite evidence to the contrary? While a part of this answer might lie, as I have suggested, in the strategic location of the 'place' and its concentration of brahmin settlements, there are two consequent factors that contributed to an optics of scale around the otherwise individualised pursuit of *brahmacharya*.

The first lies in the Vedic precept that only brahmin scholars could teach the Vedas, and that a failure to study it on the part of any of the three castes deemed worthy of its pursuit would lead to their violation of dharma (righteous conduct) – and eventually result in a loss of caste identity. That the preservation of social privilege was made incumbent on the 'prescribed' course of study forced parents to compulsorily send off their wards to the households of brahmin teachers. It was thus through conventions of social propriety and associated threats of ostracism that huge numbers of *antevasins* were forced to travel to the settlements of potential brahmin *acharyas*. Furthermore, the second condition for Takshashila's popularity derived from the fact that the Vedic *samhitas* and *dharma-shastras* were all part of an oral tradition (*sruti* and *smriti*) – which necessitated for its transmission the physical coincidence of the teacher and the taught. Because no part of the study in the *ashramas* of Takshashila consisted in the reading of written texts, even boys of brahmin families residing in faraway lands could not but be apprenticed to masters of the doctrine by journeying to their households. The method for the teaching of the Vedic *shlokas* involved an incantatory exercise, joined in by the chorus of the *antevasins*, and subsequently committed to memory over a period of time. In order to aid the process of memorisation, the Vedas were divided into sections and their chanting routinised through alternating modes of *pada-patha* and *samhita-patha*. Writing, or the use of written texts, was however not part of the foundational course of study, since the word of the scripture was believed to have been conceived by the *rishi*'s supernal vision and then transmitted through the ages in sound and memory. Inasmuch as the teachers of Takshashila were conduits of that tradition, they had to directly entrust the word to posterity through repeatable acts of communal utterance – which would not be possible except in the immediate and proximal presence of students.

Nalanda: A Buddhist *Higher* Education?

If in the brahminical transmission of Vedic systems of knowledge, there was never an integrative consciousness of a 'place' (for the 'gathering of the world') – constitutive of the outward form and inner being of the 'university' or the *vishwavidyalaya* – what about the history of Buddhist education in Nalanda, Vallabhi or Vikramshila? I will take them up in that specific order, for my analysis here. To begin with: is it possible, or prudent, to imagine the monastic complex at Nalanda as a 'university'? It is true that, unlike Takshashila, there happened to be an infrastructural enclosure to the 'premises' of Nalanda, which – despite continuous efforts at extension through newer and newer endowments from a series of rulers – were nonetheless incorporated into a *mahavihara* layout. Seventh-century accounts of the 'place' document, as in the words of the Chinese visitor Hiuen Tsang,

> its six wings, each built by a king, all enclosed in the privacy of solid brick[.] One gate opens into the great college, from which are separated eight other halls, standing in the middle (of the monastery). The richly adorned towers, and the fairy-like turrets, like pointed hilltops, are congregated together. The observatories seem to be lost in the mists (of the morning), and the upper rooms tower above the clouds. From the windows one may see how the winds and the clouds produce new forms, and above the soaring eaves the conjunctions of the sun and moon may be observed. And then we may add how the deep, translucent ponds bear on their surface the blue lotus intermingled with the Kanaka flower, of deep red colour, and at intervals the Amra groves spread over all, their shade. All the outside courts, in which are the priests' chambers, are of four stages. The stages have dragon projections and coloured eaves, the pearl-red pillars, carved and ornamented, the richly adorned balustrades, and the roofs covered with tiles that reflect the light in a thousand shades, these things add to the beauty of the scene. (*Life* ix–x)

The near-literary picturesqueness of the 'scene' at Nalanda aside, what emerges from Hiuen Tsang's enthralled portrait is the indisputable existence of a plan underlying the growth and evolution of Nalanda. More recent archaeological finds, especially Spooner's report of 1916–17, have contested the marking of the outer limits of the *mahavihara* in any clear 'boundary' wall. But, the fact that successive foreign visitors to the 'place' – including I-Tsing, who travelled into the country nearly three decades after Hiuen Tsang – have recorded identical structures in terms of the number of *viharas* or halls testifies to the communal maintenance of an inhabited institution. The question is: might this institution be called a 'university'?

On the face of it, a clinching factor in favour of the *world-ness* of Nalanda lies in that our most authoritative knowledge about it comes from the accounts of two foreign travellers named above. If indeed, as we are told, Buddhist scholars from China, Tibet, Korea and Nepal were often received as guests at Nalanda as well as those training in Nalanda invited over to these countries, there remained a distinct possibility for 'gathering' the knowledges of the world. Interestingly, the stories around the naming of Nalanda also bear traces of a popular folklore, combining supernatural belief and material circuits of patronage. One of these origin-myths borrows from a Buddhist insistence on serpent-worship, contending that the name of the monastery owed to an ancient coiled *naga* (snake), whose propitiation ensured the prosperity of the village. The second theory took cue from the fact of Nalanda's burgeoning prosperity instead, to root its lexical form in a compound '*na-alam-da*' – meaning, an unrepayable surplus of charity. Whatever may be the reality or credibility of these accounts, it strikes the modern reader of Buddhist education as particularly relevant that the Nalanda *mahavihara* had its patrons and audiences spread across a range of classes, sects and regions.

Despite this massive expanse of its imaginative charm, it is worth repeating that almost all of the contemporary acclaim of Nalanda can be sourced first-hand from the 'outsider' representations of Hiuen Tsang and I-Tsing alone. Both these memoirs, situating a richness of eyewitness detail in the early- and late-seventh-century India, are preceded by a fifth-century Chinese monk Fa-Hien's complete silence and disregard of Nalanda as a 'place' of Buddhist learning. The latter is supposed to have arrived in India in 399 AD, leaving more than ten years later in 409–410 AD. It is improbable that Fa-Hien would have missed the renown of Nalanda and its stately experience, in his decade-long sojourns through the breadth of India's monastic map. Archaeological excavations have come in handy here, to attribute the rise of the Nalanda monastery complex to the endowment of Sakraditya (or Kumaragupta I) in about 425 AD (Spooner; Sastri; Page; Kuraishi; Stewart).

So, did Nalanda become a 'place' of learning – and subsequently achieve narrative felicity as a university-prototype – in the interim of two hundred years that transpired between Fa-Hien's exit and Hiuen Tsang's excursion? Not really, in as far as both *Majjhima Nikaya* and *Digha Nikaya* (as well as other scriptural commentaries) mention the 'small but prosperous village' of

Nalanda as one of the preferred sites for the Buddha's discourses and disputations with Jaina adversaries like Dighatapassi, Upali and Abhayrajakumara. A couple of monasteries around the village earned the fame of having sheltered the Buddha and his accompanying troupe of learned *bhikshus*. Even Hiuen Tsang registers the truth of this gradual (and almost millennium-long) accretion of *viharas* in Nalanda – which were built and conceived as rain-retreats for the Buddhist *sangha*. The originary purpose of the Nalanda *mahavihara* was to provide a resting-place for the wandering *bhikshus* during the monsoon season – a '*sangharama*', meaning a place where the *sangha* can retire for a seasonal hiatus or *arama* (rest). The conceptual enfolding of the *mahavihara* as ideally a '*sangharama*' predated the gift-establishments of the Gupta rulers by more than eight hundred years, and since the life and times of the Buddha. In fact, the *Cullavagga* maintains that, on the Buddha's advice, the monks taking up residence in a '*sangharama*' were grouped in lodging-quarters according to their expertise and scholarly interests:

> For those monks who were repeaters of the *suttantas* he appointed a lodging-place together, thinking, "They will be able to chant over the *suttantas* to one another." For those monks who were in charge of the *vinaya* he appointed a lodging place together, thinking, "They will be able to discuss the *vinaya* one with another." For those monks who were preachers of the dhamma he appointed a lodging-place together, thinking, "They will be able to talk over the dhamma one with another." For those monks who were given to meditation he appointed one lodging-place together, thinking, "They will not disturb one another." For those monks who were wise in worldly lore, and abounding in bodily vigor, he appointed one lodging-place together, thinking, "These venerable ones, too, will thus remain settled according to their pleasure." ('On Settlements', *Cullavagga* IV 4: 4, 75)

It was this strategic but structural curation of learned opinion that ensured a propensity in the 'gathered' *bhikshus* – escaping the rains – to form assemblies of religious debate and profess the knowledge of truths they already possessed. Quite as an accident, learning and dissemination of learned doctrine became the characteristic feature of an institution that was intended instead for an annual respite from mendicant preaching. However, having said that, the material purpose of the monastic complex was temporary escape and withdrawal from the physical inconveniences of seasons or disaster. In other words, a rain-retreat meant that substantial parts of the Buddhist *sangha* were constantly in transit at the 'place'. A careful comparison of the two foreigner accounts of the Nalanda *mahavihara*, from the seventh century, would confirm this point.

While Hiuen Tsang wrote of ten thousand monks (including 1510 teachers and the rest trainees) residing in the six monasteries of Nalanda, I-Tsing's count of residents – coming only about thirty years later – pegged the figure at three thousand. These could not have been rough approximations, since both are otherwise very punctilious in their counts of the different gradations of monks. Also, they stayed at Nalanda for five and ten years respectively, to not be aware of its demographic scale with relative precision. Even if we imagine the figures as rounded off for purposes of documentation, the reported hollowing out of such a renowned 'university' into less than one-third of its strength within a space of three decades is too huge a statistical oversight to be ignored. Or, did the haloed status of Nalanda suffer such a great 'crisis' (or decline) in these intervening years? Far from it, as Radhakumud Mookerji collates from the two accounts, '[i]n Hiuen Tsang's time, "the king of the country remitted the revenues of about 100 villages for the endowment of the convent." (*Life*, p. 112) In I-tsing's time, "the lands in its possession bestowed upon the monastery by kings of many generations contained more than 200 villages" (p. 65)' (Mookerji 561–62). If anything, Nalanda had only grown in fame, finances and favour. The 'miraculous' fall in the strength of the Buddhist *sangha* at Nalanda can therefore only be explained by the nature of the 'place' as a temporary resting-site – something that the imagination of a '*sangharama*' (and not a 'university') already indicates. That the Buddhist *mahavihara* was actually designed more as a rain-retreat than as a centre for education is also borne out by the radically differing accounts of monastic census that a reader finds in the successive travelogues of Fa-Hien, Hiuen Tsang and I-Tsing. For example, while Fa-Hien noticed only two monasteries in Kanyakubja on his visit, Hieun Tsang encountered a hundred with more than ten thousand monks. Sravasti, on the other hand, boasted of ninety-eight *viharas* during Fa-Hien's travels through the land, whereas Hiuen Tsang found only one of them peopled in his own time. The recurring images of abandoned or forsaken *vihara*-structures in Hiuen Tsang's first-person catalogue of more than 5000 Buddhist sites visited by him – the Jetavana-*vihara* being one of the most prominent of such deserted complexes – are, in all likelihood, a result of the constant movement of the religious mendicants from their resting-places.

A *Bhikshu* Curriculum

Let me now attempt a brief overview of the various stages of progression, through which the Buddhist ideal of monkhood was produced in *viharas* like Nalanda.[3] While a child was to begin education with elementary grammar and Panini's *sutras* between the ages of six and eight, the initiation into religious scripture (*vinayas*, *suttantas* and *abhidharma*) would have to wait till the *samanera* (trainee-monks) were fifteen to twenty years of age. The initiation-ritual for the *samanera* consisted in an act of leaving the home (*pabbajja*) and taking residence with a preceptor (*upajjheya*) in the monastery. From that point onwards, the trainee would unconditionally surrender for his spiritual nourishment and physical protection (*nissaya*) to the *upajjheya*, who would eventually lead the former into salvation (*moksha*). There would be daily routines of instruction in the Buddha's word, followed by the practice of alms-begging (*bhiksha*) from nearby householders. It was not as if the alms collected by the *samanera* would contribute to their material upkeep, since the finances of the monastery were separately maintained through royal grants and donations from the laity. Yet, the ritual of begging

[3] All references to formal procedures of Buddhist education are taken from *Mahavagga* and *Cullavagga*.

was an absolutely necessary part of the monk's training into the order, insofar as it would teach the inmate both an attitude of renunciatory humility and an awareness of material value. The final ordination of the *samanera* into *bhikshu*-status was called *upasampada*, which signified the taking up of a stance of complete disaffection towards worldly desire.

It is here that one may notice a difference in teleological orientation between the Buddhist and brahminical models of religious indoctrination. In the former, the ordination confers on the apprentice (*sramana*) a complete break with the world, while for the brahmin student (*antevasin*) the period of ascetic austerity (*brahmacharya*) was a compulsory rite of passage into worldly life (*garhasthya*). In either case, education was about the successful abnegation of the world – whether to eventually earn the privilege of retiring from it or the right to return to it. In Nalanda *mahavihara*, the subjects of study for the *samanera* mandatorily included the Mahayana doctrine and all the eighteen sects. Among these, there was special emphasis laid on the academic pursuit of theology – and the philosophies of *sunyavada* (nihilism) and *vijnanavada* (idealism) as the essence of the Mahayana school (Sankalia 67). Other secular fields of learning were also on offer, but only as optional trajectories available to the interested scholar after the process of religious interpellation. These 'miscellaneous' subjects encompassed, as Hiuen Tsang names, 'the *Vedas* and other books, the Hetuvidya, Sabdavidya, the Chikitsavidya, the works on Magic or Atharvaveda, the Samkhya' (Tsang 112).

Members of the laity (breaking away from worldly careers) and seekers of secular knowledge (training in the professional disciplines) were however treated differently within the daily organisation of the *mahavihara*, by being left to fend for their own needs at their own expense. They were, for all purposes, treated as external to the order and therefore ineligible as claimants on the permanent property of the monastery, unlike the *samanera*. I-Tsing documents this fact very succinctly, when he notes:

> Those white-robed (laymen) who come to the residence of a priest, and read chiefly Buddhist scriptures with the intention that they

> may one day become tonsured and black-robed, are called 'children' (*Manava*). Those who (coming to a priest) want to learn secular literature only, without having any intention of quitting the world, are called 'students' (*Brahmacharin*). These two groups of persons (though residing in a monastery) have to subsist at their own expense. (I-Tsing 105)

The differential hierarchies of value and norms of treatment attached to the different courses of study, classes of students and presumed uses of such studies already prove, beyond the scope of much doubt, the primacy of religious training over professional careers. That the worldliness of the student's origins or the potential instrumentalisation of his studies in the cause of future material prospects was not the 'vocation' of Buddhist education, even if it was not frowned upon, is important to note – especially when we test the validity of a 'university'-thesis against a *mahavihara* like Nalanda. Concisely put, an education governed by worldly origins or ends – that is, a utilitarian consciousness – was distinguished from the cognate character of the *vihara*, which consisted in the furtherance of a religious zeal. In terms of the two meanings of *world-ness* implicated in our inaugural framing of the university's ontological being, Nalanda seems to falter on one front. But, to repeat a point I hinted at earlier, what does one make of its enduring hospitability towards the rest of the world – as traveller testimonies of the welcome accorded to Hiuen Tsang or I-Tsing and their long (and pleasant) periods of stay at the monastery would have us believe?

Intellectuals or Evangelists?

In this context, it needs to be emphatically stated that neither of these travellers – whose accounts we rely on for a historical reconstruction of Buddhist education – had visited India with the explicit purpose of documenting intellectual practices within its 'institutions' or enabling a process of cultural exchange through a 'give-and-take' of knowledge traditions. The mission of the Chinese, Tibetan or Javanese monks was more than negotiating with cultural difference, or a mutually enriching dialogue with otherness; in other words, a hubristic desire for knowledge or intellectual fervour was only incidental to their difficult journeys into a foreign land. Their primary purpose was never lost sight of, and in fact unapologetically maintained through all their observations about the Buddhist (or Indian) way of life. Theirs was a training into religious evangelism, the force of which could then steer the life of Buddhism as a world-religion in their own home countries. It is amply clear from the records left behind by Fa-Hien to I-Tsing that they saw themselves as conduits for the spread of the Buddha's word and bearers of the correct interpretation of scripture. Even though it is famously known that Hiuen Tsang studied the *yoga-shastras* under the coveted guidance of the chief of the Nalanda monastery, Silabhadra, it was all driven by the need to acquire virtuous competence in the reading and exegesis of Sanskrit texts for their accurate transmission back at home. As Mookerji notes from Watters' edition of Tsang's *Life*, the 'object of his travels was . . . to procure the sacred books of [the Buddha's] religion in their original language and to learn the true meaning of their doctrines from orthodox pundits in India' (503). Also, L. Cranmer-Byng notes in his 'Preface' to the *Life of Hiuen Tsang* that 'no less than 657 volumes of the sacred books, seventy-four of which [Tsang] translated into Chinese, while 150 relics of the Buddha, borne by twenty horses, formed the spoil reverently gathered from the many lands we call India' (xiv). Returning again to Mookerji's survey, 'like Fa-Hien, I-Tsing's object was to study and gather the genuine texts of the *Vinaya* rules, to correct their misrepresentations in China, and to combat the erroneous views held by the *Vinayadharas* there in those days' (535).

Fuelled by an evangelist instinct to collect the *vinaya*-texts in their original and subsequently translate them into the languages of their home-countries, all these foreigners' travelogues contain passages which record the painstaking labour of copying the *shastras* available at several different monasteries. For example, when Hiuen Tsang reached Kashmir and toured its 'religious foundations', the resident priests of the Buddhist temple he was staying in received a divine command in a dream – to help the

'Master of the Law' to 'study the sacred books, and to adore the sacred traces in India' (*Life* 68). Thus summoned to the task providentially, the king of Kashmir arranged for his reception and residence at the Jayendra monastery:

> Observing his readiness (joy), and finding that having come from far, fired by a desire to learn, he had no original texts from whence to read (the king) gave him twenty men to copy the Sacred Books and *Sastras*; moreover, he ordered five men to wait on him and obey his orders, and to furnish him, free of expense, with whatever things he required. The chief of the priests of that establishment was a man of high moral character. He observed with the greatest strictness the religious rules and ordinances. . . . Thus he was pleased to invite the illustrious stranger and to honour him as a guest. The Master of the Law likewise with all his heart respectfully questioned him, and night and day begged him ceaselessly to explain and give into his keeping the various *shastras*. (ibid. 69–70)

At Nalanda, Chinese scholar Hiuan Chao met a fellow traveller from Ceylon, for whose generosity and assistance he copied the *Yogachara* and other sacred texts. A Korean student, Aryavarma, is known to have copied several *sutras* while residing in Nalanda; so did his peer and fellow countryman Hwui Yieh. Similarly, the most learned expounders of Buddhist doctrine in Nalanda – like Silabhadra, Dharmapala, Chandragomin, Padmasambhava, Sthiramati and Buddhakirti – had their Sanskrit works copied and translated into Tibetan by different visiting scholars at different points of time. It is indeed a little surprising that such frenzied writing activity was happening at the Buddhist monasteries at a time when the teaching of religious precepts was however entirely confined to oral instruction. The pedagogic methods assumed by the teachers of the faith were persistently rooted in routines of recitation and repetition. From Hiuen Tsang's comprehensive detailing of the educational activities at a few thousands of Buddhist *viharas*, we come to know that '[i]nstruction was imparted orally and characterized by much earnestness and painstaking labour on the part of the teacher. The pedagogic method followed was that of trying to quicken and rouse the latent powers of thinking in the student and lead him on to conclusions' (Mookerji 505–506). As long as the practice of writing was wedded to the purpose of disseminating the word of the Buddha - and therefore, the propagation of religious faith in other neighbouring countries - it did not pose a challenge to the primordial orality of doctrine.

What emerges from the preceding discussion is Nalanda's 'place' in bringing about a confluence of learned minds - not in the interests of intellectual curiosity (or comradeship), but of intense religious proselytism. And, it is this truth of Nalanda's vocation, despite its habitual hospitality for the 'world' and foreignness, that makes it little more than an ecclesiastical guild. To that extent, it might seem to share a kinship of spirit with the medieval European *universitas* - which was nonetheless far from what we now understand as the idea of the 'university'.

Vallabhi, Vikramshila, and the 'University'-Consciousness

Next named in the catalogue of 'ancient Indian universities', Vallabhi, grew out of endowments made by the local Maitraka rulers around the sixth century AD. While Hiuen Tsang documented the existence of 'some hundred *Sangharamas*' around this part of the western coast, a concatenation of monastery-structures identified as the 'Dudda-*vihara-mandala*' came to attract attention over time. The fame of the learned priests at Vallabhi rose to such great heights and in such a short span of time that both Hiuen Tsang and I-Tsing spoke of it as the 'main rival' of Nalanda. In fact, it was an erstwhile student of Nalanda, Gunamati, who opened a centre for the teaching of *Yogachara* here - which, with the help of generous benefactions and sustained royal patronage, eventually branched out. Both Gunamati and his devoted apprentice in Sthiramati lent their respective reputations to this 'place', composed their own religious commentaries here and accounted for much of the public prestige that 'gathered' interested scholars at this site.

An allusion in *Katha Sarit Sagara* to 'Vallabhi' proves that the monastery extended its appeal even to brahmin families, who were willing to have their children travel to this distant part of the country as soon as they were sixteen years of age (Somadeva 283). I-Tsing dwelt further on the kinds of students invited within its fold, when he noted that some of the trainees joined the services of the royal court after their stint in Vallabhi. This has been taken as a significant clue to the nature of studies conducted in the *vihara-mandala*, which must have included some secular professional components in law, medicine or the military arts. But what comes through with great clarity and complete certainty is the secondary nature of these secular pursuits – insofar as Vallabhi's institutional rivalry with Nalanda consisted in its primary dedication to the rival school of Hinayana Buddhism. Religion, and the spread of the doctrines of the 'little vehicle', were the reigning rationale for the founding and flourishing of Vallabhi. This truth is abundantly in evidence, even though the rest of this monastery's history is shrouded in the mist of insufficient information available from a few scattered sources alone.

The story of Vikramshila, situated in northern Magadha (not very far from Nalanda), is similar – except that 'its main orientation was Mahayanist, with an even stronger emphasis on Tantric beliefs and practices' (Scharfe 155–56). Established and maintained from the treasury of King Dharmapala, the monastic complex of Vikramshila was built around a centrally planned design and enclosed on the outside by what Mookerji calls a 'strong wall' (587). In its outward form therefore, it preserved the sense of a 'place' where students could 'gather' for their studies in the Buddhist curriculum. The physical architecture included a wide assembly hall with six gates leading to the six teaching spaces (subsequently referred to as the 'colleges'). Apart from this structural resemblance with Nalanda, it is believed that the two *mahaviharas* even shared some part of their administrative personnel. The learned monks too travelled between these two sites, thus encouraging some form of exchange of scholarly expertise (ibid.)

What really stands out from the archive on Vikramshila, most of which is recoverable in Taranatha's *History of Buddhism*, is the range and extent of its correspondence with Tibet and its scholars. Again, akin to the Nalanda-character, it appears that this Magadhan *mahavihara* was on its course to becoming an international 'centre' of collaboration and conviviality. This spirit of interaction was so intense that most of Vikramshila's teachers not only learnt the Tibetan language, but also translated several Sanskrit *sutras* and Tantric works (including their own commentaries) for audiences in Tibet. As demonstrative examples, Prajnakaramati wrote two treatises in Tibetan, Jnana Sri Mitra translated one of his own *tikas* (commentaries), Ratnavajra translated fourteen Buddhist texts, and Atisa both wrote and translated more than two hundred texts (mostly on Vajrayana). But, all of this tapestry of manuscripts and texts woven around the act of translation was finally intended to 'purge Tibetan Buddhism of its many corruptions' (Mookerji 591), through a cult of scholarly exegesis. Vikramshila's missionary activities in Tibet were so strongly engirded by diplomatic diktat and a bilateral agenda for religious purism that the subsequent course of Tibetan Buddhism was almost redrawn with exclusive reference to these Indian visitors. That the scholars of a 'university' had effectively become the patron-evangelists of a world religion does indeed take away from the apparent openness of the institution's negotiations with the 'world' – as we have already seen in the case of Nalanda.

(A)voiding Truth, Making Belief

If a critical exhumation of historical fact, as we have attempted so far, prevents the 'great Indian tradition' (NEP 34) from claiming an 'original' custody of the *name* of the 'university', why does a policy vision for the contemporary Indian university beg legitimation from such sleight of focus? Phrased more succinctly, why do we need the crutch of a myth in order to steer the course of independent India's history? The answer lies not far from how the NEP 2020 – with which I set out my argument in this chapter – seeks to re-signify the very terms of the debate. Unless words like 'history', 'ancient', 'tradition', 'liberal', 'world' and 'university' are torn from their own contexts of signification and tied to completely different points of reference, a mythical 'greatness' would not become the cause for belief (and even jubilation and complacency). Hence, it becomes the task of policy to first evolve a substantive glossary of cross-sampled 'ideas' – carrying the carcass of one word and the meaning of another. Semiotic accidents are produced in a controlled narrative environment, till 'history' becomes synonymous with national 'fantasy', the 'ancient' a measure of the 'eternal', 'tradition' circumscribes a range of disconnected 'pasts', 'liberal' passes off as the analogue for a caste-based economy of intellectual rights, or the 'world' and the 'university' are brought together to disturb the historical resonances in their relationship. Take one example from the policy-text that I have already cited: the recalibration of the term 'liberal arts' as 'a liberal notion of the arts' (36). Nothing can be further from the truth. The Greek *artes liberales* – the etymological root for the coinage – consisted of seven distinct divisions of knowledge spanning from grammar to music, but this taxonomy was not about defining the nature of the 'arts'. Instead, it was about mandating the fit subject for the study of these arts – which, in being called 'liberal', was to be the sole prerogative of the free male citizen, and not the women, slaves and children. In short, the question of the 'liberal arts' is not pitched around 'what' constitutes art, but 'who' possesses the right to artistic knowledge. The entire hubris of the liberal tradition, and its history of exclusions, is underwritten in this Greek root; and that a current-day Indian policy-testament chooses to ignore this bears more intention than ignorance.

In veering towards a conclusive teasing out of the implications of my argument here, the historical truth about the 'ancient Indian university' does not need to be restated. But, a related query follows from it. If the two meanings of *world-ness* evoked by the idea of the university are where the Indian 'precedent' falls short, how does the latter project its own relationship with the 'world'? I would suggest that this effect of a self-projection is achieved by a semiotic accident, similar to the one I detailed in the previous paragraph.

The first move towards re-signifying the 'world' – via the 'ancient Indian university' and its enrolment within a 'great Indian tradition' – happens through the discourse of the 'world-class' institution. According to a World Bank report of 2009, which first provided a referential matrix for the 'world-class university',

> [T]he term 'world-class university' has become a catch phrase, not simply for improving the quality of learning and research in tertiary education but also, more important, for developing the capacity to compete in the global tertiary education marketplace through the acquisition and creation of advanced knowledge. With students looking to attend the best possible institution that they can afford, often regardless of national borders, and with governments keen on maximizing the returns on their investments in universities, global standing is becoming an increasingly important concern for institutions around the world. (Salmi 15)

In this revealing definition of the 'world-class', one profound secret of educational policy-making is bequeathed to all 'governments' and 'institutions around the world': that the 'market' is the only truly global 'place'. On that note, it proceeds to proclaim the 'capacity to compete' as the only claim to 'global standing' – and 'league tables and rankings . . . as global comparison indicators' (Bhattacharya 13) are naturally the instruments for calibrating the 'value' of the 'world-class'. The NEP 2020's anointing of 'Takshashila, Nalanda, Vallabhi, Vikramshila' as 'world-class institutions of ancient India' appropriates the 'world' in such a genetic claim to origins that we are finally made to believe that India was always on the market, and at the top of it. Alternatively put, India's auctioning of its institutions in a 'global tertiary education marketplace' goes back to ancient times; and if it could then rank as the 'best' in 'global standing', what is wrong with our current-day universities being pushed towards world-class ratings? I have analysed elsewhere, in some detail, how the World Bank and UNESCO's compound fictions of the 'world-class university' create the grounds for rating higher education institutions as investable assets for profits in the future – and how the 'fictitious capital' generated and circulated in the process make for the conditions of an unpayable debt (ibid. 12–18).

Seen against this backdrop, it is not surprising that soon after the University Grants Commission (UGC) – India's higher education regulator – released the conditions for 'recognition' and 'establishment' of 'World Class Institutions' in 2016, the Indian government announced the setting up of a non-banking finance company called the 'Higher Education Funding Agency' to sanction ten-year infrastructural loans to 'top institutions' (GoI 2017). The NEP 2020, by re-attaching the meaning of the 'world' to the race for the 'world-class', hurls the destiny of the Indian university towards the market – as a constant, even *sanatan* ('ancient and eternal'), force. Again, the implication is: if we, as a nation and our institutions, could host the 'world' by being hostage to the 'market' since our mythical beginnings, the fear of a free market of competitive bidding among 'ranked' and 'rated' institutions today must surely be unfounded. The UGC's most recent invitation to foreign universities for setting up offshore campuses in India is yet another step towards realising the meaning of the 'world'-as-market in the making of 'world class universities' of NEP-vintage.[4]

In a section on the 'internationalization' of higher education, the text of NEP 2020 carries over this refrain: 'India will be promoted as a global study destination providing premium education at affordable costs thereby helping to restore its role as a Vishwa Guru' (Section 12.8, 39). The campaign for the 'restoration' of ancient India as 'Vishwa Guru' – meaning the 'teacher of the world' – is the second tweaking of the *world-ness* of the university-idea, which references to a 'great Indian tradition' perform. Contra the world as a market for competition, the symbolism of the 'vishwa guru' interprets the 'world' through the superior self-imagination of a master (and mastery). If the 'world-class' is an index of the 'capacity to compete', the 'vishwa guru' is the announcement of always-already winning that competition. The latter imagines the

[4] Refer to the "UGC (Setting up and Operation of Campuses of Foreign Higher Educational Institutions in India) Regulations, 2023."

'world' as a supplicant for intellectual enlightenment – exactly miming the operations of colonial conquest and its conjoined histories of epistemological violence.

In sum, it turns out that the two registers of re-signifying the *world-ness* of the Indian university – in the 'world-class' and as the 'world's teacher' – are both tools of an ahistorical consciousness, parading as national destiny. One beckons the market, the other behaves like the master. And in this performative semiosis of history, the script is one: the self-bidding of false nationalist pride for a great Indian sale of the university.

References

Altekar, A.S. *Education in Ancient India.* Nand Kishore and Bros., 1944.

Apte, D.G. *Universities in Ancient India.* Maharaja Sayajirao University of Baroda, 1961.

Bhattacharya, Debaditya. "The University in History: From 'Idea' to Impossibility." *The Idea of the University: Histories and Contexts*, edited by Bhattacharya. Routledge, 2019.

Bose, Phanindra Nath. *Indian Teachers of Buddhist Universities.* Adyar, 1923.

DeGraff, Geoffrey, ed. and trans. *The Buddhist Monastic Code I: The Patimokkha Rules.* Metta Forest Monastery, 2013.

Devy, Ganesh N. "An Amnesiac Policy that Falls Flat on its Face: Ganesh N. Devy's Take on NEP 2020." *Chalk Circle*, vol. 1, no. 1, 2022, pp. 5–15.

Durkheim, Emile. *The Evolution of Educational Thought: Lectures on the Formation and Development of Secondary Education in France*, translated by Peter Collins. Routledge and Kegan Paul, 1977 [1938].

Dutt, Nalinaksha. *Early History of the Spread of Buddhism and the Buddhist Schools.* Luzac and Company, 1925.

Dutt, Sukumar. *Buddhist Monks and Monasteries in India.* George Allen & Unwin Limited, 1962.

Fa-hien. *The Travels of Fa-hsien (399–414 A.D.)*, translated by H. Giles. Cambridge, 1923.

Ghurye, K.G. *Preservation of Learned Tradition in India.* Popular Book Depot, 1950.

Government of India. "Higher Education Funding Agency (HEFA) Credit Policy Framework (F. No. 16-2/2017-TC)." Ministry of Human Resource Development, 2017.

Haskins, Charles Homer. *The Renaissance of the Twelfth Century.* Harvard UP, 1927.

I-Tsing. *A Record of the Buddhist Religion as Practised in India and the Malay Archipelago* (A.D. 671–695), translated by J. Takakusu. New Delhi, 1982.

Kane, P.V. *History of Dharmasastra: Ancient and Medieval Religious and Civil Law*, Volumes I–V. Bhandarkar Oriental Research Institute, 1930–1962.

Keay, F.E. *Ancient Indian Education: An Inquiry into Its Origin, Development and Ideals*. Oxford University Press, 1918.

———. *Indian Education in Ancient and Later Times: An Inquiry into Its Origin, Development and Ideals*. Oxford University Press, 1938.

Kimura, Ryukan. *A Historical Study of the Terms Hinayana and Mahayana and the Origin of Mahayana Buddhism*. University of Calcutta Press, 1927.

Kosambi, D.D. *Ancient India: A History of Its Culture and Civilization*. Pantheon, 1965.

Kuraishi, M.H. *A Short Guide to the Buddhist Remains Excavated at Nalanda*. Government of India Central Publications Branch, 1931.

Mahabharata, edited by Sukthankar et al. Poona, 1933–1966.

Manava-dharmasastra (Sacred Books of the East Series, vol. XXV), translated by Georg Buhler, edited by J. Jolly. Oxford University Press, 1887.

Marshall, John. *Taxila: An Illustrated Account of Archaeological Excavations, In Three Volumes*. Motilal Banarsidass, 1975.

Milindapanha (Sacred Books of the East Series, vol. XXXVI), translated by T.W. Rhys Davids, edited by V. Trenckner. Oxford University Press, 1894.

Misra, B.N. *Nalanda*. Buddhist World Press, 1998.

Mookerji, Radha Kumud. *Ancient Indian Education: Brahmanical and Buddhist*. Macmillan, 1947.

National Education Policy (NEP) 2020. Ministry of Human Resource Development, 2020.

Norman, K.R. *Pali Literature*. Wiesbaden, 1983.

Olivelle, Patrick. *The* Asrama *System: The History and Hermeneutics of a Religious Institution*. Oxford University Press, 1993.

"On Settlements." *Cullavagga* IV, translated by I.B. Horner. The Book of the Discipline (Vinaya Pitaka, Volume V). Luzac and Company Limited, 1963.

Page, J.A. "Nalanda." *Archaeological Survey of India Annual Reports*, 1921–28.

Pedersen, Olaf. *The First Universities: Studium Generale and the Origins of University Education in Europe*, translated by Richard North. Cambridge UP, 1997.

Raja, C. Kunhan. *Some Aspects of Education in Ancient India*. Adyar Library, 1950.

Ramayana, edited by G.H. Bhatt et al. Baroda, 1960–1975.

Rashdall, Hastings. *The Universities of Europe in the Middle Ages. Volume 1: Salerno–Bologna–Paris*. The Clarendon Press, 1895.

Salmi, Jamil. *The Challenge of Establishing World-Class Universities*. World Bank, 2009.

Sankalia, Hasmukh D. *The University of Nalanda*. B.G. Paul and Company, 1934.

Sastri, Hirananda. *Nalanda and Its Epigraphical Material*, Memoirs of the Archaeological Survey of India, no. 66, 1942.

Satapatha-brahmana, edited by A. Weber, translated by J. Eggeling. Varanasi, 1964.

Scharfe, Hartmut. *Education in Ancient India* (Volume Sixteen). Brill, 2002.

Singh, Upinder. *A History of Ancient and Early Medieval India: From the Stone Age to the 12th Century*. Pearson, 2016.

Somadeva. *Katha Sarit Sagara, or Ocean of the Streams of Story*, Volume I, translated by C.H. Tawney. Asiatic Society, 1880.

Spooner, D.B. "Nalanda." *Archaeological Survey of India Annual Reports (Eastern Circle)* I–II, 1915–19.

Stewart, Mary L. "Nalanda Mahavihara: A study of an Indian Pala Period Buddhist Site and British Historical Archaeology, 1861–1938." *BAR International Series* 529, 1989.

Taittiriya-brahmana, edited by Mahadeva Sastri, R. Shama Sastry, L. Srinivasacharya. Delhi, 1985

Taranatha. *History of Buddhism in India*, translated by Lama Chimpa and Alaka Chattopadhyaya, edited by Debiprasad Chattopadhyaya. Calcutta, 1970.

The Jataka, or Stories of the Buddha's Former Births, Volume I, translated by Robert Chalmers, edited by E.B. Cowell. Luzac and Company Limited, 1957.

The Jataka, or Stories of the Buddha's Former Births, Volume II, translated by W.H.D. Rouse, edited by E.B. Cowell. Luzac and Company Limited, 1957.

The Jataka, or Stories of the Buddha's Former Births, Volume III, translated by H.T. Francis, edited by E.B. Cowell. Luzac and Company Limited, 1957.

The Jataka, or Stories of the Buddha's Former Births, Volume IV, translated by W.H.D. Rouse, edited by E.B. Cowell. Luzac and Company Limited, 1957.

The Jataka, or Stories of the Buddha's Former Births, Volume V, translated by H.T. Francis, edited by E.B. Cowell. Motilal Banarsidass, 1994.

The Jataka, or Stories of the Buddha's Former Births, Volume VI, translated by E.B. Cowell and W.H.D. Rouse, edited by E.B. Cowell. Motilal Banarsidass, 1994.

The Jatakas: Birth Stories of the Bodhisatta, translated by Sarah Shaw. Penguin, 2006.

The Long Discourses of the Buddha: A Translation of the Digha Nikaya, translated by Maurice Walshe. Wisdom Publications, 1987.

The Middle Length Discourses of the Buddha: A New Translation of the Majjhima Nikaya, translated by Bhikkhu Nanamoli and Bhikkhu Bodhi. Buddhist Publication Society, 1995.

Tsang, Hiuen. *The Life of Hiuen-tsiang by the Shaman Hwui Li*, translated by Samuel Beal. Kegan Paul, Trench, Trubner & Company Limited, 1914.

University Grants Commission (Declaration of Government Educational Institutions as World Class Institutions) Guidelines and (World Class Institutions Deemed to Be Universities) Regulations. University Grants Commission, 2016.

"University Grants Commission (Setting up and Operation of Campuses of Foreign Higher Educational Institutions in India) Regulations, 2023." *The Gazette of India: Extraordinary* (Part III, Sec. 4), 7 Nov. 2023, https://www.ugc.gov.in/pdfnews/Setting%20up%20and%20Operation%20of%20Campuses%20of%20Foreign%20Higher%20Educational%20Institutions%20in%20India.pdf

Upasek, C.S. ed. *Nalanda: Past and Present*. Nava Nalanda Mahavihara, 1977.

Wittrock, Bjorn. 1993. "The Modern University: The Three Transformations." *The European and American University since 1800: Historical and Sociological Essays*, edited by Sheldon Rothblatt and Bjorn Wittrock. Cambridge UP, 1997, pp. 303–62.

Two

The Long Nineteenth Century: Caste and Collegiate Life in Colonial India

University as Community: A Promise or Threat?

I have argued in the previous chapter that what lent the university its 'idea' – or, in other words, its institutional character – was a certain *will to world-ness*, both in terms of who was taught and what was taught within it. The university, in its necessary openness to people from the world and knowledges of the world, was thus to be shaped as the corporative consciousness of a 'community'. But crucially, this was a community imagined in contradistinction to extant practices of sociality in caste, religion, ethnicity, provinciality and even the modern nation-state. It was this imaginative charter for the *being* of the university that disqualified, in our historical scrutiny, the ancient brahminical and Buddhist efforts at organising systems of learning from either a story of origins or the charge of precedence. This is how we began by debunking the myth of 'ancient Indian *universities*'.

What then accounts for the birth of an idea of *collegiate education* in India, and when exactly does this turn to a community (as corporation) of secular scholarship happen? Historical chronicles of the development of Indian education have typically situated this turn in the colonial measures introduced through the length of the nineteenth century – from an amendment in the East India Company Act of 1813, which stipulated the setting aside of public funds for the instruction of natives through institutional means of encouragement,[1] to the Indian Universities Act of 1904,

[1] Following Lord Minto's Minute of 1811, which lamented the 'progressive state of decay' that had overtaken educational efforts among native Indians (Sharp 19), there was a renewed interest in the East India Company's

which proposed to convert universities from mere examining bodies into residential teaching institutions (*IUA*, Section 3, 60). In the process, the story of India's waking into a university-*idea* is bundled in the form of a debate between the Anglicists and the Orientalists, revolving around what contents of knowledge were best suited to the intellectual needs of a colonised population. In the end, it is English-language education that decidedly emerges the winner – with Lord Bentinck's Resolution of 1835 (Sharp 130–31), Macaulay's *Minute* from the same year (ibid. 107–17) and the eventual establishment in 1857 of the first three English-language universities modelled on the University of London. We are made to believe that the colonial intention of creating a class of lower functionaries for the business of local administration, and the liberality of learning enabled by the teaching of European literature and science, are what effectively paved way for a secular educational system in India. This chapter would vehemently disagree with this narrative, long in circulation, by insisting that the secularity of outlook championed by English-language instruction was a carefully stitched-up veneer for protecting the feudality of social relations in caste. What an attribution of the history of Indian university-building to a colonial archive of legislation and policy does is that it distracts us from what I have elsewhere called a 'secular feudal complex of interests' (Bhattacharya 157) extending

representatives about means to address questions of intellectual-moral improvement. When the Company's charter came up for renewal in 1813, a new 'Section 43' was incorporated which provided for 'a sum not less than one lac of rupees in each year' for the education of 'natives' (22). This clause, as H. Sharp contends, was 'justly famous as containing the first legislative admission of the right of education in India to participate in the public revenues' (18) – and therefore, the first acknowledgment of the need for 'public colleges' as crucial to a large-scale educational reform-agenda in colonial India. The subsequent debates – often termed as the Anglicist-Orientalist controversy – devolved into questions about how this 'public collegiate' culture was to be achieved, whether through an encouragement of existing village schools and oriental seminaries or through the establishment of new institutions for English-language instruction.

across the teaching and learning of English in nineteenth-century India. It might serve us better instead to look for the *world-ness* of a university-idea, and India's passage into a secular collegiate order of learning, not in colonial bureaucratic reason but in the indigenous systems of vernacular schooling already in existence at the time and subsequently pushed out of relevance.

I will take as the site of my historical inquiry the case of Bengal, for more than the sake of simple convenience. From the establishment of the Hindu College in Calcutta in early 1817, as an effort to institutionalise English-language education for moral-practical dividends, to the Indian Universities Act (1904) immediately leading to the British administration's attempt at clipping the wings of the educated Bengali elite through the Partition of Bengal (1905) and the subsequent debate (1909–11) on shifting the administrative capital from Calcutta to Delhi, there is much to notice in this chronology of Bengal's growth and decline in significance. A careful reading holds up a mirror to the twinned fortunes of colonial educational reform and the emergence of the figure of the Bengali *bhadralok*,[2] as containing all the symptoms of an imported modernity. Let me list out these intersections, one by one. First, the status of the Province of Bengal as containing the administrative capital of the colonial state (in Calcutta) created an economy of professional aspirations that could only be breached through an initiation into the English language. Second, the history of land ownership in Bengal had already positioned its elite upper-caste populations in a unique relationship with the *mofussil* towns[3] and rural estates. Through tenured land-contracts and the rent returns on them, the absentee land-owner did not have to

[2] The word '*bhadralok*' – literally translating into a 'virtuous-civil man' – has entered the vocabulary of Indian social sciences, as distilling the civilisational benefits of colonial 'mimicry'.

[3] The term '*mofussil*' (alternatively, '*mufassil*') refers to the suburban outskirts of the administrative limits of a colonial city. Historically, the imagination of the '*mofussil*' – counterposed to the immediate benefits of colonial modernity – has also inhabited the outsides of the civilisational project.

directly engage in agriculture and yet could channel agricultural profits into a training for respectable urban employment or petty bureaucratic careers.[4] Add to this the interest-income on debts that tied the landless farm workers for life to these estates, run by proxy from the city. Third, the strategic coincidence of these historical circumstances conferred a specific currency of moral distinction on the caste elite of Bengal – that goes by the name of the *bhadralok* (or, the 'virtuous civil man'). Put differently, and perhaps more accurately, the *bhadralok* was he who could mask the hereditary entitlements of caste privilege with the humanist acquisition of a secular intelligence and a life of 'respectable' city-professions.[5] To that extent, *bhadrata* (virtuous civility) became the precise postulation of a 'secular feudal complex of interests' that the history of English education in India was enjoined to. It is therefore not difficult to understand why I choose to turn my focus to colonial Bengal as the representative allegory of the intended (but often concealed) effects of nineteenth-century educational policy making. In the course of my argument, I will refer to the conjoined fortunes of Bihar among the Lower Provinces, as well as the distinctly different trajectories of the North West Provinces. There will also be occasional references to the Bombay and Madras Presidencies, as comparable instances for examining the progress of education in colonial India.

4 For a deeper analysis of how colonial modernity interacted with histories of land ownership and agrarian arrangements in Bengal, see Partha Chatterjee, *The Present History of West Bengal.*

5 For an account of the historical mutations that produced the figure of the '*bhadralok*' vis-à-vis the theoretical postulation of the 'colonial modern', refer to J.H. Broomfield, *Elite Conflict in a Plural Society*; Partha Chatterjee, "The Nationalist Elite"; Rajat Kanta Ray, *Social Conflict and Political Unrest in Bengal*; Tapan Raychaudhuri, *Europe Reconsidered*; S.N. Mukherjee, *Calcutta: Essays in Urban History*; Mrinalini Sinha, *Colonial Masculinity*; Ashis Nandy, *The Intimate Enemy*; Parimal Ghosh, *What Happened to the Bhadralok*; Debraj Bhattacharya ed. *Of Matters Modern*; Swati Chattopadhyay, *Representing Calcutta.*

What to Teach, and Where: The Distractions of Colonial Reform

The 1813 Charter of the East India Company, in one of its most widely-debated sections, ordained that the colonial government was committed to providing public funds for 'the revival and improvement of literature, and the encouragement of the learned natives of India, and for the introduction and promotion of a knowledge of the sciences among the inhabitants of the British territories in India' (Sharp 22). Understood as espousing a definite middle-ground between the 'revival' of learned classical traditions and an 'introduction' of European knowledges, this Act started off a flurry of often-acrimonious bargains between advocates of Orientalist and Anglicist education. The Company's Court of Directors jumped in the fray with a letter to the Governor General in Council of Fort William in Bengal, dated 3 June 1814, and urging a policy of cautious non-intervention on the question of native education:

> Neither of these [two] objects is, we apprehend, to be obtained through the medium of public colleges, if established under the rules, and upon a plan similar to those that have been founded at our universities, because the natives of caste and of reputation will not submit to the subordination and discipline of a college; and we doubt whether it would be practicable to devise any specific plan which would promise the successful accomplishment of the objects under consideration. (ibid.)

Collegiate life, it is feared by the directors, will be prevented by the hierarchies of caste ordination and reputation prevalent among the natives. The secularity of a public college, if taken in its true spirit by the Company's Act, is assumed to be in fundamental opposition to the feudality of social life in India – and therefore, the question of education would be better left to the 'usages and habits of the natives' (ibid. 23). The same letter, a few paragraphs further, goes on to exuberantly commend a 'mode of instruction' provided by village teachers, who double up as 'public servants of the community' (ibid.). It is to the operation of these local schools, particularly suited to instruction in the vernacular language, that the 'general intelligence of the natives as scribes and accountants' is attributed (ibid.). So, clearly, the preliminary scepticism of the Company directors and the presumed indisposition of natives towards collegiate instruction as well as secular subjects of learning are both belied by the 'highest tribute of praise' reserved for the vernacular schools in the country (ibid.). The latter is also hailed as the example that 'Reverend Dr. Bell, formerly chaplain at Madras' had subsequently adopted in England with great hope of felicity and success.

The Bell method, alternatively known as the Madras system of monitorial instruction, consisted in distributing the work of teaching among different grades of students, alongside the masters. With the teachers of village schools being recruited from the local population, there was always a dearth of adequately qualified persons fit to take up such positions. Furthermore, the poor rates and informal modes of payment to the teachers meant that most of those entrusted with the intensive work of instruction in reading, writing and arithmetic had, in addition to a bare minimum of competence, the burden of very difficult financial circumstances. Supplementing their income through other sources of support and means of employment was a dire necessity for these teachers; and therefore, having the most advanced students in the class supervise the incremental process of education in their not-so-advanced compatriots turned out to be a very effective way of dealing with the challenges of the local village situation (Bell 1807; 1808; 1823). The form of this schooling was largely inspired by self-sufficient village communities in early-nineteenth-century India, where everything – from the master's school-house to his subsistence and the learning material in use – was provided for by the immediate population. In fact, the increasing popularity of the village vernacular school made it the preferred recourse for emulation by private colonial initiative in the field of education. As Reverend J. Long documents in his "Brief View of the Past and Present State of Vernacular Education in Bengal":

> Mr. Ellerton at Malda established some Vernacular Schools in the beginning of this [nineteenth] century, and in the leisure of his Factory composed various Bengali books for the use of his scholars. In 1814, Mr. May, a Missionary, began his first Vernacular School in the Dutch Fort of Chinsura. In June 1815 he had 16 schools and 951 pupils, which soon increased to twenty-six schools, besides some ten others six miles below Chinsura, visited by him and his assistants sixty times every three months. In 1815 Lord Hastings made a monthly grant of Rupees 600 to the schools, and stated in a minute on the Schools, "the humble, but valuable, class of village schoolmasters claim the first place in this discussion." In 1816 there were 2,136 pupils, and a school for instructing teachers was commenced. In 1818 there were thirty-six schools and 3,000 pupils – but Mr. May was cut off by death, and Mr. Pearson then took charge. Mr. May's labors excited such interest, that after his death money arrived in Bengal from friends in America for the support of his schools. (1)

The establishment of the Calcutta School Society in 1818, owing to the impassioned efforts of David Hare and William Carey, was geared towards two ends: the improvement and superintendence of existing vernacular schools in the Provinces under Fort William, as well as the setting up of a few new model schools with the purpose of training teachers who could then resume the work of superior instruction in the districts. By 1821, the School Society network extended as far as supervising 115 vernacular schools with 3828 students under their tutelage (ibid. 8). A monthly grant of 500 Rupees was allocated to the Society by the government, which continued to sponsor the costs of sending thirty scholars trained in the vernacular elementary schools to Hindu College. Students from all castes were allowed into the School Society institutions, following the example of the native village schools – through which, as Marshman noted, 'a peasant, or an artificer, thus rendered capable of writing as well as reading his own language with propriety, and made acquainted with the principles of arithmetic, would be less liable to become a prey to fraud among his countrymen, and far better able to claim for himself... protection from oppression' (ibid. 5). By 1833, the School Society had however fallen on bad times, with its finances drying up and the burgeoning desire for English education among the native elites working to the detriment of the cause of vernacular schooling.

Language and Pathologies of Social Desire

That the dissemination of and desire for English education among the 'higher classes of Natives under the Presidency of Bengal' had gathered exemplary force is already evident in 1830, from the way the Company's Court of Directors set it up in polemical opposition to the Madras government's contrary attention to native schools and the preparation of vernacular textbooks. In a letter despatch to the Governor in Council of Fort St. George of Madras, the Directors vehemently insist:

> The improvements in education, however, which most effectually contribute to elevate the moral and intellectual condition of a people, are those which concern the education of the higher classes; of the persons possessing leisure, and natural influence over the minds of their countrymen. By raising the standard of instruction among these classes, you would eventually produce a much greater and beneficial change in the ideas and feelings of the community than you can hope to produce by acting directly on the more numerous class. (Zastoupil and Moir 126)

By early 1835, this design of the colonial government had become a repeated refrain in the deliberations and official correspondence made by the General Committee of Public Instruction (GCPI) – but not without active support and abetment from 'the Hindoos of Calcutta, the Sirkars and their connexions and the descendants and relations of the Sirkars of former days, those who have risen through their connexion with the English and with public offices, men who hold or seek employments in which a knowledge of English is a necessary qualification' ("Note by H.T. Prinsep to the Government of India", Zastoupil and Moir 182). What followed was the Resolution passed by the Governor General of India, Lord Bentinck, on 7 March 1835, mandating that 'all the funds appropriated for the purpose of education would be best employed on English education alone' (Zastoupil and Moir 195). Less than two months prior to this notification, and just one day before the Governor General received 'the two letters from the Secretary to the Committee of Public Instruction dated the 21st and 22nd January' (ibid. 196) – which he cites in his Resolution as the immediate grounds for the legislative order – there was some other correspondence sent from his own office. At this point in the chapter, it might be useful to shift focus to this other development and track the story that it tells.

As indicated, on 20 January 1835, Bentinck appointed a certain Mr William Adam on a salary of Rupees 1000, to enquire into the 'actual state of Native education, that is, of that which is carried on . . . entirely under Native management' (Long 13). Quite in opposition to what had already become known as the official scheme of the government in 'winning the desired confidence of the enlightened classes of the Indian public' (Zastoupil and Moir 150), Bentinck's 20 January *Minute* seemed curiously to defer to 'the establishment of education upon the largest and most useful basis [as has] become the object of universal solicitude' (Long 10). The officer he deputes for the purpose of this investigation had spent seventeen long years in residence in India, was distinguished for 'his knowledge of the languages, and his habits of intercourse with the Natives' (ibid. 13), and had lately been made Editor of the *India Gazette*.

What William Adam reported in the next three years – and through the minute insights afforded by fifteen to sixteen months of travelling (1836–37) across the several districts of Bengal and Bihar – is a monumental achievement. His three *Reports* remain the most punctilious testament of, and the firmest edifice on which, the strength and spread of indigenous systems of schooling may be confirmed. There has not been any other document that plumbs the expanse of field and the wealth of detail which Adam's *Reports* bring to bear upon our knowledge of the native village-schools – silently carrying the charge of mass education in the districts, beyond public glare or government support.

The Indigenous Vernacular: Adam's Caste Census

The first *Report*, already drafted and submitted within days of his appointment to the task, limits itself to a survey of the state of education in Bengal – as apparent from reports commissioned by the colonial government, the GCPI or archives of related institutional records. Registering the numerical vastness and density of the network of elementary schools in Bengal's villages, all of which were opened and supported by local inhabitants, Adam hazards a rough calculation:

> [T]here are 100,000 such schools in Bengal and Behar, and assuming the population of those two Provinces to be 40,000,000, there would be a village school for every 400 persons.... Taking, therefore, eleven-thirtieths of the above-mentioned 400 persons, and three-sevenths of the result, it will follow that in Bengal and Behar there is on an average a village school for every sixty-three children of the school-going age. These children, however, include girls as well as boys, and as there are no indigenous girls' schools, if we take the male and female children to be in equal or nearly equal proportions, there will appear to be *an indigenous elementary school for every thirty-one or thirty-two boys.* (Long 18–19, emphasis mine)

Adam's second *Report*, submitted in the following year, demonstrated great depth in laying out the state of native schooling systems within the district of Rajshahi. However, it was the third and final of his *Reports* that made the most lasting contribution to the avowed purpose of the exercise, in that it ethnographically documented the situation of these schools through direct references to field visits and first-person records of observation. Following his laborious encounters with school teachers and students (and often with the aid of assistants deputed to different *thanas*), Adam compiled the mass of data collected from three districts of Bengal and two of Bihar into the "Third Report on the State of Education in Bengal, including Some Account of the State of Education in Behar" in 1838. He surveyed both Oriental schools (Sanskrit, Persian and Arabic) as well as vernacular schools (mostly, Bengali and Hindi with some reliance on Oriya in specific instances) in the city and district of Moorshedabad, alongside the districts of

Beerbhoom, Burdwan, South Bihar and Tirhoot. Some startling revelations are made, particularly in the case of the vernacular schools in Bengal – in terms of the number of schools in each *thana*, the caste backgrounds of both teachers and students, the sources and means of material or infrastructural support, the average income of teachers, the mean age of admission and school-leaving, the rough duration of study and the proportions of scholars graduating to the final stages of study. Let me now devote my critical labours to placing some of this statistical mass in perspective.

In the twenty *thanas* comprising the city and district of Moorshedabad, Adam notes the presence of some 67 one-teacher vernacular schools conducting instruction in the Bengali and Hindi languages. The 67 teachers in these schools included two from the Sunri caste, and even one Chandal pundit. Both of these castes were, by Vedic Hindu diktat and the social proscription of caste-labour, otherwise forbidden from an indulgence in the life of the mind. Furthermore, there happened to be a Bengali school run by a Muslim teacher in the district. Adam clarifies:

> Parents of good caste do not hesitate to send their children to schools conducted by teachers of an inferior caste and even of a different religion. For instance, the Musalman teacher above-mentioned have [sic.] Hindus of good caste among his scholars, and this is equally true of the Chandal and other low-caste teachers enumerated. (Long 158–59)

Some of these teachers offered their lessons in the schools for free, while others barely managed to secure subsistence wages from the voluntary and uncoerced contributions of students in the form of fees or weekly doles of uncooked rice and farm produce or annual gifts during the festive season. In several cases, the teachers themselves were so poor that they had to look for alternative means of fixed employment as weavers or neighbourhood retailers. Despite struggling against such trying circumstances, 'these instances of unostentatious benevolence in the humblest ranks of native society' (159) were what marked the communitarian spirit of the village vernacular schools. The same feeling of mutuality could be noticed in the provisioning of physical infrastructures for the school-house – where, in most cases, the teacher himself would build it at his own cost, while being supplemented by some minimal subscription from the locals and the labour of his potential students.

The average age of attending students at the time of Adam's visit was about 10 years, while most parents seeking the benefits of education for their sons would send them at around six years of age and allow them to continue until they were sixteen or seventeen. Looking at the caste composition of students in the Moorshedabad schools, one will be surprised to note that there were 181 brahmins co-educated in physical proximity with 39 Sunris, 24 Kurmis, 19 Goalas, 16 Malas, 15 Napits, 13 Sutars, 9 Kamars, 4 Malis and Chandals each, 2 each of Kahars, Jalias, Laharis and Bagdis, and one each from the Dhoba, Kairi and Muchi castes – all of these belonging to social groups outside of the dominant Hindu *chaturvarna* system.[6] While all students of all castes received the same practical instruction – reading, writing and a combination of agricultural and commercial accounting, with an occasional inclusion of printed school-texts or Chanakya's verses – almost half of the total attendance did graduate to the final stage of study (which involved writing on paper, as opposed to palm or plantain-leaves) and must have therefore continued in school for close to ten years of their lives.

When plotted against population census data – which too is provided by Adam's survey, for one *thana* in each district, as an index of the exact percolation of the schooling systems under analysis – some more astounding aspects come into view. Taking the example of only Daulatbazar *thana* in the district of Moorshedabad, it appears that about 370 students of a range

[6] Those outside the *chaturvarna* (four-fold caste grouping) system would refer to the *panchamas* (the fifth caste group) or the *atishudras* – later severally termed as the Dalits, untouchables, depressed classes or the scheduled castes. The *panchamas* are, in this theological sense, outside the caste system altogether (that is, outcastes) and therefore the lowest social grouping according to Vedic Hindu precepts.

of high and low castes are in attendance in its 23 schools. This amounts to 5.4 per cent of the total male population of school-going age (five to fourteen years), even though there were about 21 in every 100 men who could potentially be brought within the ambit of school education. While, on the face of it, these figures would seem to leave much to be desired, the fact that nearly one-third of the actually-enrolled fraction were non-upper caste and Dalit-*bahujan* students is indeed a marvellous secret of the system in place.

In the 412 vernacular schools of Beerbhoom district, though the majority of teachers hailed from the caste Hindu communities (especially Kayasthas), there was a substantial number of Goala, Sunri, Napit, Dhoba, Kalu, Mala and Chandal teachers offering their services. At least eleven of these teachers did not charge a fee, of whom one had only taken in the sons of the working poor. The average age of students was the same as in Moorshedabad, while the adivasi populations of Beerbhoom had gained rights of access to intellectual training even outside of missionary initiative in these vernacular schools: 'Of the whole number of scholars, 3 are Dhangars, a tribe of Coles; 3 are Sonthals, another forest tribe' (Long 165). The Hindu student-force included, alongside 1853 brahmins, 560 Goalas, 258 Kalus, 164 Sunris, 79 Napits, 50 Sutars, 28 Dhobas, 23 Doms, 14 Bagdis, 12 Mals, and less than ten each from Lahari, Mali, Muchi, Dhanuk, Bauri, Duliya, Byadh and Chandal castes. Of these, almost one-third of the total number was on the verge of completing their instruction and therefore would have had a decade of schooling to support their professional prospects. Taking Nanglia *thana* as its census sample, Adam's data helps us ascertain enrolment rates in the district – which was about 8.3 per cent of the existing male children between five and fourteen years of age. Juxtaposing this against 23.4 per cent of the total male population which was fit to avail the benefits of school education, it seems laudatory that nearly two-thirds of the actual enrolments had successfully battled the stigma of non-upper-caste lineage.

The district of Burdwan presented the most promising case, with its largest coverage of 629 Bengali vernacular schools. Focusing on Culna *thana* as a sample, 13.5 per cent of appropriately aged male children were in attendance at one or the other of these schools – demonstrating the highest rate of school admissions for potential beneficiaries in the population. Of the Hindu teachers associated with the schools, there were at least four from the Chandal caste. Those from Napit, Goala, Bagdi, Naga, Dhoba, Kalu and Sunri communities had also made inroads into the teaching workforce. Two instructors were even suffering from leprosy – a disease which rural folklore had long mired in superstitious injunctions and ordained as resulting from a curse of the gods. One of the Chandal teachers and a Muslim *peer* shunned the practice of charging fees for their profession. Of the 12,408 Hindu students in attendance at the vernacular institutions, more than half came from non-upper-caste backgrounds, registering substantial numbers of admission from the Goala, Kamar, Kalu, Napit, Sunri, Bagdi, Sutar, Dom, Chandal, Mali, Dhoba, Muchi, Kurmi, Tior, Garar and Mal communities. In recounting the caste affiliations of scholars, Adam maintains with amazement:

> The number of scholars of low caste is so considerable that, without explanation, it might be supposed that they were chiefly found in the Missionary schools which are more numerous in this district than in any other I have visited, and which, of course, do not recognize distinctions of caste. The fact, however, is otherwise, for the number of scholars belonging to sixteen of the lowest castes amounts to 760, of whom only 86 are found in Missionary schools, and the remaining number in native schools. (170)

Again, nearly half of the students in Burdwan's Bengali schools had graduated to the final two stages, and were therefore under tutelage for six to eleven years by then.

Moving to the province of Bihar, the numbers dwindle in relative proportions – though South Bihar exhibits far greater social acceptance for and access to native schooling in Hindi than the district of Tirhoot. The latter, with its 80 vernacular schools spread across sixteen *thanas* and taking Bhawara *thana* as a representative field-site, had an average enrolment of only 0.4 per cent among males of school-going age. But, what prevents such a miniscule fraction from fading into insignificance, and instead spells hope, is the fact that even a less than one per cent schooling ratio features the maximum number of enrolments from the Sunri caste. In fact, the Sunris here are equal to the combined strength of brahmins and Kayasthas enrolled in the schools. The other lower castes – namely, Luniar, Goala, Dhanuk, Napit, Lahari, Sutar – are similarly represented and form part of a non-upper-caste majority in terms of student demography.

Orientalist Education

Having documented the impact of the vernacular schools in Bengal and Bihar on rural economic relations and Hindu ritual practices of social organisation, Adam's third *Report* turns to the Sanskrit schools to show quite a contrary situation. These native Oriental schools teaching Sanskrit grammar, law, logic and Hindu mythology had only brahmin teachers and students (with a very few exceptions from the Vaidya or medical caste) in all five districts under scrutiny. The case with the Arabic schools was much the same, with an overwhelming majority of Muslims engaged in the giving and receiving of instruction. The Persian schools however registered a departure, by enrolling a far more diverse constituency of students ranging across religious faiths and even admitting the Hindu outcastes in significant numbers. The reasons for the relative popularity and accessibility of Persian schools were twofold: first, the Persian language almost worked as a Muslim vernacular in certain areas, in the absence of any kind of extant schooling in the Urdu language; and second, Persian continued to be the language of local administrative records for the most part and some knowledge of it was essential for honing professional ambition.

Another important detail that emerges from a comparison of the monthly incomes of teachers in the vernacular schools as opposed to those in the Oriental schools (especially the Sanskrit *tols*), is the gross disproportionality ranged against the interests of the former. While an instructor in a vernacular school, having compounded his income from all sources and in all kinds, earned between one and four rupees per month, the *gurus* of the Sanskrit *tols* received nearly four to ten times of that sum and often with additional endowments from native *zamindars* or pensions from the colonial government.

The careful partitioning of the 'great Indian education debate' into a controversy between Orientalists and Anglicists – while completely side-stepping the vernacular means by which the bulk of instructional delivery was happening at the time – would appear a calculated move. It was about making the question of education begin from a premise of class and caste entitlement – which both factions in the debate were already the inheritors of. Demonstrably, if there was indeed a real antagonist to the social filtering effects of Oriental learning, it was to be found within vernacular instructional models and not in the fabled loaning of colonial knowledge or pedagogy. In the false binarism erected around Orientalist-Anglicist education, or at least the discourse of it found in colonial archives, lay an instrument for extending class/caste apartheid.

William Adam was alive to the potential of the vernacular schools, both managed and financed by local native populations who were for the largest part extremely poor. And yet, the latter not only sought social mobility by partaking of such a system of instruction, but also paid petty subscriptions from their already-meagre resources to keep that dream alive. A form of collegiate life was already springing up in these indigenous schools for secular pursuits, in stark contrast to the caste-rules of social association and intercourse. The seeds of the 'Indian university' were sown in these villages and districts, insofar as a *will to world-ness* was carefully reared in a practice of vernacular modernity within schools. Adam commented early on, in cataloguing the numbers of 'outcaste' scholars in Moorshedabad schools:

> This enumeration shows in what classes of Hindu society vernacular instruction is chiefly found, and in what classes it becomes increasingly

> deficient. It would be a mistake, however, to suppose that the latter, as compared with the former, are losing ground. The fact is quite the reverse: they are gaining ground, and are almost imperceptibly acquiring a sense of the value even of that humble instruction which is within their reach, but from which, by the customs of society, they were formerly almost wholly debarred. The time is not distant when it would have been considered contrary to all the maxims of Hindu civilization that individuals of the Mala, Chandal, Kahar, Jalia, Lahari, Bagdhi, Dhoba, and Muchi castes should learn to read, write, and keep accounts; and if some aged and venerable brahman who has passed his life removed from European contamination were told that these low castes are now raising their aspirations so high, he would deplore it as one of the many proofs of the gross and increasing degeneracy of the age. The encroachment of these castes on the outskirts of learning is a spontaneous movement in native society. . . . (161–62)

We had already seen that, by 1833, the sudden and premature closure of the Calcutta School Society and several of its vernacular schools (among them, the most acclaimed in Arpuly) signalled concerted efforts at a planned sabotaging of this 'spontaneous movement' in Hindu society. Despite clear signs of an ascendant interest in English-language instruction by impoverishing the vernaculars, and the colonial state's backing of it through the GCPI's determined stakes and Bentinck's 1835 Resolution, Adam's ethnographic excursions through 1836–37 bear testimony to the resilient potential contained within the system of indigenous vernacular schooling. That pedagogic practices in the districts of Bengal stood resolutely opposed to the growing climate of disapprobation (and misapprehensions) surrounding the benefits of vernacular schooling comes through in the extensive evidence of popular subscription that was still current in the day. In fact, having witnessed the degrees of success and extent of vindication enjoyed by these village schools, Adam was convinced of the misdirected nature of colonial education policy under Bentinck. He pointed out the fallacy in such a mediated estimate of native interests and ill-informed understanding of general welfare, in the final *Report* of 1838:

> . . . the desire to know English is found in fewer instances in the Behar than in the Bengal districts. In both it is chiefly learned and wealthy men that have sought it for themselves or their children; and, with a view to purposes of practical utility, it is to those classes in the present condition of native society that it is most suitable. (219)

Following from 'impressions which fact and observation may produce' (218), Adam persuasively recommended that public finances at the disposal of the British government, and those earmarked for spending on native education, might only be most judiciously employed in supporting and improving the existing systems of vernacular schooling in the country's districts and *pergunnahs*. He commended the strides made on that front by the then-extinct School Society, and held that a similarly resuscitated agenda was the most urgent call of the contemporary moment. Not surprisingly, Lord Auckland – the then Governor General and successor to Bentinck – issued a *Minute* on 24 November 1839, in responding to the 'dissatisfaction occasioned by Lord Bentinck's Resolution, and by the uncompromising spirit in which it was carried into effect by the Educational Committee' (Kerr 10). Here, while attempting a course-correction through renewed emphasis on combined instruction in English and the vernaculars, Auckland nonetheless clears any misgivings about the intended beneficiaries of colonial policy-reform:

> The Governor General's views, so far as they are favourable to combined instruction in English and vernacular, will not be fairly understood, unless it be borne in mind that the object kept chiefly in view was, in the first instance, the extension of education among the upper and middle classes of the people. His Lordship was prepared to admit that he saw little prospect of education in this form extending beyond a small portion of the population, the greater part of whom must be content with a less complete education through the medium of their own language. (ibid. 13)

Notwithstanding the dubbing of vernacular schooling as a 'less complete education' – which, on the contrary, had proved inordinately successful in preparing the largest numbers for a fortune otherwise forbidden to them by caste-precept – Auckland's

Minute drove home the truth that colonial administrative efforts were unpretentiously tailored 'to win the confidence of the educated and influential classes of the people' ("Letter to H.T. Prinsep", Zastoupil and Moir 149). The object was clear: to secure the legitimacy of foreign rule by making the native elite serve as conduits of class hegemony. Adam's painstaking documentary labour was to remain a scholarly relic commissioned by colonial magnanimity and consigned to useless co-optation within an order of bureaucratic-statistical record-keeping.

Bhadralok Agendas

Through the 1840s and 50s, Bengal's thriving village schooling systems were gradually impoverished and allowed to languish away into insignificance, while in the North West Provinces a radically different policy saw the government actively taking on the management and financial onus of vernacular schools and shutting down the minor English schools. This happened owing to a jurisdictional separation of education in the north from under the control of Bengal, and enlisting the former to the charge of the Lieutenant Governor of Agra, Mr Thomason, in 1843. In a letter to the government of Bengal, Thomason impressed upon the need to distinguish between the demographies and cultural life-worlds of the two provinces – maintaining that the desire for English education cannot be assumed as a universal charge, even among the classes of landed gentry (Long 13–14). Furthermore, he consulted objective assessments of the educational infrastructures current in the region in order to conclude that the self-supported 'native schools' in Agra district were not frequented by more than five per cent of the teachable male populations from among the highest classes. Therefore, it was incumbent on the government – in recognition of the potentially wider benefits of vernacular education and the limited reach of the native schools in that regard – to open and sponsor more and more institutions for vernacular instruction among those 'from a lower rank, and from the hangers-on of our public offices, the inferior shop-keepers, the children of our *burkendaz*, and of individuals with whom the respectable classes would not desire their children to associate' (Kerr 151). Accordingly, a system of village schooling was instituted in the north western parts in 1852, called *hulkabandi*, which aimed at providing massive access to government initiatives in vernacular education through lateral geographical expanse and the imposition of an educational cess towards that end.

The Wood's Despatch of 1854 also claimed to have fulfilled the founding commitment of the colonial administration to providing education for the wealthy, and now urged a channelling of public resources into educational provisioning for those who had thus far been left out ("Lord Stanley's Despatch of 1859", Long 18). To that extent, it envisioned the setting up of English-model universities in the three Presidencies as a nudge to those privileged enough to seek higher education at their own cost; while a necessary push for vernacular schools could now reorient colonial policy towards general welfare through mass education. But, nothing changed in Bengal. The once-vibrant village schooling arrangements continued on their decline, until – as Reverend Long cites in his prefatory essay to a collection of Adam's *Reports* – the Inspector of Schools in 1861 observed that 'in the richest and most populous portion of Bengal, there are about three persons in every hundred under education' (12). From having a vernacular village school for every thirty-two boys in 1835 to recording a shameful three per cent enrolment in all schools combined in the early 1860s, education in Bengal had undergone a sea-change in a little over two decades.

The alarming starkness of the transformation is held out in fact and statistic, by an exhaustive missive sent by the Secretary to the Government of India, Mr Bayley, in April 1868 (and quoted by Long):

> While there is no Province in India which can bear comparison with Bengal in respect of the progress made in the higher branches of education by a considerable section of the upper classes of the community, the Governor General in Council has long observed with regret the almost total absence of proper means of provision for the elementary education of the agricultural classes which form the great mass of the population. The contrast in this respect between

> Bengal and other Provinces is striking. In Bengal, with a population that probably exceeds forty millions, the total number of pupils in the lower class Government and Aided Schools was, in 1866–67, only 39,104. In the North-Western Provinces, with a population under thirty millions, the number of pupils in Schools of a similar class was 125,394. In Bombay, with a population of sixteen millions, the number was 79,189. In the Punjab, with a population of fifteen millions, it was 62,355. In the Central Provinces, with a population of eight-and-a-half millions, it was 22,600. Nor does there seem to be any probability that these proportions will hereafter become more favourable to Bengal, although the measures that have lately been taken for the encouragement of vernacular education by means of the system of training Masters in the so-called indigenous Schools have been more or less successful. The means of affording elementary instruction appear to be increasing with far greater rapidity in other Provinces. (25)

Bayley prolongs his lament by adding to it the complaint that a people which once supported thousands of vernacular schools by voluntary subscriptions of land, labour and money must now be so ill-supported by the aversion of its land-owning classes towards the levying of a government cess for public utilities like education. In contrast, he recounts that in all the other Provinces of the country, the *zamindars* – who, in Bengal, happened to be the greatest beneficiaries of the Permanent Settlement Act of 1793 – paid between one to more than three per cent of an educational cess in proportion to their land-holdings.

But the Bengali *zamindars* and Hindu caste-elite had, for half a century by then, invested their fortunes in and pinned their hopes on advanced English-language instruction in higher colleges and seminaries – with more restricted rights of entry. The Hindu College, willed into existence in early 1817, was a pioneer and prime example of such an economy for redistributing intellectual goods. In the rest of this chapter, I will detail how this was achieved and what effects it had on the encounter between systems of knowledge and the question of caste – something that had worried the proponents of Vedic Hindu doctrine since the historical vintage of Takshashila.

Anglicist Education, Caste Honour and Hindu College

In a series of meetings through 1816, a plan for the establishment of Hindu College was drawn up - for the 'tuition of the sons of respectable Hindoos, in the English and Indian languages; and in the literature and science of Europe' ("Rules of the Hindu College" 2) - and a committee of native managers was formed for the nascent institution. Rammohun Roy, by then a vocal seeker of Hindu religious reform through legislative controls, was invited at these meetings by David Hare; but he thought it better to abstain for fear of offending, by association, those 'respectable Hindoos' whose caste-respect consisted in their opposition to Roy's reform-attempts (Mitra 122). Soon after, in 1823, on learning of the government's intention to set up a Sanskrit College in Calcutta, Roy petitioned to Lord Amherst seeking instead a collaboration between the colonial government and native elites for the institutionalisation of European knowledges (Zastoupil and Moir 110–14). It was around the same time that the native management of Hindu College ran into financial trouble, and had to seek support from the British administration (and its General Committee of Public Instruction) for funds to ensure survival (Mitra 124). The latter happily agreed to share a part of the college's establishment costs and annual expenditure, but in the process bargained for the supervisory entry of government nominees on the managing committee (*Presidency College Register* 6–7). Of this development, the Secretary of GCPI, J. Sutherland, later remarked with self-congratulatory glee in a letter to H.T. Prinsep - as demonstration of how sensitive colonial policy has been to the cause of defending the caste-interests of a native Hindu population:

> The Committee are proud to say that they have hitherto been entirely successful in winning the desired confidence of the enlightened classes of the Indian public. Of this they have many proofs and there is none more conclusive or more satisfactory than the manner in which the Hindoo College of Calcutta was placed by the spontaneous act of its managers under their fostering care and supervision. If the Committee have accomplished this great object there can be no doubt that their

> success is owing not only to their having refrained from measures of a religious tendency but likewise to the jealous watchfulness with which they have checked in others and themselves avoided the offensive obtrusion of schemes and notions of pure European growth opposed to and uncalled for by the state of feeling amongst the people they have had to deal with. (Zastoupil and Moir 150)

In the late 1820s and early 30s, when the young Derozians – schooled in the philosophies of Hume and Bentham (Coomer 41) – started calling into question the regressive and exclusionary caste-practices in Bengali society, all hell broke loose. This was a maiden instance of public outrage caused by students of a 'liberal' Hindu College education, and it hardly found a parallel in the college's history through a more heightened anti-colonial nationalism of the late nineteenth century. I will return to this point later, but it definitely does not need reiterating that the popular alarm against Derozio and the Young Bengalees stemmed from their being a cautionary tale for those caste Hindu adults who were trained into Western thought (Chakraborty 47–56; Mitra 133–34). That was exactly the tenor in which popular Bengali newspapers (like *Samachar Chandrika*) held up the 'offenders' as targets of moral censure (Banerjea I & II). In fact, the resolution passed by the managing committee, dismissing Derozio from employment on 23 April 1831, echoes the same 'state of public feeling among the Hindu community of Calcutta' (*The Calcutta Christian Observer* 126). It alluded to the class pride and religious anxieties of the founding patrons, chief among them being Radhakanta Deb and Ram Comul Sen – both of whom were leaders of conservative Hindu associations like the Dharma Sabha and Gaudiya Sabha respectively (*Presidency College Magazine* vol. 41). Later historians have contended that the charges brought against Derozio, of hurting Hindu caste-sentiment, was actually a cover for something else. The withdrawals of students from Hindu College in 1830–31 was, on the face of it, not as alarming as it was made out to be – and there was no deep damage portended by the Derozians' activity in specific. There was already a slump in enrolments in Hindu College around that time, owing to the large-scale economic duress caused by the failure of the Company's richest trading and banking agency, Palmer and Company (Wilson's "Report"; *Accounts Book*). The personal losses sustained by many among the native gentry, due to a general climate of financial uncertainty, had some corresponding impact on college admissions and drop-outs. The injured class-position of the Bengali intelligentsia could be safely avenged in the name of caste-pride – because the two went hand-in-hand – and, in the process, the blame of it could be disposed on to the liberality of a Derozian imagination (Coomer 51–52).

Derozio being scapegoated and the Hindu conscience appeased, enrolments at Hindu College rose up again. In 1835, while the chorus against subsidising oriental studies through stipendiary payments had already gained strength and a consensus on the propriety of English-language training was emergent, there was a plan mooted for the creation of a Medical College – 'in which Medical science was to be taught on European principles; through the medium of the English language' (GCPI "Report" 33). The first Principal of the new institution, Dr Bramley, noted in his "Report" that most of the youths admitted to the College had undertaken courses in general instruction from the adjacent Hindu College – but their relative competence in the different subjects contained the hint of a larger phenomenon:

> They could all speak and read English with ease and fluency, and could write from dictation with tolerable rapidity and correctness. . . . In Bengalee their acquirements (as remarked by Mr Sutherland and the Pundit Moodusoodan) were, with two or three exceptions, slender. They could read and translate, but to do either seemed rather a business of labour than ease. (ibid. 64)

How the 'respectable Hindu youths' of Hindu College had, within the space of a year of Bentinck's *Resolution*, shifted the force of educational credentialling away from a learning of the vernaculars does not beg any more proof.

In 1838, a controversy broke out when the managers of Hindu College feared a reprise of the perception of religious hurt caused by Derozio a few years ago – this time, owing to the proposed erection of a new church right across the college building. It had come to the knowledge of the college's founder-patrons that Rev. Krishna Mohan Banerjea – a Christian convert from the brahminical classes and a once-ardent Derozian, now intent upon attacking the mindless prejudices and rituals of Hindus – had been appointed the pastor of the church (*Asiatic Intelligence* 140). There was immediate alarm among the parents of those studying at the college, all upper-caste residents of Calcutta, about an ulterior conspiracy to proselytise Bengali youth away from their caste-vocation. Insofar as Banerjea's exit from the fold of his inherited religion carried such rich rewards and material gains, many of the contemporary students of European liberalism might be allured into similar predicaments. A report in *Asiatic Intelligence* quoted extensively from *The Reformer*:

> The generality of those who send their children to this institution [Hindu College] have been brought up in the strict observance of the Hindu religion, and with all those notions of caste which have been known to operate so powerfully against any change of sentiment among them. It must be well known to all, that conversion is yet tantamount to expulsion from family and society. Whatever might hereafter be the notions of the enlightened portion of the Hindu community of the rising generation, that generation which entertains the notions we have mentioned has not yet passed away; its doctrines, absurd as they may be, are devotedly believed by millions, whose prejudices, however unreasonable, are pertinaciously adhered to. (140)

The fear of inviting the ire of Hindu conservative elites was so strong, and the desire to protect what I had earlier called a 'secular feudal complex of interests' at work within the English-language institution so intense, that the management came up with an expensive alternative. It was decided that the Hindu College trustees would provide a substitute ground of 'equal quantity and value' for the setting up of the church, and 'pay all expenses and law charges that have been incurred by the trustees and members of the Evangelical Fund' (141) – only in return for an assurance of being left alone. Even the teachers and Secretary of the Medical College joined in the chorus, and submitted a petition to the

Bishop, with the stated object of preventing a 'powerful re-action . . . among the Hindu priesthood, and the parents and guardians of these pupils' (278). Keeping the brahmins – that is, the 'Hindu priesthood' – pacified was crucial to the peaceful running of any of these liberal institutions, ironically insisting at the same time on a relentless exercise of scholarly reason.

The Making of a 'Secular-Feudal' Consensus: Education against Employment

From the very beginning, one of the explicit aims of allowing members of the superior castes alone into the higher educational institutions was the creation of a middle-class intelligentsia – who could forsake their degenerate life-styles as rural landlords and instead invest their social prestige in seeking public offices of profit. This was spelt out as early as in 1830 by the East India Company's Court of Directors to the Governor-in-Council of Madras Presidency, thus maintaining that the moral sobering effected by education cannot be enough recompense for the colonial government's massive investments in it (*IOR*, "No. 34"). Instead, the *bhadralok*-subjectivity produced by the ennobling influence of European scholarship was to be reaped through *babu*-entitlements in the civil administration of the country. Put differently, the moral-filtering potential of a college diploma had to be effectively combined with native systems of social benchmarking via caste – each validating and vindicating the other – in order to sculpt out positions of economic profit. Lord Hardinge, who passed a similar-spirited *Resolution* in 1844, knew that such an arrangement would ensure not just the interests of the Empire, but help it survive at the lowest costs (Richey 90–91) – in as far as it steered clear of the transformative labour of any kind of social reorganisation, otherwise avowed as the principle of liberal learning.

In trying to smooth the entry of educated natives into the uncovenanted services – namely, the Native Judicial Service, the Native Educational Service and the Native Medical Service – it was decided that every institution would prepare returns of the most distinguished students on the basis of which employments could be made (ibid.). In addition, certificates of merit were also to be issued to exceptionally gifted diploma-holders by the Local Committees of institutions, for ease of their finding favour with colonial officials. However, by 1850, this policy had failed to make good on its promises – twenty-five out of forty-one distinguished diploma-holders, in a period of five years, remained 'either unemployed, or [in] situations of inferior value' (Kerr 191). Those who landed jobs were also not in greatly improved situations of professional worth. Writing in 1852, the Principal of Hooghly College, J. Kerr, finds it necessary to reinstate the mutually beneficial pact between colonial intention and the native elite's desire for moral elevation. He observes that, no matter how delayed the fruits of such collaboration might be, the edification of native character – and a heightening of his claim to 'honour' – is definitely a direct consequence of 'English principles' in instruction, and must therefore be made practical use of by the government:

> It may be asked, are the educated Natives more likely to prove "honest men," and consequently more useful servants of the State, than the rest of their countrymen? I believe they are. The universal impression among themselves is that they are; and of this distinction they are not a little proud. At our Colleges and Schools, they acquire, to some extent, the habit of truthfulness. English principles are to a certain extent engrafted in their hearts. They acquire also a taste for what is true and beautiful in speculation, which, so far as it goes, is favourable to upright and honourable conduct. It may also be observed, that it is becoming a point of honour with those Natives who have received a good education, to be more truthful and trustworthy than the uneducated classes. It would give them more pain to be detected in a falsehood or in any dishonest practice. A public feeling favourable to integrity is growing up among them. (195)

That advanced moral instruction in 'English principles . . . [of] what is true and beautiful' had, by the 1850s, only come to benefit the upper-caste Hindus – both in terms of social distinction as well as whatever opportunities for professional enlargement went with it – became the cause of another kind of 'public feeling' instead. This 'feeling' had taken root among the privileged classes of Muslims in Bengal, who complained of the unsatisfactory progress of the Calcutta Madrassa and the slender profits derivable from its Anglo-Arabic bent. By 1853–54, it began to be argued by the Secretary of the Council of Education, Fred. J. Mouat, that the colonial government's pact with the founders of Hindu College and its continued financial assistance for the learning of a chosen community-elite were liable to be perceived as partisan. Also, the targeted spending of Education Funds on a miniscule and already-advantaged cross-section of Bengali society ran counter to the principles of equitable governance and political justice ("Papers" 21). Mouat recommended the opening up of Hindu College, if the government was still to be involved in its functioning, to youths of all faiths and creeds. But he was nonetheless apprehensive of the reactions of the native managers – who, as a certain Baboo Ausootosh Dey commented, 'would not willingly place their children to be instructed under the same roof with the children of all castes and creeds . . .' (ibid. 24). As a result, the Council of Education, in conferring with the Secretary to the Government of Bengal, came up with a plan: the senior collegiate department of Hindu College was henceforth to be reinstituted as Presidency College, and opened for admission to all communities, even as the junior department was to remain reserved for upper-caste Hindu youths under the name of 'Hindu School'. The justification for this was furnished as below:

> It is obvious that in this, as in other countries, the prejudices of rank, caste, and station, oppose themselves more strongly to the association of boys of tender years, than to that of youths of more advanced standing. The latter, whose character and habits are in some degree formed, are naturally less likely to suffer by contact with persons of a lower class. On the other hand, the student of humbler origin, will generally, as he advances in intellectual cultivation, become more refined, and throw off much of what in his former manners or mode of thinking, may have been objectionable. As a general rule, the mixture of ranks is greater at our English Universities than at our Schools, and nobody complains of it. (26)

The ground reality in India had been just the opposite, in that its vernacular schools allowed a 'mixture of ranks' that advancement in 'intellectual cultivation' only sought to decidedly block and forestall the effects of. But, even this higher training at Presidency College, now a government institution and officially declared as free for common pursuit, could not be brought within everybody's reach. There had to be successive barriers of entry, designed to filter out the corruptive influence and potentially contaminating presence of the 'student of humbler origin'. Two ways of achieving this were at hand: first, the levying of an annual admission fee of ten rupees in addition to a monthly fee fixed at five rupees – which was 'more than the fee as yet paid at any Mofussil College, which does not exceed three rupees a month' (46–47); and second, a far more stringent scholarship examination directly supervised by the Council of Education and capable of sieving in the most distinguished among all social ranks (*Presidency College Register* 15–18). Since its early years, Hindu College had provided an example of the scholarship system as an effective substitute for stipendiary grants from the government, which the colonial administration only adopted as declared policy for disbursal of its public purse much later in 1835.

Sieving out the *Mofussil*: Confounding 'Caste' and 'Class'

The annual revenue raised from tuition fees of paying scholars alone (as opposed to scholarship holders) at Hindu College had grown nearly eight-fold between 1823 and 1828, indicating the increased number of considerably wealthy people admitting their sons for an English education (Mitra 128–29). By the time the plan for Presidency College came into being in 1854, the fee receipts amounted to more than Rupees 30,000 annually (ibid. 129). In the next decade of its history as a government college, the monthly fee was hiked from a proposed founding rate of five rupees to ten (as the "Bengal Education Report 1863–64" noted), 'yielding an income of Rs. 32,000 per annum' (Mitra 137). It was further increased to Rupees 12 per mensem in the immediately following years, standing at an exorbitant annual fee-claim of 14.8

British pounds on account of tuition expenses by 1868 – which, as the Director of Public Instruction W.S. Atkinson maintained, was 'already larger than any corresponding rates in any country in the world' ("Statistical Statement" 13). On being informed in July 1868 of the government's plan for yet another fee revision in Presidency College, Atkinson urged the then-Principal of the College J. Sutcliffe to prepare a report on the 'social position and incomes of the parents and guardians of the students of the College' (ibid. 15) – and sent it off to the Lieutenant Governor of Bengal, making an extraordinarily passionate case against the proposal. Atkinson's correspondence, which is a salutary defence of the virtues of free public education and holds tremendous value even for our own day and time, reported on the misjudged economic prosperity of the Bengali middle classes and the city-exiled *zamindars* thus:

> The Zemindars of Bengal in particular, instead of rolling in wealth, as appears to be popularly believed, are, in reality, as a body, possessed of very moderate means, and large numbers of them are actually poor. Under the permanent settlement the Sub-division of beneficiary interests in land has been carried out with extraordinary minuteness, under a variety of most complicated tenures, and the result is that the wealth derived from proprietory rights in the soil is distributed amongst enormous masses of the population. These constitute the bulk of the large middle class of Bengal, and there is, probably, no country in the world where this class is so numerous, in proportion to the entire mass of the community at large. It is this middle class which almost exclusively supplies the population of our schools and colleges of every rank and standard, and it is in behalf of this class that I venture to plead, most earnestly, against the views which seem to be now in the ascendant in the Supreme Government of India. (12)

The above plea, having etched out the aspirational economy and the historical concatenation of desire that produced the figure of the metropolitan Bengali *bhadralok* – as the 'actually poor' city-bred *zamindar* now seeking cultural capital to compensate for the loss of feudal prestige – carries sociological value. In the attached survey report from Sutcliffe, we get a sense of how this abstract historical estimate plays out in real economic terms: 57 per cent of scholars enrolled in Presidency (across all five years, and hailing from both Calcutta and *mofussil* circles) were paying students, with the proportion of scholarships dwindling as one moved up the stages of instruction (15). And yet in the final fourth year of undergraduate instruction (barring the optional fifth year, catering to students preparing for a Masters education), more than eighty per cent of those enrolled were financially self-supporting and therefore from families of the native gentlemen. This is corroborated by the fact that about 81 per cent of total students in the General Department had their parents' occupational status registered under the following heads: *zamindars*, house owners and fund holders, government pensioners, merchants, *banias*, tradesmen, judicial officers, sub-assistant surgeons, professors, school masters, police officers and clerks (ibid.).

How these aspirational claims to a respectable city-life, among the Bengali middle classes, were soon to be invigorated by the opening of the Indian Civil Services (ICS) to men of native origin in 1869 – and in preparing for which the government was seeking to increase the price of a 'good' education – is not difficult to guess. But it is not a little ironic that the same Mr Atkinson, who had so vociferously fought for the public subsidising of Presidency College, had a few years ago – in 1863 and while in the same office – provoked a snub from the Secretary of State for India Charles Wood for demanding a reservation of 'the means of education for the higher classes [alone]' (Long 19).

The Wood's Despatch to Lord Dalhousie (1854) had set in motion the process of creating inaugural universities in the three major Presidencies of Calcutta, Bombay and Madras. Coming into being in 1857, these universities were intended as controlling agencies to oversee examinations in the English-language colleges and seminaries, without directly offering courses of study. The growing *bhadralok*-monopoly over questions of both academic merit and social standing in terms of professional opportunities – the twin gifts of English education to an exclusive caste-elite – had hardly been disturbed (let alone abated!) by the transformation of

Hindu College into Presidency. Repeatedly, through the 1880s and 1890s, there was a simmering disgruntlement among parents of Presidency scholars over the inefficient handling of examinations and arbitrary marking of scripts by the University of Calcutta. For example, the *Bangabasi* of 9 February 1884 angrily remarks: 'There were never such confusion and delay in the publication of results of examinations. Many good students have been plucked, and many bad ones have passed' (*RNP* 16 Feb 1884, 180). A week later, the same paper rues that 'Calcutta University has lost the reverence of the people' (*RNP* 23 Feb 1884, 210), and alleges a host of irregularities in the matter of examinations and results under the then-Registrar – who, as a rule, happened to be the Principal of Presidency College. Alongside these, there were reports in the contemporary press about a submission before the Education Commission, which maintained that the native students of Presidency College 'do not like to be taught English by native professors' (*Dacca Prakash*, 26 Mar 1882, qtd. in *RNP* 1 April 1882, 111). Complaints about racist and politically incendiary comments made by Professor Rowe, teaching English literature to Presidency students, also abound in newspapers of the time like *Pratinidhi* (*RNP* 7 Jul 1883, 383). While anxieties about the academic-administrative affairs of the University of Calcutta, and their disproportionate impact on the *bhadralok*-sensibilities of those studying at Presidency, were most vocally expressed in the native press, there was an occasional alarm about the moral rearing of caste Hindu students – who, for example, were the only ones allowed to stay at the Eden Hindu Hostel. The Bengali paper *Prabhat*, at the turn of the century, voiced much anguish about how 'brothels at the south-west corner of the bustee in front of the Eden Hindu Hostel [are] . . . polluting the morals of the inmates . . .' (*RNP* 18 Aug 1900, 635).

Containing the Nationalist Elite

When Lord Curzon assumed charge as the Viceroy of India in 1899, he was quite worried about the strengthening clout – and under the shadow of the revised Indian Councils Act (1892), the growing political self-representation – of the college-educated Bengali *bhadralok*. They had now seamlessly started making their passage from the university to membership of the provincial Legislative Councils, and something needed to be done urgently. For a decisive beginning, Curzon commissioned a revision in the governing bodies of all five universities, stocking them up with more representatives from the colonial government. The Indian Universities Commission of 1902, leading to the promulgation of the Indian Universities Act (1904), also proposed the setting up of teaching departments in the universities under direct control of these reconstituted governing bodies. A stated justification for this change in the fundamental character of the Indian university – becoming, for the first time, a collegiate space itself – was a familiar story of *mofussil* neglect (*IUA* 72–76), owing to the undue concentration of attention and resources on the *bhadralok*-breeding potential of Presidency College. The historical angst and disaffection of the *mofussil* colleges in Patna, Cuttack, Hooghly and Krishnagar were statistically mustered in the *Third Quinquennial Review* of "Progress of Education in Bengal (1902–1907)" thus:

> In 1882–83 the four mufassal colleges, viz. Patna, Cuttack, Hooghly and Krishnagar cost Government Rs. 1,05,142 and the Presidency College cost Government Rs. 78,850. In 1890–91 the Presidency College cost about Rs. 79,836, while the four mufassal colleges cost about Rs. 96,982. From that year the nett cost of the mufassal colleges steadily declined, and in 1899–1900 it amounted to Rs. 55,441 only. It has since risen, but the nett cost in 1905–06 was less than the nett cost in 1882–83 by about Rs. 24,000. The nett cost of the Presidency College on the other hand has been increasing steadily since 1886–87, though there was a slight set back between 1896–97 and 1899–1900. During the last six years the annual rate of increase has been about Rs. 10,000 and the nett cost during 1905–06 was Rs. 1,14,702, which was nearly double that of the four mufassal colleges put together. . . . These facts are to a large extent due to the policy of attempting to maintain a single college in a high state of efficiency. . . . Undoubtedly, the Presidency College has to some extent grown at the expense of colleges in the mufassal. . . . [T]he proportion of the total expenditure

> which was borne by fees at the Presidency College and the average mufassal college respectively was 51.2 and 33.4 percent. (19)

The fee revenue registered by Presidency College, relative to its substantially higher outlay of expenditure, is conclusive proof of the unchanged caste–class consensus driving metropolitan English education through the whole of the nineteenth century. Close on the heels of reforms suggested by the 1904 Act, Curzon finally unveiled his master plan for curbing the historical accumulation of Bengali *bhadralok*-aura: the Partition of Bengal, announced on 16 October 1905.

There was something far more insidious in the announcement than what met the eye, and occasioned general public outrage – which was taken to be the religious 'divide-and-rule' policy, territorially separating Hindu and Muslim populations in the province. The logic cited by the Governor General was administrative convenience. But the exact cultural-economic implications of the division call for a deeper look at the maps in the making: the metropolitan Bengali intelligentsia of Calcutta was collapsed into a single unit with a Bihari-Oriya majority, neither speaking the language of the former nor sharing the same history of caste mobility as the English-educated elite. The Muslim-Namashudra coalition from the Bengali *mofussils* – who had so far been a ready public sphere, refracting the glories of Calcutta – was welded together with an Assamese-speaking population. Neither of the non-Bengali demographic constituencies, with which the Hindu and Muslim majorities of Bengal were attached, had any traffic with the by-then celebrated mantle of Bengali 'culture'. On the contrary, they were deeply resentful of the Bengali *bhadralok's* sphere of influence within both the public life of culture and the professional dividends promised by colonial bureaucracy.

What Curzon's attempt at dealing a death-stroke to the 'secular feudal complex of interests' – which, as I have shown here, kept up India's tryst with English-language education in the nineteenth century – did to the country's new universities is a story that must spill over into the next chapter.

References

Accounts Book of Hindu College, 1830–1832.

Annual Reports of the Hindu College and others for 1846–47. Military Orphan Press, 1848.

Annual Reports of the Hindu College and others for 1850–51. Military Orphan Press, 1851.

Bandyopadhyay, Krishnamohun. "Dharmer Dwesha-dweshi." *Nabajiban*, vol. 4, no. 2, 1887, pp. 72–85.

Banerjea, B., ed. *Sambadpatre Sekaler Katha*, Vols. I & II. Calcutta, 1937.

Basu, Rajnarayan. *Hindu Athaba Presidency College-er Itibritta*. Calcutta, 1875.

Bell, Andrew. *An Analysis of the Experiment in Education Made at Egmore Near Madras*, 3rd ed. Cadell and Davis, 1807 [1797].

———. *Mutual Tuition and Moral Discipline; or, Manual of Instructions for Conducting Schools*, 7th ed. G. Roake, 1823.

———. *The Madras School, or Elements of Tuition*. Cadell and Davis, 1808.

Bhattacharya, Debraj, ed. *Of Matters Modern: The Experience of Modernity in Colonial and Postcolonial South Asia*. Seagull, 2008.

Bhattacharya, Debaditya. "Of Feudal Intellectual Capital: The History of the New Provincial Universities." *The Idea of the University: Histories and Contexts*, edited by Bhattacharya. Routledge, 2019.

Broomfield, J.H. *Elite Conflict in a Plural Society: Twentieth-Century Bengal*. University of California Press, 1968.

"Brothels near the Eden Hindu Hostel." *Prabhat*, 15 Aug. 1900. *Report on Native Papers, for the week ending the 18th August 1900* [No. 33 of 1900].

Chakraborty, Manotosh. *Hindu College O Unish Shataker Banglar Samaj*. Subarnarekha, 1979.

Chatterjee, Partha. "The Nationalist Elite." *The Nation and Its Fragments: Colonial and Postcolonial Histories*. Princeton University Press, 1993, pp. 35–75.

———. *The Present History of West Bengal: Essays in Political Criticism*. Oxford University Press, 1997.

Chattopadhyay, Swati. *Representing Calcutta: Modernity, Nationalism, and the Colonial Uncanny*. Routledge, 2005.

Coomer, Anita. "H.H. Wilson and the Hindu College (1823–1832)." *Calcutta Historical Journal*, vol. 6, no. 1, 1981, pp. 30–59.

General Committee of Public Instruction (GCPI) of the Presidency of Fort William in Bengal. "Report for the Year 1836." Baptist Mission Press, 1837.

Ghose, Subarna and Ashokelal Ghose. "Hindu College Samparkita." *Desh Patrika*, 1972, pp. 1289–96.

———. "Hindu College Samparkita: Dwitiya Baktabya." *Desh Patrika*, 1973, pp. 1277–82.

Ghosh, Parimal. *What Happened to the Bhadralok*. Primus Books, 2016.

India Office Records: Dispatches to Madras, E/4/939, "No. 34. Court of Directors' Public Department Dispatch, 29 Sep. 1830." pp. 263–83.

Kerr, J. *Review of Public Instruction in the Bengal Presidency, From 1835 to 1851*. Baptist Mission Press, 1852.

Long, J., ed. *Adam's Reports on Vernacular Education in Bengal and Behar (1835–38)*. Home Secretariat Press, 1868.

Mitra, Kissory Chand. "The Presidency College." *The Bengal Magazine*, October 1873, pp. 120–39.

"Mr. Bellett's incompetency." *Bangabasi*, 9 Feb. 1884. *Report on Native Papers, for the week ending the 16th February 1884* [No. 7 of 1884].

"Mr. Rowe of the Presidency College." *Pratinidhi*, 5 Jul. 1883. *Report on Native Papers, for the week ending the 7th July 1883* [No. 28 of 1883].

"Mr. Tawney before the Education Commission." *Dacca Prakash*, 26 Mar. 1882. *Report on Native Papers, for the week ending the 1st April 1882* [No. 13 of 1882].

Mukherjee, S.N. *Calcutta: Essays in Urban History*. Subarnarekha, 1993.

Nandy, Ashis. *The Intimate Enemy: Loss and Recovery of Self under Colonialism*. Oxford University Press, 1989.

"New Church - Proselytism" and "The New Church." *Asiatic Intelligence*, Nov.–Dec. 1838, Calcutta, pp. 140–41, 278–79.

"Papers Relating to the Establishment of the Presidency College of Bengal." *Selections from the Records of the Bengal Government*, No. XIV. Bengal Military Orphan Press, 1854.

Presidency College Centenary Volume (1955). West Bengal Government Press, 1956.

Presidency College Register, edited by Surendrachandra Majumdar and Gokulnath Dhar. Education Department, Government of Bengal, 1927.

"Proceedings for the Dismissal of Derozio." *Presidency College Magazine*, vol. 41, April 1959.

"Progress of Education in Bengal (1902–1907)." *Third Quinquennial Review*. Bengal Secretariat Book Depot, 1907.

Ray, Rajat Kanta. *Social Conflict and Political Unrest in Bengal, 1875–1914*. Oxford University Press, 1984.

Raychaudhuri, Tapan. *Europe Reconsidered: Perceptions of the West in Nineteenth-Century Bengal*. Oxford University Press, 1988.

Richey, J.A. *Selections from Educational Records Part II (1840–1859)*. Office of the Superintendent of Government Printing, 1922.

"Rules of the Hindu College." *Presidency College Register*, edited by Surendrachandra Majumdar and Gokulnath Dhar. Education Department, Government of Bengal, 1927, pp. 2–4.

Sharp, H. *Selections from Educational Records, Part I (1781–1839)*. Calcutta, 1920.

Sinha, Mrinalini. *Colonial Masculinity: The Manly Englishman and the Effeminate Bengali in the Late Nineteenth Century*. Manchester University Press, 1995.

"Statistical Statement Regarding Social Position of Parents and Guardians." Education Department, Fort William, May 1869.

The Calcutta Christian Observer, Volume 1 (June–December). Baptist Mission Press, 1832.

The Indian Universities Act 1904 (IUA), Papers Relating to the Act VIII of 1904, 57–82, Calcutta.

"The University." *Bangabasi*, 16 Feb. 1884. *Report on Native Papers, for the week ending the 23rd February 1884* [No. 8 of 1884].

Wilson, H.H. "Report, dated 14 January 1830." *G.C.P.I Copybook of Letters* (January–December 1830).

Zastoupil, Lynn and Martin Moir, eds. *The Great Indian Education Debate: Documents Relating to the Orientalist-Anglicist Controversy, 1781–1843*. Routledge, 1999.

175th Anniversary Commemoration Volume: Presidency College, edited by Amal Kumar Mukhopadhyay. Presidency College, 1996.

THREE

Pre-Independence Youth Movements (1905–47): The Force of Religion and the Making of a Nationalist Student Subject

The Souring Fruits of Colonial 'Mimicry'

I have tried demonstrating in the previous chapter how the benefits of English-language education in India were almost exclusively appropriated by a metropolitan caste-elite, under the aegis of nineteenth-century colonial educational reform. Taking Bengal as an instructive example for understanding the distributive economy of social and cultural capital, it was apparent that such policy-reform alternated between a structural neglect of existing systems of vernacular education and the growing prominence of institutional monoliths like the Hindu (later Presidency) College. What I proposed as the ideological rationale behind this slow congealment of structures of privilege is a 'secular-feudal' consensus, which sought to specifically prevent opportunities of social-professional mobility for the lower castes. But, the resulting harvest of institutionally reared (Bengali) *bhadralok* youths did not always gain much beyond the metaphysical dividends of 'honour' – insofar as their education hardly translated into promised jobs within the urban colonial bureaucracy or its recent spawn of learned professions.

This chapter deals with the political effects of such disaffection within a college-educated Hindu caste-elite. It chronicles how this initial push for a comprador bourgeoisie threatened the goal of 'secularity' in the later period of anti-colonial resistance, leading up to India's independence in 1947. The way colonial systems of education encountered the charge of 'community' in India lay in their appropriation of cultural logics of 'caste' and 'religion', in order to mould a certain nationalist subjectivity of the student. Such nationalist self-making in the early twentieth century thrived on political-juridical proscriptions of any alternative sense of 'community' – except for religion – as irrelevant and potentially communistic.

The exact period under analysis here would roughly span the first half of the twentieth century – from the sub-text of colonial intentions underlying the Indian Universities Act of 1904 to the veritable symptoms of a transfer of power to the national bourgeoisie soon after the Second World War. Though the chapter will proceed through a signposting of significance in monumental 'events' and periods of churning that followed each, the larger purpose here is to provide a genealogy of political subjectification for the college-going nationalist youth of these times. In this, there are two effects that I hope to make apparent, in the cause of understanding the current postcolonial trajectories of Indian higher education: first, the utterly inadequate encounters between *religion* and *class* as well as the critiques of each emerging from the educated intelligentsia; and second, the historical production of affects suited to the student subjectivity and their potential (ab)uses in an indefinite future.

When Viceroy Curzon proposed a redefinition of the Indian university through a blanket amendment of its founding Acts in 1904, he probably expected more durable resistance than he met. Issuing forth from the resolutions of a Shimla conference on education in 1901 and the subsequent recommendations made by the Universities Commission (1902), the "Act No. VIII of 1904" – as passed by the Governor General in Council and published in the government's *Gazette* – enjoined the university to the 'purpose (among others) of making provision for the instruction of students, with power to appoint University Professors and Lecturers' (*IUA* Section 3, 60). This was in stark contrast to the erstwhile-legislated 'idea' of the university for nearly half a century until then, which regarded the institution as merely an examining and overseeing authority for the growing network of colleges in the country. With the suggested introduction of teaching activities within the immediate physical precinct of the Indian university, it was expected that students from *mofussil* colleges could now breach the metropolitan disconnect by travelling to Calcutta, Bombay, Madras, Lahore or Allahabad for a life of higher intellectual pursuits. But, again, the theoretical possibilities for such intellectual emancipation – contained in the lure of the big colonial city – were undergirded by regulatory conditions, where every college had to satisfy far stricter norms and procedures for 'affiliation' before allowing students into the credentialling economy of a university (ibid. 72–76). The onus of 'qualifying' for a life at the university was thus passed on to the *mofussil* institution which a student would be enrolled in, rather than the individual 'mettle' of the potential entrant. In this way, the division of interests between the metropolitan elites and the *mofussil* elites was far from being dismantled, even as these constituencies were played against each other in competitive statistics of access ("Progress of Education" 19). Understandably, the hint of transforming universities into teaching institutions appeased the mobility-aspirations of an increasingly ambitious (and caste-advantaged) non-urban youth accessing college education through family legacies of intermediate land-tenures.

But, at the same time, the Act of 1904 proposed something way more insidious in terms of the 'Body Corporate' – that is, the administrative arms – of the university. The Senate, which was to be the conduit of interactions between the colonial government and the university, was recomposed through an overwhelming proportion of its member-'Fellows' being 'nominees' of the lieutenant-governor of the province, acting as Chancellor of the respective university. In the case of the three oldest universities, the number of Fellows was fixed between fifty and hundred, of whom a maximum of twenty could be elected by students and teachers, and all the rest were to be 'nominated by the Chancellor' for life (*IUA* Section 6[1], 62). For the remaining two universities in Lahore and Allahabad, a maximum of fifteen elected Fellows could be vetoed by the sixty nominees installed by the government (ibid., Section 6[2]). The eventual rein over university affairs, ranging from which teaching departments to open, who to appoint as faculty and which colleges to be affiliated and how, was thus to remain secured in the hands of the British administration through overarching veto powers. The university's Senate and Syndicate – seemingly empowered with the work of executive governance in everyday contexts – were finally reconfigured as puppets of grander political designs and working at the behest of imperial interests.

Bengal Partition and Nationalist Self-Fashioning

There was some resistance to the bureaucratic and ideological intrigues planned by the 1904 Act, though most of it was expressed in the form of recorded dissent notes (for example, by Justice Gooroodas Banerjee of the Universities Commission of 1902) or newspaper articles written by Congress leaders (Ghosh, "The Genesis of Curzon's University Reform" 475). Emboldened by what Sumit Sarkar refers to as the 'mendicant' methods of the moderate nationalist leadership (*The Swadeshi Movement in Bengal* 29), Curzon went a step ahead and toyed with other administrative blueprints for a decisive alienation of the Bengali *bhadralok's* influence from over a section of increasingly impatient anti-colonial audience. The Bengali nationalists had already become sufficiently notorious for their reformist initiatives, and a sustained production of anti-British literature; and even people like Surendranath Banerjee, despite their adherence to constitutional modes of struggle, were gaining tremendous popularity among the youth of Bengal.

As early as in 1903, the Central Provinces commissioner in Andrew Fraser had suggested a redrawing of Bengal's territorial borders through the transfer of Chittagong, Dacca and Mymensingh divisions to a non-Bengali speaking province of Assam (Broomfield; Bishui). Curzon saw merit in this idea, insofar as it promised a fracturing of the nationalist leadership from its audiences – primarily through an accentuation of linguistic and religious differences. The 1905 Partition of Bengal, with the creation of a Muslim-majority East Bengal, was initially expected to generate a spurt of frenzied petitioning over logistical and bureaucratic inconveniences of land-and-revenue distribution and then eventually die out like the protests over the 1904 Universities Act.

The reality, as it unfolded, was however radically estranged from colonial apprehensions of damage and dissent. Almost all districts of Bengal erupted in sporadic, but increasingly consolidated, scenes of protest – decrying the imperialist attempt at driving a cultural wedge between the Hindu and Muslim Bengalis. The primary addressees of the movement were the educated youth in different parts of the erstwhile united province, who were made to see in this communal plot a consummation of economic theories of imperialist 'drain of wealth'. The mass disaffection caused by unemployment or underpaid underemployment, despite English-language education, was attributed to the colonial government's deliberate plunder of resources by seeking ready Indian markets for British factory produce. The corollary of such import-based profits made from native markets lay in a simultaneous destruction of conditions for setting up indigenous industry. The answer to the Partition was therefore sought in an economic programme for the use of *swadeshi* (home-grown) goods and boycott of foreign products – from salt and sugar to textile-made cloth and leather boots and cigarettes and alcohol (Sarkar, *The Swadeshi Movement in Bengal* 92–148).

Use(s) of Religion: The Forging of a *Swadeshi* 'Mass'

That the *swadeshi* movement in Bengal – as it has come to be called in the historical annals of Indian nationalism – was largely tethered to the class-character of upper-caste Hindu educated youth and worked by mobilising their thwarted passions becomes apparent on a deeper analysis of its political tactics. This is not to say that it assumed the dimensions of a youth movement, by precluding the involvement or collaboration of adult leaders. Quite on the contrary, the leadership of the upsurge was resolutely in the grasp of a relatively seasoned and strategically militant class of public figures (most often ensconced in the liberal professions of law or teaching) like Aurobindo Ghose, Bipinchandra Pal, Aswinikumar Dutta, Prafulla Chandra Ray, Chittaranjan Das or Aswinicoomar Banerjee. But, significantly, the private appeal of the movement rested on an inner consciousness of student angst and potential. The government's repressive attempts at forestalling student participation through the issuing of the Carlyle and Lyon Circulars (October 1905), at the very moment of the Partition announcement, further indexed the colonial state's fear of the nationalist student-subject. These circulars threatened institutions with withdrawal of affiliation if their students were found indulging in political agitations and anti-government public programmes, including the use of slogans like 'Bande Mataram'.[1] In response, hordes of school- and college-going students embarked on an active educational boycott, which corresponded with the demand for a substitutive system of national education cohering under a 'national university' (ibid. 149–75). Imaginatively therefore, the cultural literacies and physical energies contained in young crowds could not but be the means to Bengal's regenerative fantasy. I will touch upon four specific aspects of the public mobilisations that constituted the 'upsurge', in order to point at how a sly seductive incorporation of militant vigour was achieved through the political tools of the movement.

---

[1] 'Bande Mataram' – literally translatable as 'I bow to thee, Mother' – was the refrain of a song appearing in the Bengali litterateur Bankim Chandra Chattopadhyay's novel *Anandamath* (1882). Unfolding in the context of an armed insurgency of Hindu monks against Company rule, the novel contained the nascent war-cry of an anti-imperialist struggle and subsequently exerted a massive imaginative influence on the future of India's struggle for independence. The undertones of a religious uprising, coupled with subtle emphases on a regimentation of the rebels' bodily strength against the military might of a colonial state, made the novel stand in as a handbook for Hindu nationalist mobilisation. The forceful imagining of the nation as 'mother goddess' – demanding obeisance from the sons [of the soil] in the form of masculine sacrifice – also sought to transform nationalism into both sacral duty and devotional creed.

First, the constant anxiety about mass appeal that proponents of *swadeshi* laboured under was the result of an acute self-consciousness about the class/caste-character of the movement. That bands of upper-caste Hindu youth, in order to reach out to constituencies radically separated by age and social status, needed the glue of religion to both accommodate their own interests as well as those of their detractors or interlocutors is not surprising. What resulted of this was a distinct tenor of Hindu revivalism that projected a past of self-sufficiency against the economic-spiritual impoverishments of the colonial present. References to Ma Bhawani, worshipping the cult of 'Shakti' in the form of a Mother India, the observance of Shivaji or Birastami festivals, popular deprecation of Mughal rule and Muslim rulers as symptomatic of foreign defilement – were all part of the public itinerary of *swadeshi* articulations, in the cause of connecting with Hindu 'mass' sentiment (Pal; Banerjea; Kanungo; Guha). Alongside these discursive entanglements, the rituals for induction into the *swadeshi* fold were deliberately made to mirror the form of religious vows or gestures, just as the penalty for non-compliance replicated rules of caste-based association in techniques of social excommunication[2] (Ghose; RSDD). Unsurprisingly, the Hindu religious fervour through which a caste-marked literate 'populace'

[2] See, for example, the *Report on Native Papers in Bengal* (No. 5 of 1906, for the week ending 3 February 1906) which cites excerpts from an article titled "Punishment of the enemies of the country" published in the 28 January edition of the Bengali *Hitavarta*: 'We shall have to punish those wicked men who, cowards as they are, first adopted the vow of boycotting English-made goods, but are now violating it. . . . Cannot the society teach those a lesson who do not care for the good of their class but are bent on attaining their own selfish ends. . . . [T]hey will have to seek with downcast tail their own society's assistance and protection at the time of marriage of their sons and daughters, at the manes of their father and mother: society will then be in a position to punish these wretches in the following manner:- (1) That none shall eat and drink with them./ (2) That none shall intermarry with them./ (3) That washerman shall not wash their clothes./ (4) That barbers shall not shave them./ (5) That none shall buy from or sell to them./ (6) That boys and girls shall be instructed not to play with their children' (97).

sought to achieve a commonality of purpose (and identity) with the 'masses' only ended up divorcing the fortunes of *swadeshi* from the quotidian economic interests of Muslim and lower-caste peasantry (Tagore). The latter, when forced into boycotting cheaper factory-made foreign items of essential use by Hindu *zamindars* (or their intermediaries) supporting the *swadeshi* cause, rose up in revolt. Scenes of rioting in Comilla or Mymensingh during 1906–07 confirmed the ironies of the anti-Partition movement's 'mass'-character (Sarkar, *The Swadeshi Movement in Bengal* 405–64).

Second, the most favoured instrument for propagation of *swadeshi* ideology and declaration of its goals or programmes was the newspaper or periodical – which again points at the young educated 'core' of the movement and the ill-fated ironies of their plans for mass-contact. Newspapers like *Bande Mataram* (operated during its peak by Aurobindo Ghose and Bipinchandra Pal), *Sandhya* (edited by Brahmabandhab Upadhyay), *Jugantar* (founded by Barindra Kumar Ghosh) or magazines like Satishchandra Mukherjee's *Dawn* (which was the mouthpiece of Dawn Society for students of University of Calcutta) forged communities of *swadeshi* activism through print-networks. The excessive reliance on literacy and literate modes of political address betrays contemporary anxieties about tapping into a student base, capable of being ideologised through routines of intellectual grooming and indoctrination.

Third, because Curzon's Partition was perceived as an assault on the cultural oneness of Bengal, the response to the colonial move saw a historic rise in literary and performative expressions of protest. A reinvigorated genre of nationalist literature took shape around the singular event of the 1905 Partition, with songs, poems, plays and prose-fiction cementing the textual-literate solidarities that lay at the root of the movement. The cultural aura mustered by Bengali writers active in that period (1905–10) remains unparalleled, despite the relatively consistent production of nationalist texts by subsequent authors. The successive adaptations of 'high' literary forms of creative expression into popular performance-genres like *jatra* or *pala-gaan* – or seeking dissemination through first-person storytelling formats in the *melas* (fairs) and magic lantern lectures – once again required the participation of student squads, without whom the 'mass' transmission of Bengali cultural injury was hardly imaginable.

Fourth, and finally, the actual action-programmes of picketing, strikes or bonfires of *bideshi* (foreign) goods called for an intensive order of coordination and disciplining. This was not possible in any motley group of people, and therefore necessitated a practice of harnessing youthful ebullience and enthusiasm through regimes of bodily control. The extant *akhara* tradition, with its insistence on physical training and a sacrificial cult of masculine aggression, was best suited to provide the resources for *swadeshi's* honing of Bengali youth. Long considered unfit for vocations that required physical labour, the intellectually-oriented Bengali student-force now became the centre of a growing network of volunteer associations (or *samitis*) like the Anushilan Samiti, Suhrid Samiti, Swadesh Bandhab Samiti or the Anti-Circular Society. It was through the everyday life of self-consecration within these *samitis* that the *swadeshi* movement effectively reoriented nationalist militancy towards the form (and practice) of a religious associationism. Often dropping out of government schools and colleges in heeding the call for an extended boycott of foreign institutions, the *samiti*-youth were re-schooled into behavioural idioms of *seva* (selfless service) as the restitutive basis of bonding with the 'masses'. It is this ethic of service that is then postulated as the elite upper-caste intellectual's bid at losing oneself in the nation, via the medium of Hindu religiosity (ibid. 336–404).

Resistance as (Mother) Worship: A Tale of Contradictions

A Bengali play, performed at the Star Theatre on 25 December 1905 and published soon after, documented the early mood of the *swadeshi* agitation as entirely impelled by the initiative of these Hindu upper-caste students – taking huge pride in their precolonial ancestral 'tradition' as much as miming a language of mystical surrender to the nation transfigured as mother goddess. Scripted by Amritalal Basu, *Shabaash Bangali* (Bravo Bengalees!) – as the play is called – carries the subtitle *Samajik Naksha* (meaning 'social sketch'), and does live up to its self-proclaimed representational status as a record of the times. There is simply no plot or dramatic intrigue in the text, except a series of portraits – each rounded in the form of an independent stage-scene with no binding logic beyond the historical frame. Sets of unrelated *swadeshi* characters people the scenes, to give the audience discrete glimpses into the 'social character' of the movement – where, of course, the major body-force derives from groups of student activists. Alongside them are choric constellations of unnamed working-class 'followers' – who are never individualised, but nonetheless identified by their professions as 'cobbler-folk' (*muchigon*), 'bangle-seller folk' (*churiwaligon*) or 'washerwomen folk' (*dhopanigon*).

By interspersing scenes of student revolt with musically-rehearsed collective effusions of worker-sentiment, Basu's play points at both the fictions of 'mass' mobilisation conjured by *swadeshi* youth as well as the rather tenuous assumption of political agency by such 'masses'. It is also interesting that a text which roots the *swadeshi* outrage in the 'bravery' of the Bengalis alone deliberately projects the working classes of the province as speaking a Hindustani dialect, and therefore automatically exempted from the self-imagination of the 'brave Bengalee'. The class imprints of not just the movement, but of the whole of 'educated' Bengal, are thus etched out at the same time as the *swadeshi* 'mass'-following is itself dubbed as *bideshi* (foreign) to the spirit of Bengal. The movement is successfully reclaimed as Bengali heritage, even while its outreach among Hindi/Hindustani-speaking migrant labour is critically understood as a tactic of social mimicry. In all of this, it is made demonstrably clear that what holds together the class-pride of the caste Hindu student and the dialect-marked illiterate itinerant 'mass' is their common inheritance of religion – where a visual semiotics of the *swadesh* (home/nation) can seamlessly give way to an incarnate mother of Hindu idolatry.

All the episodes of confrontation in the play – between student volunteers given to the cause of the nation and their parents or the Anglicised wife of a government college professor or the local *zamindar* – are strung with appeals to subscribe to a Hindu cult of *maatri-bhakti* or mother-worship. For example, Motilal resolves to give up his training in colonial law and join the nationalist-educational ranks of technical skill-training in order to contribute towards a 'poor' mother India's industrial rehabilitation programme (14). This reference echoes the divide within the *swadeshi* demand for national institutions – where, on the one hand, ideologues like Satishchandra Mukherjee argued for a curriculum rooted in national cultural tradition, while on the other the likes of Nilratan Sarkar started the Society for the Promotion of Technical Education (1906) as the true antidote to an imperialist collegiate model (Mukherjee and Mukherjee). But, when Motilal explains his preference for an indigenous cult of 'technique' over an imported tradition of legal 'theory' (which, in his own words, ironically thrives on the perpetuation of civil conflicts between local populations) to his mother Bhabatarini, the clear-sightedness of his political critique slides into the muddied sentimentality of a stock transcendentalism:

> . . . [B]ut ma, if you ever fall sick, is it not my duty to forget about attending college and sit by your side through days and nights, giving you care and love? Just like that, Mother Bengal (*Banga Mata*) too is now in a state of deep crisis and disease; and in this moment all I can say is my studies and my career and my future are all irrelevant. I must give of my life to revive my mother and get her back to a life of peace and tranquillity; only after that may I devote my mind to any other work. Ma, when you're dying, how can I turn the other way and keep plotting about how to wear the lawyer's wig? (17–18, translation mine)

Motilal goes on to privilege the imagined 'mother' in the 'nation' (alternating as the 'motherland' of Bengal) over the real mother's anxious and helpless pleas about his future. In the process, he crafts a ritualistic idiom of compulsory self-sacrifice as the 'sacred duty' of all sons of a (Hindu) mother-nation. *Banga Mata* (Mother Bengal), inspired as it is by Bankim Chandra's nationalist war-cry in 'Bande Mataram', is also the prototype of the *Bharat Mata*

(Mother India); and this chain of idiomatic overlaps effectively fuses the nation and home and family into a singular register of selfless devotion. The appeal to religion is thus folded into the imaginative activism of nationalist *dharma* (duty), now embodied in the soul- and body-force of the educated upper-caste student.

By around 1908–09, the exceptional charge of the *swadeshi* movement started tottering away into the occasional 'actions' – as they were called – of secret society volunteers. But by then, the strategic bulwarks of religion and communal sentiment, which had held the movement together in its heyday, also ended up exposing the fault-lines of an assumed mass-action helmed by student vanguards. The scaling up of repression by the colonial police and government led to the disappearance of many of the volunteer associations (while the others shifted base or went underground), and their print organs of mass propaganda in newspapers and periodicals were mostly banned. The Indian Councils Act of 1909, with its promise of increased representation of the native elite on legislative councils as well as the introduction of separate electoral quotas for Muslim populations, hardened the division of political interests along communal lines even as the Partition of Bengal was already on its course to being annulled in 1911. The National Council of Education, started in 1905–06 in response to the demand for a self-supported system of national schools and colleges, had also failed to ensure financial and curricular means for a viable education tailored to professional ends. Most students who had dropped out of their institutions, riding on the fervour of an extended boycott programme, were now without recourse to either government jobs or hope of gainful employment in a *swadeshi* entrepreneurial establishment that never quite took off. The economic impact of the programme, which was initially predicted to have been the most damning for British industrial capital and export markets, portended no less of a debacle. In fact, as Sumit Sarkar accounts, the nature and range of commodity-consumption patterns through the *swadeshi* years testify to the deeply class-inflected truths about the movement:

> [T]aken as a whole, the gap between expectation and achievement seems even wider in the boycott movement than in other aspects of the swadeshi age. . . . The indigenous substitute was simply not available in adequate quantity or quality in many cases, and it was usually more expensive, too. In cotton textile, for instance, the Bombay mills could not yet manufacture the finer types of yarn and cloth, while the handloom product was inevitably costlier than the Manchester article. In salt, there was in Bengal a real displacement of Liverpool in favour of karkatch, but the latter too generally came from foreign sources like Spain. It is also a significant commentary on the social character of the movement that the boycott should have achieved its most spectacular early success in boots and shoes and cigarettes; as Morshead commented, the demand for such commodities came mainly from "Indian gentlemen of the middle class such as clerks, pleaders, etc., and they are the class who really take an interest in and are opposed to the partition". (*The Swadeshi Movement in Bengal* 147–48)

Exceeding Religion from Within: World War I and Student Movements

While the Bengali youth's political apprenticeship through the first decade of the twentieth century was marred by a collaboration of class and religious interests, how were students in the rest of the country – and particularly in the north western or central provinces – responding to the political currents of nationalism? It appears, from an attentive historical analysis, that in the decade immediately following the *swadeshi* upsurge in Bengal, nationalist youths elsewhere were gradually extending their networks beyond the geographical limits of the 'nation'. The 1910s was understandably a period of great social hope and worldwide transformation, insofar as it led to the Bolshevik spectre of an October revolution in 1917 and the formation of the first Communist International (Comintern) in 1919. The communist influence compounded the anti-imperialist vigour of Indian student-populations outside of Bengal and structured strategic collaborations and exchanges with the Ghadar Party operating along the American West Coast, and Khilafatist demands surrounding the fate of Ottoman Turkey.

The steady flows of Sikh immigrant labour into the farms and factories of California and the Pacific Northwest, from around the turn of the century, helped politicise them through an exposure to trade unions and workers' associations. Most of these diasporic working-class Sikhs had prior military experience as part of the British Army, while at home. Around 1913, a sufficiently massive expatriate community of the Punjabi Sikhs gave Lala Har Dayal the opportunity to work out a curious political compound of armed revolutionary nationalism and socialist sympathies in the founding of the Ghadar Party (Dayal; Josh; Ramnath). The party used the religious egalitarianism of the Sikhs to foment discontent about British rule in India and the economic injustices of forced immigration, until the outbreak of the First World War provided a chance for military action along Punjab. A staple audience for party propaganda as well as for armed volunteerism, students at both Berkeley and in the colleges of north India responded to the Ghadarite call. Much of the party's literature found its way into student study circles and secret societies of nationalist youth, thus establishing trans-continental channels of revolutionary communication and influence. As J. Daniel Elam has posited, the Russian-born anarchist Emma Goldman – who travelled with Ghadarite leaders along the West Coast in 1912–13 – left behind the marks of a radical political consciousness on young Bhagat Singh and the public articulations of the Hindustan Socialist Republican Association (HSRA), which were to come to fruition more than a decade later (Elam 46–64). Singh's resuscitation of the transformative valence of the 'crowd' as an agent of meaningful political action – a category long derided in the nationalist imagination and in a classic Gandhian suspicion of violent mass action – owes, as Elam contends, to Goldman's variety of anarchism.[3] In this, the thought-encounters made

[3] Elam explains the nuances in Bhagat Singh's response to Gandhi's "Cult of the Bomb" (1930) through discursive detours into Har Dayal and Emma Goldman: 'Singh's argument against Gandhi here might align the masses with violent revolutionary action. Indeed, the "Philosophy of the Bomb" purposely

possible by the Ghadar Party's austere anti-imperialism and its intercontinental collisions with communism were indeed the most lasting legacy for a future of Indian youth movements. The form of the Sikh religious 'pledge' again had a peculiar charm for student revolutionaries at home and abroad, and in the process reaffirmed the role of religion within student experiments with anti-colonial nationalism (Hesse 55).

The Khilafat movement among the Indian Muslims, which was a reaction to the British dismemberment of the Ottoman Empire at the close of the First World War and therefore represented the restitutive forces of a pan-Islamic political world order, could – among other things – be traced back to an aborted demand for 'university'-status to the Muslim college in Aligarh as early as in 1912 (Minault; Jalal). Patrick Hesse makes this suggestion, in his dissertation on the relationship between subcontinental communism and processes of religious claims-making. The *muhajirin* (emigres), who left India in protest against British oppression of Muslims on a global scale and in search of a promised land of Islam, were very often mobilised into a militant anti-imperialism through the efforts of communist emissaries like M.N. Roy. As Hesse contends, the early lineaments of a Khilafatist revolutionary spirit may be discerned '[a]lready in 1915, [when] a party of Muslim students had left Lahore in order to foment a revolution among the tribes in Afghanistan and the NWFP (North West Frontier Province). Several of them joined Obeidullah Sindhi's "army of god." It was to fight for the subcontinent's liberation under pan-Islamist auspices' (58). The historian goes further to document the *muhajirin's* enlistment within the

sets out to argue that the bomb is available to large masses (as opposed to small cults). The two texts' primary debate hinges on their respective ability to better represent the masses and their desires; the philosophy of the bomb is the philosophy of mass revolutionary action. Bhagat Singh's title comes from Har Dayal's 1912 pamphlet of the same name, where Har Dayal grandly proclaimed that the bomb was "the Esperanto of revolution". Indeed, for Har Dayal, Emma Goldman, and Bhagat Singh, violence was mass communication' (52–53).

Communist University of the Toilers of the East (KUTV), when the latter came up in Moscow in 1921. Paralleling the fortunes of the Khalifatists in India, these KUTV students were trained into espousing a version of political Islam that foregrounded its anti-imperialist stance, and even saw the movement at home as seeking a socialist integration of the world *contra* the forces of colonial capitalism (ibid. 67–70; Alavi 1–16). Muslim students joining the Khilafat fold in post-1919 India, and under the leadership of the Ali brothers, carried on this quasi-communist legacy of the Soviet-trained *muhajirin* – in that they saw the rule of the Caliphate as granting a geopolitical form to the economic redressal of British imperial crimes.

Religion's Return: Gandhi and the Making of a 'Hindu' Soul Force

Through the years of the First World War, the simmering passions and tensions of a nationalist youth were in the process of being moulded by global political events into a revolutionary anti-colonialism. There were constant local attempts to overthrow the yoke of foreign rule, embodied in repressive institutions of the government like the army and the police; most often, these sporadic spurts of popular outrage were dubbed as 'conspiracies' in government intelligence reports and immediately suppressed through an application of emergency provisions codified in the Defence of India Act 1915. However, by the time M.K. Gandhi returned to India in early-1915, it was clear that the Congress party's grasp over the struggle for independence was increasingly slackening. There was deep dissatisfaction over the learned civilities of protest, resorted to by the moderate leadership of the Congress who believed in the righteousness of the British liberal conscience and nauseously appealed to it for intervention. It was particularly the young populations, studying in colleges of northern India and the Punjab, whose impatience foreshadowed a distinct legacy of militant action and armed rebellion against the colonial state – often in conversation with communist ideals shaping up elsewhere in the world, as outlined above (Chand; Hardiman; NJBS; Bamford). Gandhi realised that the time was ripe for coordinated mass action, but not until the belligerence of youthful crowds was re-schooled into radically alternative registers of a moral-religious subjectification.

Predictably enough (and in borrowing from the lessons afforded by Bengal's *swadeshi* movement), the resources for a Gandhian production of (nationalist) selfhood were to be found in Hindu spiritual doctrines and ritual practices of abnegation. The principles of *ahimsa* (non-violence) and *satyagraha* (insistence on truth) became the twin instruments for a turning of the critical anti-imperialist gaze inward, rather than fixating on the outward apparatuses (and agents) of political rule. Gandhi insisted that the capacity for political self-rule rested on a prior constructive reorganisation of local resources and institutions, as much as a subjective surrender to an economy of controlled affects. The making of the nationalist self was thus an ascetic preparatory ritual for a higher moral consciousness, where resistance no longer consisted in retaliation but in the sheer soul-force of *converting* the other (Gandhi, *Hind Swaraj*; *An Autobiography*; Hardiman 19–64). This is what came to typify the *dharmic* (duty-bound) insistence on non-violence, quite in contradistinction to the effervescence of militant student-hood which had already become the most popular (and immediate) mode of nationalist engagement by around the end of the War in 1919.

In responding to these extremist strategies of political expression, the Rowlatt Act passed by the Imperial Legislative Council in March 1919 – more fully (and suggestively) titled as the 'Anarchical and Revolutionary Crimes Act' – extended the war-time emergency provisions for summary arrests of anti-government collaborators and their imprisonment without trial. Gandhi worked his way into the centre-stage of Congress politics, at this opportune moment of mass disillusionment and desperation, and called for a nationwide *hartal* (strike) to embark on his non-violent programme of individual *satyagraha*. The *hartal* turned violent in several parts of northern India (including Delhi and Punjab) owing to passionate conflagrations of the participating youth, and Gandhi had to immediately withdraw his pledge – but not before expressing his growing distrust of youthful patriotism and what he believed was its unthinking advocacy of terror (Gandhi, "Speech at Khilafat Conference"; *An Autobiography*; Kumar, *Essays on Gandhian Politics*; Ray 249–55). The Jallianwala Bagh tragedy of April 1919, which has come to be regarded as the bloodiest example of British terror on unsuspecting civilians, followed soon after. The Montagu-Chelmsford (Mont-Ford) reforms, promulgated around the same time, offered a parliamentary optics of compromise by extending franchise at the level of provincial council elections.

But, the predominant nationalist mood reflected a resolute desire for political non-collaboration, and instead demanded the concrete announcement of an action programme. In September 1920, just a few months before the first council elections were to be held under the Mont-Ford plan, the annual Congress session in Calcutta resolved – under the leadership of Gandhi – to embark on a non-cooperation movement directed against the British government and its institutions (Gordon 443–73). This was declared to be the means for mounting pressure on the colonial administration to concede to the nationalists' demand for *swaraj*, through at least a grant of Dominion Status if not complete home rule. In this, Gandhi joined ranks with the Khilafatists and brought the charge of Islamist anti-imperialism to bear on an otherwise pronounced symbolism of Hindu self-cultivation. Obviously, this was not an innocuous move aimed simply at incrementing nationalist sentiment; instead, Gandhi hoped that the wealth of religious codes and tools of spiritual self-making within both the Hindu and Muslim faiths could potentially deflect the tendency towards violence (Gandhi, "Noncooperation"; "Speech at Idgah"; "Hinduism"; Brown). Once again, the youth was exhorted to adopt (and regiment) a 'mass'-character through insidious recourse to religion (Devji).

Non-Cooperation, and the Bursting Forth of a Communal Unconscious

In its initial *avatar*, the non-cooperation movement was to proceed by making an example of the renunciation of colonial structures of privilege by the educated elite. Hence, its earliest charters called for a surrender of government-bestowed honours and titles, boycott of legislatures and government-run educational institutions and civil courts, as well as a refusal to participate in government ceremonies (Gandhi, "Noncooperation"). Clearly, the political charge of this nascent phase was to devolve onto the exclusive beneficiaries of colonial modernity – which ranged from the rural elite in *zamindar* classes to those engaged in the learned professions of the city. There was sustained resistance in particular to demands for boycotting schools and colleges and courts of law, insofar as that would have meant a direct assault on the historical alliance between class-caste advantage and the opportunities for social-economic mobility enabled by colonialism. For Gandhi, on the contrary, the full boycott of colonial institutions was the only condition of possibility for a constructive programme of local self-government through alternative structures of civic and spiritual education. The Bengal variety of prominent nationalists, still revelling in the memory of a decades-old *swadeshi* activism, was in no mood to submit to a resolutely non-violent programme and instead argued for a strategic mobilisation of the country's burgeoning youth in *hartals* and public demonstrations and picketing rallies (Ray). It was owing to pressure from the Bengali intelligentsia, and specifically Chittaranjan Das, that Gandhi included a boycott of foreign items of everyday use in the early non-cooperation manifesto. This meant an unleashing of public squads of young volunteers to ensure adherence to boycott principles, in fear of whose penchant for violence Gandhi decided on one of the most effective symbolisations of *swadeshi* self-building: the compulsory daily manual labour of spinning the *charkha* (cotton spinning-wheel). The astuteness of this political-symbolic move was at once directed at re-incorporating (and containing) the corrosive energies of young nationalists as well as breaking out of the middle-class character of mainstream nationalist articulations of Congress-vintage.

The *baniya* (trader-caste) roots of Gandhi were alert to the fact that trusting the political benevolence of the urban educated classes – while at the same time alienating them from historically accrued caste-privileges – could not in itself guarantee the longevity of this movement. A concurrent moral gesture of edifying the dignity of labour, in routines of hand-spinning, was also not enough. He thus reached out to Marwari and Parsi communities of domestic industrial capital, by aligning the agendas of boycott with a greater encouragement for indigenous entrepreneurialism (ibid. 228–30). But, none of this strategic political sagacity could counteract the communal tensions simmering beneath class and caste inequalities, between landholding/landlordist Hindus and Muslim peasants and landless tenants (Siddiqi; Kumar, *Peasants in Revolt*; Henningham; Sarkar, "The Conditions and Nature of Subaltern Militancy"; Pati). The inner pathologies of violence that Gandhi tried extremely hard to divert into regimes of spiritual affect-production, by co-opting a quotidian experience of popular religion, could not be neutralised. The ghosts of religion, insofar as they were hardly ever frontally questioned in terms of their effects of social reification, erupted most fearfully in the Mapilla rebellion of 1921.

The Mapillas, a community of poor Muslim tenants settled in the Malabar district, had long been oppressed by the extortionist tactics of Hindu *zamindars* and their revenue collectors. There had been reports of forceful evictions from their land under the auspices of the local *zamindars* at times, and the Khilafat platform provided a space for collectivising and politicising the aggrieved Mapillas to sporadically rise in revolt (Menon; Tottenham; Namboodiripad). The August 1921 rioting gave an outlet to these pent-up perceptions of communal persecution among the peasantry, and was provoked by rumours of desecration of a mosque by the local police. There was a serious outbreak of violence, largely meditated along religious lines. The nationalist response to the Mappila violence is summed up by David Hardiman:

> Both the Congress and Khilafat leaders disowned the rebels. They said that the issue was primarily an economic one, rather than a result of nationalist propaganda and Khilafat activity. The Mappilas had, they said, gravely misunderstood the movement. If the noncooperators had been allowed to work in the area freely, they could have propagated nonviolence. A.K. Azad and Abdul Bari expressed horror at the forcible conversions, pointing out that proselytising with the sword was against Islamic law. The insurgents, for their part, denounced Gandhi and the Ali brothers as infidels when they appealed for them to renounce violence. Many Hindus were alarmed by the revolt, seeing in it a pattern of supposed Muslim fanaticism and lack of commitment to the nationalist cause, and went on to argue that Muslims could not be trusted. (51)

When Gandhi abruptly called off the non-cooperation movement in February 1922, following a spate of anti-colonial violence by young picketers which killed twenty-three policemen,[4] it was largely the Indian students who felt utterly betrayed by the old guard of the Congress. In the general sense of frustration that thus crept in, a new crop of youth politics was being imaginatively forged as an antidote to religious nationalism. For this non-Gandhian variant of political activism, the resort to armed violence had to be philosophically recalibrated into an anti-imperialist manifesto. The resources for this intellectual exercise, by the country's youth, once again necessitated a detour into the Comintern's policy across the seas and the regional labour union struggles of the Workers' and Peasants' Party (WPP) units across the country. The formation of the Indian Communist Party (ICP), which was later remodelled into the Communist Party of India (CPI) in 1924–25, along with

[4] The Chauri Chaura incident, as it was called, became the immediate cause for Gandhi's suspension of the mass civil disobedience movement about to be launched from Bardoli. In the pages of *Young India*, dated 16 February 1922, Gandhi expressed his angst: 'non-violent non-cooperators can only succeed when they have succeeded in attaining control over the hooligans of India, in other words, when the latter have also learnt patriotically or religiously to refrain from their violent activities at least while the campaign of non-co-operation is going on.'

the militant trade unionism among jute mill workers of Bengal or textile workers of Bombay – were all instrumental in conjuring an alternative to Gandhian politics during the interwar years (Joshi, *Struggle for Hegemony in India*; Petrie; Ganguly).

Armed Revolutionary Youth and Class Struggle

Needless to say, the unionised 'working classes' were not a coherent political force in nationalist politics, insofar as they were prone to deep religious divisions and a consequent incorporation into radicalised communal agendas. This became apparent in recurring episodes of Hindu-Muslim riots through the 1920s, peaking with the violence on Marwari traders in 1926 in Calcutta (Roy; Dutta 38–48), or the attacks on Pathan strike-breakers by Girni Kamgar Union (GKU) members in 1929 in Bombay (Hesse 139–43). In the despairing aftermath of the failed non-cooperation movement and against the backdrop of continued communal fear-mongering, the revolutionary-spirited youth of northern India persisted in their quest for a determinedly secular socialist front for anti-colonial action.

Their efforts panned across a series of organisational offshoots – like the Hindustan Republican Association (HRA, 1924), Naujawan Bharat Sabha (NJBS, 1926) and Hindustan Socialist Republican Association/Army (HSRA, 1928) – each of which left behind a distinct footprint in the silting up of interwar nationalism. With their membership overlapping across subsequent formations, it is from this harvest of revolutionary youth movements that the likes of Bhagat Singh, Chandrasekhar Azad, Sukhdev Thapar, Shivram Rajguru and Batukeshwar Dutt tirelessly attempted to align the currents of subcontinental nationalism to the forces of communist internationalism.

The HRA's early organisational successes were thrown off-gear by the conviction of its leaders in a *swadeshi* dacoity, now famously termed as the Kakori Conspiracy Case (1925–26). Filling the vacuum thus created, Bhagat Singh's Naujawan Bharat Sabha made an impassioned plea to the youth of the nation to break out of the mists of indecision created by a national-level leadership and plunge headlong into a militant movement ("Manifesto" 530). The NJBS manifesto was careful in qualifying this brand of militancy as a philosophy of deep immersive 'work' with the masses. Alongside this, the force of religion had to be kept at an arm's length or more, in order to prove one's suitability for the cause. It begins by declaiming:

> We have appealed to the young only. Because the young bear the most inhuman tortures smilingly and face death without hesitation. Because the whole history of human progress is written with the blood of young men and young women. And because the reforms are ever made by the vigour, courage, self-sacrifice and emotional conviction of the young men who do not know enough to be afraid and who feel much more than they think. . . . (ibid. 527)

For Singh, it was only the youth – and concurrently, the nationalist student-subject – who might structure anti-imperialism's passage into the 'masses'. This itself was the substance of 'revolution' – the means for which lay not in a routing through sectarian ties of identity and commonality, but in a universalist desire for community beyond the 'form' of the nation. Such community, the NJBS manifesto maintained, cannot but force a realisation of the shared truth of injustice – fighting against which, for all peoples of all nations, is also what binds them together.

> Do you know the wonders worked by the Young Turks? Do you not daily read what the young Chinese are doing? Were it not the young Russians who sacrificed their lives for Russia's emancipation? Throughout the last century hundreds and thousands of them were exiled to Siberia for the mere distribution of socialist pamphlets or, like Dostoyevsky, for merely belonging to a socialist debating society. Again and again they faced the storm of oppression. But they did not lose courage. It were they, the young only, who fought. And everywhere the young can fight without hope, without fear and without hesitation. And we find today in the great Russia, the emancipation of the world.
>
> While, we Indians, what are we doing? A branch of peepal tree is cut and religious feelings of the Hindus are injured. A corner of a

> paper idol, tazia, of the idol-breaker Mohammedans is broken, and "Allah" gets enraged, who cannot be satisfied with anything less than the blood of the infidel Hindus. Man ought to be attached more importance than animals and, yet, here in India, they break each other's heads in the name of "sacred animals". (ibid. 527–28)

It is not the violence incipient within religion (and its concomitant demands for allegiance) that can connect the fortunes of the 'young' and the 'masses', though history has been witness to such attempts since the early *swadeshi* days. Instead, the anarchist oeuvre in Bhagat Singh's career holds that the invisible structures of violence animating governmental instances/exercises of political rule can only be made palpable by unravelling a potential 'physical force' that inheres in all masses without differentiation. It is to this extent that revolutionary violence belonged to the 'mass', while religious strife characterised the 'sect'; alternatively, it is this same political potential shared by the youth and the masses that makes one a revolutionary conduit into the other. Singh's communism, along with that of his HSRA comrades, was perhaps one of India's earliest debates on a structural analysis of violence and its strategic/activistic uses.

Understanding Structural Violence: An Other 'Mass'

When Bhagat–Rajguru–Sukhdev–Azad sought to avenge Lajpat Rai's death by killing a British police officer J.P. Saunders (mistakenly assumed to be James Scott) in Lahore in December 1928, the philosophical secret of revolutionary violence was postulated in the HSRA's claim that 'this man was a part of [a] cruel, despicable and unjust system' (Lal 137–38). That Rai, on the other hand, was a member of the Hindu Mahasabha and had explicitly antagonised the HSRA's brand of revolutionary politics is significant, in that the revolution against structural injustice was reaffirmed as defeating the violence endemic to religion. The NJBS manifesto continued on a similar strain:

> The future programme of preparing the country will begin with the motto: "Revolution by the masses and for the masses." In other words,

> Swaraj for the 90%; Swaraj not only attained by the masses but also for the masses. This is a very difficult task. Though our leaders have offered many suggestions, none had the courage to put forward and carry out successfully a concrete scheme of awakening the masses. Without going into details, we can safely assert that to achieve our object, thousands of our most brilliant young men, like the Russian youth, will have to pass their precious lives in village and make the people understand what the Indian revolution would really mean. They must be made to realise that the revolution which is to come will mean more than a change of masters. It will, above all, mean the birth of a new order of things, a new state. This is not the work of a day or a year. Decades of matchless self-sacrifice will prepare the masses for the accomplishment of that great work and only the revolutionary young men will be able to do that. A revolutionary does not necessarily mean a man of bombs and revolvers. (ibid. 530)

The 'Indian revolution' – which consisted in 'the birth of a new order of things' – called on young student revolutionaries to commit themselves to an ethic of deindividuation. That was the communist path; it involved a passage from the 'precious' propriety of a name to a community of unnamed 'masses'. This was not social service of the extremist-nationalist or constructive *swadeshi* variety – gestures that demanded either an austere sacrificiality or a messianic disposition towards charity. In both these bourgeois-nationalist versions of *seva*-ideology, revolution is muddled with devotion (for gods or essences). The NJBS–HSRA's cult of 'matchless self-sacrifice' lay in slow processes of structural overhaul that went far beyond 'bombs and revolvers'. The latter could only 'make the deaf hear', as Singh and Dutt's bombing in the gallery of the Central Legislative Assembly intended to do, at the precise moment when the Public Safety Bill and the Trade Disputes Bill were being tabled on 8 April 1929 (Lal 139). The work of the revolutionary, Singh clarified in "Philosophy of the Bomb" (1930) as well as in his public despatches as an under-trial in the sessions court, lay contrarily in forcing one to see the invisible under-prints of structural violence and injustice.[5]

---

[5] See, for example, Sanyal et al., "Statement of the Undefended Accused"

It was this same revolutionary ideal – committed not to a programme of symbolic mass-contact, but to the relentless labour of unveiling structures of naturalised oppression – that led Singh to launch a mass hunger strike in the Central Jail of Mianwali in mid-1929. Otherwise disavowed by Congress circles as a 'man of bombs and revolvers', the hunger strike was Singh's means of forcing nationalist public opinion to wake up to the experience of racial discrimination within colonial prison systems, in terms of the specific treatment of 'political prisoners'. Given the British government's determined reluctance to grant legislative credence to the category of 'political prisoners', Singh issued a call to his fellow Indian jail inmates to self-identify as such and join in the fast against custodial indignity. The hunger strike claimed the life of an HSRA comrade in Jatindra Nath Das in September 1929, which granted renewed public visibility to the revolutionary strand of nationalist activism. The death of Das provoked massive student unrest across the country, which again forced the Indian National Congress to review its political demands and eventually launch a movement for *purna swaraj* (complete independence) – as opposed to Dominion Status – in late 1929 and early 1930. In pursuance of the Congress' new-found stridency and the general mood for some decisive action-plan among the nation's youth, Gandhi announced the start of a civil disobedience movement by marching against the government's salt tax laws and issuing a public call for a countrywide 'salt *satyagraha*' in March 1930.

Meanwhile, Singh and the HSRA's troupe of young jailed revolutionaries were first sentenced for life in the Assembly Bomb case and then awarded the death penalty in court hearings that went on through 1930. Gandhi too had courted arrest at that time, following his Dandi march, and was in a jail near Poona.

(drafted by Bhagat Singh of behalf of the Lahore Conspiracy Case [LCC] signatories, 5 May 1930, https://www.marxists.org/archive/bhagat-singh/1930/05/05.htm. See also Bhagat Singh and B.K. Dutt, "Joint Statement", 8 June 1929, https://www.marxists.org/archive/bhagat-singh/1929/06/06.htm; Bhagat Singh, "Statement before the Lahore High Court Bench", 1930, https://www.marxists.org/archive/bhagat-singh/1930/x01/x01.htm

Days before the hanging of the HSRA trio in March 1931, owing to widespread condemnation of British repressive policies in the international press, Gandhi was released from jail and allowed the confidence of a meeting with the Viceroy Lord Irwin. Signing an agreement for truce (now memorialised as the 'Gandhi-Irwin Pact' of 5 March 1931), the 'Mahatma' prevailed on the colonial state to release all political prisoners except those convicted of the use of violence. There was thus no clemency sought for the HSRA activists, even on the privileged occasion of a private negotiation, and this was construed as Gandhi's definitive disavowal of the revolutionary student cause as methodologically (and ideologically) alienated from the nationalist crusade.

Profaning Religion: Pitting the 'Nationalist' against the 'Internationalist'

It was at this precise conjuncture that an elaborately public trial was concocted and staged at the sessions court in Meerut, in order to juridically seal the Gandhian – and, by inference, Congressite – separation between anti-colonial and anti-capitalist forms of political struggle in India. The trial, commenced in June 1929 and now widely remembered as the 'Meerut Conspiracy Case', dragged on for four years in order to substantially polarise the nationalist public imagination against the work of the Comintern and its regional branches of youth leagues, trade unions and Workers' and Peasants' Parties (WPPs). The 32 accused individuals – who ranged from being members of the Communist Parties of Great Britain and India to non-party political workers and non-communist youth leaders or trade unionists – were named along with a list of 63 associate organisations and private supporters, as having 'conspired with each other and with other persons known or unknown within or without British India, to deprive the King Emperor of the sovereignty of British India' (*MCCC* 3), under assumed instructions from the Communist International. The immediate cause of their crime was ascertained as a 'meeting for conspiracy' at Meerut, followed by the formation of a local WPP unit. British radicals like Philip Spratt, Benjamin Francis Bradley and Hugh Lester Hutchinson were charged with leading the Indian revolutionaries, towards an 'incitement of antagonism between Capital and Labour' (ibid.) as ordained by Comintern policy.

As is evident from the nature and the statement of charges, the trial became an excuse for provoking (and manipulating) a public referendum on Marxism and Leninism via calculated detours into party literature and propaganda, through the long hours and days of a courtroom drama. The final judgment, pronounced in January 1933, maintains that 'the accused have from time to time raised numerous objections to the alleged vague nature of the complaint', but then surprisingly relies on 'persons as well read and well informed on Communist theory and practice as the bulk of the accused' to infer the justifiability of the charges (ibid. 4). Laughable though it may sound for a verdict on 'criminal conspiracy' to base its grounds for conviction on the scholarly competence of the accused, this is only one of the many glaring sleights of judicial reason that the Meerut case carefully crafted. The government prosecutor, R. Langford James, opened his argument in the case thus:

> The accused in this case stand charged with a conspiracy to deprive His Majesty of the sovereignty of India, and the case for the prosecution is that they have sought to do that by means of a revolution. Now the slogan, which most satisfactorily, to my mind, sums up their intentions, is "Long Live Revolution." A revolution is ordinarily an incident in time. It happens. It is done away with, and it gives place to that brighter and better state of things which, any way in the minds of its authors, it is destined to usher in. But the revolution which these accused have conspired for, and which they have visualised, is indeed a revolution that lives long. It goes on. It is a continuing and almost perpetual revolution. Now that is a point which I shall have to deal with much later on. At the moment I should like to remove one possible misunderstanding. This revolution that these accused have visualised is not a national revolution. It is an anti-national revolution. (James xx)

The injury perceived in the revolutionary slogan, when seen in the context of the Naujawan Bharat Sabha's manifesto for slow structural change, is in effect a devious rhetorical move towards privileging the symbolic over the structural. It is along these two domains of signification that a distribution of political affects is managed, through James' separation of the national(ist) revolutionary and the anti-national communist. The 'perpetuity' of change, promised by the Meerut under-trials with their links to youth and worker leagues, is itself deduced as evidence for the extension of the revolution *beyond* the nation – and almost, as if by some strange dialectical operation, *against* the immediate (non-extensive) interests of the nation. That the promissory charge of a slogan is legally equated with the application of 'criminal force' adequate for the overthrow of a government – the punitive ambit of Section 121A of the Indian Penal Code, under which charges were framed – is once again proof of a stealthy imaginative conquest. The message was succinctly sounded: legitimate (and legalised) anti-colonial politics can align with the national 'mass' by force of religion, as both the *swadeshi* and Gandhian varieties did. But, a politics which aspired to a 'mass' beyond the nation – in both length of time and extensibility of space – by bringing into sharp relief the operations of class relations was, by definition, neither anti-colonial nor nationalist. The latter smacked of a communist revolution which, by Meerut's percolation into the public memory of 1933 and after, was anti-national (Louro, "'Where National Revolutionary Ends and Communist Begins'"). Indeed, as we shall see later in this book, the imaginative aftermath of 1933 continues until this day.

Prosecutor James, by likening all the accused to Bolsheviks who wanted 'to replace the Government of His Majesty King George in India, and in its place to put the Government of the Third Communist International', went on to argue:

> [T]he object in fact which these accused had is, I repeat, anti-nationalist. They would, I think, say it was international, but the two words are really the same. . . . [I]t appears to me that to be a Bolshevik of unimpeachable character you require certain definite qualifications to which the ordinary man does not aspire. You do not love your country, you are anti-country, you are anti-God, and

> you are anti-family. In fact I think it fair to say that a Bolshevik of unimpeachable character is anti-everything which the normal man considers decent. . . . There can be no God according to the Soviet creed, and a large part of their propaganda is directed to destroying belief in God, whether he be the God of the Christian, the Jew, the Muhammadan or the Buddhist. The belief in Him is to be destroyed, and if and when the time comes that this reign of destruction comes to India, I am sure belief in the God of Hinduism will also have to be destroyed. All the religions of the world have to be destroyed, according to these gentlemen, and they have gone the length not only of murdering priests and desecrating churches but of setting up classes for the young men and young children to preach to them the gospel of anti-God. (James xx)

With the discursive circumscription of the young 'anti-national' communist who works at the behest of a Party, as opposed to those serving the nation or society (alternatively coded as 'religion' or 'national culture'), the familiar binaries of mainstream nationalism were now written in stone. Forgiving Jawaharlal Nehru's misguided excursion between these polarities of the 'party worker' versus 'social worker', the Meerut judgment nonetheless incriminates the international League Against Imperialism (LAI) that Nehru himself had helped found and officialise in 1927.[6] The LAI's natal links

[6] Louro ("'Where National Revolutionary Ends and Communist Begins'") examines the rhetorical sleights through which the magistrate's committal order separates the LAI's purported attachment to 'revolutionary violence' from Nehru's ideological subscription to 'Gandhian non-violence': 'If criminal evidence in the LAI sources was lacking, the prosecution and magistrate underscored Nehru's departures from official league policy as the essential differences between INC nationalism and LAI internationalism. Nehru's correspondence with Berlin, mostly confiscated, copied, and forwarded to the intended destination, became a central body of evidence to define the boundaries between Indian nationalism and its internationalist other. In particular, tensions in the correspondence between Nehru and Virendranath Chattopadyaya, the other co-secretary of the LAI Berlin office, served as the ammunition' (335). To demonstrate the order's accentuation of such 'tensions' with the objective of exonerating Nehru, take the example of, say, Para 270 of the MCCC judgment from 1933: 'Again in P 1644, (F. 0.620), dated the 31st October, 1928, to Mr. J. L. Nehru, Chatto mentions the fact

with the Comintern, and its imminent takeover by the Moscow line by around 1929, had already soured Nehru's relationship with the League's Berlin secretary and extraordinary student-mobiliser in Virendranath Chattopadhyay. The Meerut verdict only forced Nehru to further retreat into the Gandhian nationalist fold, and sever ties with the increasingly anti-Congress stance represented by the Comintern (Ghosh, *The Meerut Conspiracy Case*; Singh, *Meerut Conspiracy Case*; Zachariah; Gupta; Louro, "Rethinking Nehru's Internationalism) - even as he kept up his association with the communist All India Trade Union Congress (AITUC).

Internalising Religious Surrender: A *Seva* Ethic as Nationalist *Dharma*

The Meerut conspiracy case however cast a long and lingering shadow on the fate of youth mobilisations in India - with the Congress Socialist Party (CSP) breaking away from the Communist Party of India (CPI) in 1934, partly to escape public censure. The CPI's position itself was far from assured, and therefore there was a need felt for an independent student association which could both grant cover to the Party's activities as well as function as its official youth wing. The formation of the All India Students' Federation (AISF) in 1936 assumed cardinal significance in the context of the imperial war-campaign during the Second World War (Bannerjee; Joshi, *Student Revolts in India*; Rajanwale; Cross et al.; Kumar, *Indian Youth and Electoral Politics*).

---

that "The All-Russian Federation of Trade Unions (an organisation whose controlling body consists entirely of Communists[...]) has decided to affiliate to the League." In a later paragraph he writes: "The 'Modern Review' seems to have made the same mischief as the B. Chr. with regard to your speech at the Bengal Students' Conference by quoting you as having said that 'you do not believe in Communism as an ideal of society.' I have seen your contradiction of this in the daily press. But you should compel the 'Modern Review' which has become the organ of the Bengali Fascists to publish a correction." If, Chatto and the League do not believe in Communism, why this interest in the contradiction of the statement that Mr. Nehru does not believe in Communism?' (112)

In the early years of its existence, the AISF organised thousands of student activists into provincial units to demand the release of political prisoners lodged in Andaman's jails. This movement was preceded by the Andaman detenus' self-organising into Marxist cells in jail, and a subsequent hunger strike demanding freedom from incarceration was coordinated with covert support from the CPI (Chatterjee 662–69). The AISF took the reins of the movement in 1937 through mass rallies and *hartals*, thus forcing Gandhi and the Congress to give the aspect of a larger anti-imperialist struggle to these agitations. The AISF even allied with the CSP – despite Gandhi's explicit distrust for student militancy – but it was the War that changed patterns of student mobilisation in India.

The AISF tremendously grew in popularity as well as membership through its early resistance to British war-efforts, on the grounds that imperialists and fascists were both dyed in the same hue. Their student volunteers sparred with the Congress faction, over the latter's careful control by the national leadership (CC-AISF; Chandra et al.; Wilkinson). However, in the immediate aftermath of Germany's attack on the Soviet Union in mid-1941, the AISF dramatically somersaulted into a Comintern position, favouring the War as an anti-Nazi crusade. In the December conference of the association, it was decided that the Nazi forces had to be defeated by any means and the 'land of socialism' (*The Student* 6) defended against. Furthermore, the fear of a Japanese offensive on India had turned the colonial state's war-effort into a 'people's war' for the communist student volunteers.

With its popular appeal successively dwindling among the youth of the cities, the AISF soon pressed its student squads into relief-work during the deadly Bengal famine of 1943 (Wilkinson 7). The agrarian uprisings of 1946–47 – namely, the Tebhaga movement in Bengal and the Telangana movement in the south – renewed a pledge for the communist student revolutionaries to stay away from the nationalist ceremony of political independence in 1947. Instead, these young Marxists were despatched into the villages, training themselves in the rural backyards of freedom and in deep contact with peasant revolutionaries for the first time in history.

The immediate pre-independence imagination of student politics, in the wake of the Second World War and the signs of an imminent transfer of political power, consisted in sculpting out a curious amalgam of the 'nationalist' and 'communist' sign-systems. While the mode of revolutionary attachment was articulated in a gesture of self-giving – a renunciatory voiding of subjectivity shared also by spiritual *seva* routines – the 'mass' that one was donating such service to was the famine-stricken poor or the oppressed sharecropper or the landless peasant. The revivalist fantasies of religious community were thus sought to be exorcised, but often to the forceful equation between 'revolution' and a textbook secularity. In forging a critique of class, in the bodily optics of immersion and self-loss, the force of religion was imagined to have been appropriated in 'form' and in relative immunity to its 'substance'. In the process, the familiar tropes of a nationalism committed to culture and society versus a communism committed to party(-politics) were largely left undisturbed despite historical memory. It is hardly astonishing that around the eve of India's independence, none other than the would-be Prime Minister in Nehru – with his durable connections with party politics of both the Congress and socialist-unionist varieties – must thus diagnose the 'defects' of Indian student movements at a Students' Congress Conference in February 1946:

> To offer political leadership to the country is not the function of the student movements in India. They cannot recommend any action to the country. Of course, this does not apply to conditions that are created in a time of crisis. Students instead of taking active part in politics should go to the villagers when they find time and there they should try to improve the conditions of our poor countrymen. The student movements all over the world are of a non-political nature, whereas in India they are linked to politics. This is the main defect with the student's [sic] movements in India. (*ToI*, 16 February 1946)

Nehru's barbs are understandably directed at the communist student movements, but ironically offer the same appropriative fantasy that the AISF had already put into practice since 1942–43. But the stigma that this comment attaches to the 'political' in student politics will only play out in the making of the postcolonial welfare-state, and in the decades of educational policy-planning that followed after 1947. Portentously enough, Nehru here hinted at the enduring charm of an ascetic demeanour within student life – none of which might be fully outgrown by a secular-liberal training at the university, typically for the sons of a Hindu upper-caste Mother India.

This historical hindsight, writing today in an India teetering at the cusp of Hindutva, seems but plain common sense. I will probe the policy-makings of such 'common sense' in the rest of my chapters.

References

Alavi, Hamza. "Ironies of History: Contradictions of the Khilafat Movement." *Comparative Studies of South Asia, Africa and the Middle East*, vol. 17, no. 1, 1997, pp. 1–16.

Bamford, P.C. *Histories of the Non-Co-operation and Khilafat Movements.* Government of India Press, 1925.

Banerjea, Surendranath. *A Nation in Making, Being the Reminiscences of Fifty Years of Public Life.* Oxford University Press, 1925.

Bannerjee, Raman. *This is the AISF.* New Age Printing Press, 1946.

Basu, Amritalal. *Shabaash Bangali: Samajik Naksha.* Kishore Printing Works, 1905.

Bishui, Kalpana. "The Origin and Evolution of the Scheme for the First Partition of Bengal." *Quarterly Review of Historical Studies*, vol. 5, no. 2, 1966, pp. 76–96.

Broomfield, J.H. "The Partition of Bengal." *Proceedings of the Indian History Congress.* Aligarh, 1960.

Brown, Judith. *Gandhi's Rise to Power: Indian Politics 1915–1922.* Cambridge University Press, 1972.

Central Committee (CC) – AISF. "War and the World Situation: Report of the 6th AISF Conference." Delhi, 1941.

Chand, Tara. *History of the Freedom Movement in India*, Volume Three, Publications Division, Government of India, 1972.

Chandra, Bipan, Mridula Mukherjee, Aditya Mukherjee, K.N. Panikkar, and Sucheta Mahajan. *India's Struggle for Independence.* Penguin, 1989.

Chatterjee, Pranab Kumar. "The Hunger Strike Movement of the Andaman Prisoners in 1937 and National Response." *Proceedings of the Indian History Congress*, vol. 40, 1979, pp. 662–69.

Chattopadhyay, Bankim Chandra. *Anandamath*. Bangiya Sahitya Parishad, 1938.

Cross, Richard, Norry Laporte, Kevin Morgan, and Matthew Worley. *Communism and Youth (Twentieth Century Communism)*. Lawrence & Wishart, 2012.

Dayal, Har. "India in America." *The Modern Review*, vol. 10, no. 1, 1911, pp. 2–11.

Devji, Faisal. *The Impossible Indian: Gandhi and the Temptation of Violence*. Hurst and Company, 2012.

Dutta, P.K. "War over Music: The Riots of 1926 in Bengal." *Social Scientist*, vol. 18, no. 6/7, 1990, pp. 38–48.

Elam, J. Daniel. "The 'Arch Priestess of Anarchy' Visits Lahore: Violence, Love, and the Worldliness of Revolutionary Texts." *Revolutionary Lives in South Asia: Acts and Afterlives of Anticolonial Political Action*, edited by Kama Maclean and J. Daniel Elam. Routledge, 2015, pp. 46–64.

Gandhi, M.K. *Hind Swaraj, or Indian Home Rule*. G.A. Natesan & Company, 1921 [1909].

———. "Speech at Khilafat Conference, Delhi, on 24 November." *Collected Works of Mahatma Gandhi*, Vol. 16. Navajivan Press, 1970 [1919], pp. 307–12.

———. "Noncooperation." *Collected Works of Mahatma Gandhi*, Volume 18. Navajivan Press, 1970 [1920a], pp. 5–7.

———. "Speech at Idgah, Karachi, 22 July." *Collected Works of Mahatma Gandhi*, Volume 18. Navajivan Press, 1970 [1920b], pp. 80–81.

———. "The Doctrine of the Sword (published in *Young India*, 11 August)." *Collected Works of Mahatma Gandhi*, Volume 18. Navajivan Press, 1970 [1920c], pp. 131–34.

———. "Hinduism (published in *Young India*, 6 October)." *Collected Works of Mahatma Gandhi*, Volume 21. Navajivan Press, 1970 [1921], p. 248.

———. *An Autobiography, or the Story of My Experiments with Truth*, Volume 2. Navajivan Press, 1929.

———. "The Cult of the Bomb." *Collected Works of Mahatma Gandhi*, Volume 42. Navajivan Press, 1970 [1930], p. 361.

Ganguly, S.M. *Leftism in India: M.N. Roy and Indian Politics, 1920–1948*. Minerva Publications, 1984.

Ghose, Aurobindo. *The Doctrine of Passive Resistance*. Sri Aurobindo Ashram, 1948.

Ghosh, Pramita. *The Meerut Conspiracy Case and the Left Wing in India*. Papyrus, 1978.

Ghosh, Suresh Chandra. "The Genesis of Curzon's University Reform: 1899–1905." *Minerva*, vol. 26, no. 4, 1988, pp. 463–92.

Gordon, R. "Non-cooperation and Council Entry, 1919 to 1920." *Modern Asian Studies*, vol. 7, no. 3, 1973, pp. 443–73. DOI:10.1017/S0026749X00005291.

Guha, Nalinikishore. *Banglay Biplabbad*. A. Mukherjee and Company Limited, 1923.

Gupta, Sobhanlal Datta. *The Comintern and the Destiny of Communism in India, 1919–1943*. Seribaan, 2006.

Hardiman, David. *Noncooperation in India: Nonviolent Strategy and Protest, 1920–22*. Oxford University Press, 2021.

Henningham, Stephen. *Peasant Movements in Colonial India: North Bihar 1917–1942*. Australian National University, 1982.

Hesse, Patrick von. "'To the Masses.' Communism and Religion in North India, 1920–47." DPhil diss. Humboldt-Universität zu Berlin, 2015.

Jalal, Ayesha. *Self and Sovereignty: Individual and Community in South Asian Islam since 1850*. Routledge, 2000.

James, Langford. "The Speech of the Prosecutor in the Meerut Case." *The Labour Monthly (TLM)*, vol. 12, no. 1, 1930, pp. 24–29.

Josh, Sohan Singh. *Hindustan Gadar Party: A Short History*. People's Publishing House, 1977.

Joshi, Pragjee Monjee. *Student Revolts in India: Story of the Pre-independence Youth Movement*. Sirur Printing Press, 1972.

Joshi, Shashi. *Struggle for Hegemony in India 1920–47. The Colonial State, the Left and the National Movement*, Volume 1. Sage Publications, 1992.

"Judgment Delivered in the Meerut Communist Conspiracy Case (Sessions Trial No. 2 of 1930" (*MCCC*), King Emperor vs P. Spratt & Others, Volume 1. Government of India Press, 1932.

Kanungo, Hemchandra. *Banglay Biplob Procheshta*. Kamala Book Depot Limited, 1928.

Kumar, Kapil. *Peasants in Revolt: Tenants, Landlords, Congress and the Raj in Oudh 1886–1922*. Manohar Publishers, 1994.

Kumar, R., ed. *Essays on Gandhian Politics: The Rowlatt Satyagraha of 1919*. Clarendon Press, 1971.

Kumar, Sanjay. *Indian Youth and Electoral Politics: An Emerging Engagement*. SAGE Publications, 2014.

Lal, Chaman, ed. *The Bhagat Singh Reader*. Harper Collins, 2019.

Louro, Michele. "Rethinking Nehru's Internationalism: The League against Imperialism and Anti-Imperial Networks, 1929–1939." *Third Frame: Literature, Culture, Society*, vol. 2, 2009, pp. 79–94.

———. "'Where National Revolutionary Ends and Communist Begins': The League against Imperialism and the Meerut Conspiracy Case." *Comparative Studies of South Asia, Africa and the Middle East*, vol. 33, no. 3, 2013, pp. 331–44, DOI: 10.1215/1089201x-2378121

"Manifesto of Naujawan Bharat Sabha [NJBS]." *The Bhagat Singh Reader*, edited by Chaman Lal. Harper Collins, 1928, pp. 526–31.

Menon, M. Gangadhara. *Malabar Rebellion (1921–1922)*. Vohra Publications, 1989.

Minault, Gail. *The Khilafat Movement: Religious Symbolism and Political Mobilization in India*. Columbia University Press, 1982.

Mukherjee, Haridas, and Uma Mukherjee. *The Origins of the National Education Movement (1905–1910)*. Jadavpur University, 1957.

Namboodiripad, E.M.S. "A Short History of the Peasant Movement in Malabar." *History, Society and Land Relations: Selected Essays*. LeftWord Books, 2010.

Pal, Bipinchandra. *Swadeshi & Swaraj: The Rise of New Patriotism*. Yugayatri Prakashak Limited, 1954.

Pati, Biswamoy. *Resisting Domination: Peasants, Tribals and the National Movement in Orissa 1920–50*. Manohar Publishers, 1993.

Petrie, David. *Communism in India, 1924–1927*. Editions Indian, 1972.

"Progress of Education in Bengal (1902–1907)." Third Quinquennial Review. Bengal Secretariat Book Depot, 1907.

Rajanwale, Anil. *History of the Student Movement in India*. Manak Publications, 2001.

Ramnath, Maia. *Haj to Utopia: How the Ghadar Movement Charted Global Radicalism and Attempted to Overthrow the British Empire*. University of California Press, 2011.

Ray, Rajat Kanta. *Social Conflict and Political Unrest in Bengal 1875–1927*. Oxford University Press, 1984.

Report on Native Papers in Bengal, No. 5 of 1906 [For the Week Ending the 3rd February]. Calcutta: Office of the Inspector General of Police, 1906, p. 97.

Report on Samitis in the Dacca Division Part II (RSDD). Home Political Progs Deposit, 1909.

Roy, M.N. "The Calcutta Riot." *Masses of India*, May 1926, available at https://www.marxists.org/archive/roy/1926/roy-26-riots.pdf

Sanyal, J.N., B.K. Dutt, Gayal Prasad, and Kundan Lal. "Statement of the Undefended Accused (drafted by Bhagat Singh of behalf of the Lahore

Conspiracy Case [LCC] signatories." 5 May, 1930, https://www.marxists.org/archive/bhagat-singh/1930/05/05.htm.

Sarkar, Sumit. *The Swadeshi Movement in Bengal, 1903–1908*. People's Publishing House, 1973.

———. "The Conditions and Nature of Subaltern Militancy: Bengal from Swadeshi to Non-Co-operation, c. 1905–22." *Subaltern Studies III: Writings on South Asian History and Society*, edited by Ranajit Guha. Oxford University Press, 1984, pp. 271–320.

Siddiqi, M.H. *Agrarian Unrest in North India: The United Provinces (1918–22)*. Vikas Publishers, 1978.

Singh, Bhagat, and B.K. Dutt. "Joint Statement." 8 Jun. 1929, https://www.marxists.org/archive/bhagat-singh/1929/06/06.htm.

Singh, Bhagat. "Statement before the Lahore High Court Bench." 1930, https://www.marxists.org/archive/bhagat-singh/1930/x01/x01.htm.

Singh, Devendra. *Meerut Conspiracy Case and the Communist Movement in India, 1929–1935*. Research India, 1991.

Tagore, Rabindranath. "Sadupay." *Prabashi*, Sraban 1315 (Jul.–Aug. 1908).

The Indian Universities Act 1904 (IUA). Papers Relating to the Act VIII of 1904. Calcutta, pp. 57–82.

The Student. AISF Conference Issue. Feb. 1942.

The Times of India (*ToI*). "Nehru's Speech at Students Congress Conference, Banaras, 15 February." Qtd. in Kaustubh Deka (2015), *Policy Report No. 14: Youth Activism and Democratic Politics in India's Northeast - 2014 Election in Perspective*. The Hindu Centre for Politics and Public Policy, 2015 [16 Feb. 1946].

Tottenham, G.R.F. "A Note on Events in Malabar by G. R. F. Tottenham." *The Mapilla Rebellion 1921–1922*, edited by Tottenham. Superintendent, Government Press, 1922, pp. 4–7.

Wilkinson, Tom. "Student Politics in British India and Beyond: The Rise and Fragmentation of the All India Student Federation (AISF), 1936–1950." *South Asia Multidisciplinary Academic Journal (SAMAJ)*, vol. 22, 2019, http://journals.openedition.org/samaj/6488; DOI: https://doi.org/10.4000/samaj.6488.

Zachariah, Benjamin. *Nehru*. Routledge, 2004.

PART TWO

Histories of a Re-/Un-making

Four

Post-Independence University Planning (1947–86): The Ideology of Welfare

In the Shadow of Social Service

In nearly a century of university education (1857–1947) before the official declaration of independence from British rule, we have seen how the rights of entry into collegiate life in India came to be refracted through the twin prisms of caste and religion. The two preceding chapters have attempted to exhume these historical underprints of India's inheritance of educational modernity, through both colonial and anti-colonial initiatives. Feudality and religiosity became the effective coordinates against which the university-educated adult could aspire to both social mobility (in the learned professions) as well as social service (in mass action). But what came to be shunned in no uncertain terms was the university's disposition towards the *political*, as opposed to its legitimate flirtation with the *social*. The previous chapter closed precisely on this point, with an examination of the trajectory of post-War student activism vis-à-vis Nehru's demand for a *service*-ethic of spiritual surrender.

This variety of enunciation around the most proper *form* of student subjectification in the university ended up performing a few deep imaginative manoeuvres. First, it brushed aside the historical operations of *caste* and *religion* in the making of the colonial/national(ist) university as mere *political effects*, and therefore irrelevant to the *social vocation* of higher education in an about-to-be-independent country. Second, and perhaps more cunningly, the imagined *social* priorities of the university were substituted for the official programme of 'socialism' in Nehruvian

India.[1] In other words, a strategic gesture of surrender to the 'social life' of the country, as opposed to its 'political effects', could very well pass itself off as the substance of socialist nation-building. The undeniable role of *caste* and *religion* within the distributive economies of opportunity intersecting the Indian university could now be subsumed in a policy-awareness of *class* alone. And that is exactly what happened through nearly four decades of educational policy-engineering in post-independence India, until about 1986 – the year which definitively brought fantasies of a Hindu India face-to-face with attempts at opening the university to private economic initiative.

This is the period I will survey in this chapter, largely through an attentive reading of policy archives around higher education as against brief closing vignettes of the political consequences that such policy eventually made way for. I contend, with specific reference to a series of commission reports and the first-ever policy programme for educational reform in postcolonial India, that a carefully sculpted idea of 'welfare' became the 'socialist'

[1] The newly independent nation-state's economic policy, under the leadership of the first Prime Minister (1947–1964) Jawaharlal Nehru, used the Soviet instrument of the Five Year Plan as its key to developmental agendas of social welfare. Consequently, the setting up of the Planning Commission by Nehru in 1950, and the latter's formulation of India's first Five Year Plan in 1951, were cardinally imagined as socialist state-building exercises in line with a political legacy from Soviet Russia. A lot of institutional behemoths were initiated and established during Nehru's tenure as state-funded projects – all of which aimed at addressing priorities of public provisioning in agriculture or food security, as well as creating scientific-industrial infrastructures as public sector enterprises. Some of these institutions, decidedly part of India's policy-instance of postcolonial socialism, include hydroelectric power projects, the Indian Institutes of Technology (IITs), medical colleges like All India Institute of Medical Sciences (AIIMS), the Indian Space Research Organisation (ISRO), Bhabha Atomic Research Centre, the National Institute of Virology and several others. See, for example, Ramchandra Guha, "The Multiple Agendas of Jawaharlal Nehru"; Prabhat Patnaik, "The Nehru Development Model"; Irfan Habib, "Legacy of the Freedom Struggle" and A.G. Noorani, "Nehru's Legacy to India".

shibboleth for engineering the Indian university between 1947 and 1986. Distinct from the conceptual lineaments of welfarism as understood in the Western context and yet retaining something of the Benthamite insistence on a utilitarian calculus,[2] the policy-imagining of 'welfare' – driving the Nehruvian engine of national development – was poised between the benefits of a *citizenly* education and a *workerly* education. In the process, it left untouched the deeper and more fractious truths of caste and religion – not by negating them as redundant to a 'free' polity, but instead by reinstating them as moral cover for the class-benefits of merit. Insofar as the vocational and the professional might become the class-prerogative of the socially underprivileged, the charge of a compulsory 'general' education for all – edifying the spirit of the meritorious poor – could, it was assumed, bring socialism back on the liberal track. I will explain and annotate this delicious irony in the next few sections.

Framing National Welfare: Citizenly Training

Soon after independence, in November 1948, the Government of India set up a University Education Commission under the chairmanship of Dr S. Radhakrishnan and including eminent scholars-cum-educational-thinkers like Tara Chand, Zakir Husain, A.L. Mudaliar and Meghnad Saha. The working purview of the commission was 'to report on Indian University Education and suggest improvements and extensions that may be desirable to suit present and future requirements of the country' ("Report" 1).

[2] Jeremy Bentham's postulation of a 'felicific calculus' – as essential to his theory of utilitarianism – argued that the moral value of an action depended on the calculable proportions of pleasure or pain that it could produce as consequence. Such calculus of moral determination, based as it was on the relative affinity of actions towards the production of pleasure and alleviation of pain, called for deep prior analyses of duration, expanse and intensity of 'circumstances'. How long might pleasure last and for how many people are questions factored into moral judgments; and therefore make Bentham's variety of utilitarianism depend on a 'hedonic' probability-test. Refer to Bentham, *An Introduction to the Principles of Morals and Legislation* (1781).

The stalwarts got to work and initiated a process of deliberations with different segments of university populations as well as administrative planners between December 1948 and July 1949. A hectic schedule of university tours in order to survey conditions for higher educational 'work' across the country culminated in a ranging report of over 700 pages – which noted, above everything else, 'a deep general awareness of the importance of higher education for *national welfare* and an uneasy sense of the inadequacy of the present pattern' (ibid. 5; emphasis mine).

It is crucial to remember that the work of the University Commission ran parallel to a period of intense debates in the Constituent Assembly, then still in the process of drafting the Indian constitution into its final shape.[3] While much of the wisdom from these debates percolated into the reform roadmap proposed for Indian universities – and their means of decolonising the life of the Indian mind – it is perhaps a little astonishing to discern in the Commission's Report an occasional lack of the emergent constitutional consensus. For example, the document cites from the "Preamble" of the Draft Constitution to enjoin higher education to a 'quest for democracy through the realisation of justice, liberty, equality and fraternity' (ibid. 31). But soon after, in the very next section, 'social justice' is explained as the 'freeing of the individual from poverty, unemployment, malnutrition and ignorance' (ibid.). The cardinal instruments for such 'freeing', necessary for the realisation of social justice, are assumed to result from an 'increase [of] national productivity by the larger use of scientific discoveries and technical applications' (39). Taken together, the Commission's call to social justice – as achievable through the agent of the university – consists in economic mobility alone, and its corresponding fillip to what I called a '*workerly* education'. There is rare evidence, and even rarer acknowledgment, of the

[3] An official compilation of these Assembly debates, opening up an archive of the most intense discussions and differences on what it means to be/become a 'democratic republic', may be found in twelve volumes and running into nearly 7000 pages.

historical effects of structural discrimination within spaces of intellectual instruction. Educational opportunity, measured in the humanist terms of 'talent' or 'ability' or a resilience against social odds, becomes the Radhakrishnan Commission's key to 'national welfare'.

The two most important recommendations made by the 1948–49 Report pertain to a restructuring of 'first degree' courses in Indian universities and a greater emphasis on the attuning of university-curricula to local professional needs. For the first of these, the Commission mandated a reorientation and expansion of degree programmes to include the general cognitive requirements of citizenship – through a deliberate underplaying of academic specialisations in favour of a liberal training into democracy.

> While a general understanding of the scientific method, of the history of our society and the world and literature which feeds our imagination and stabilises our emotional life is to be regarded as a part of general education for all, professional education trains the students for competence in an occupation. Education has among others this double aim of preparing for a particular vocation and also for citizenship in a democratic community. These two ends are not exclusive of each other. . . . Professional education is different from general education, not so much in its subject matter as in its method, outlook and objective. To give a basic understanding of the principles of science, history and literature is the aim of the general course; to train experts in them is the aim of the specialised course. (36–37)

The prescription of a 'general education for all' could, in the views of the members of the Commission, be implemented through an additional year of undergraduate degree-training and a gradual delinking of the intermediate examination from college education. The latter, it was argued, would free up higher educational resources for a more focussed emphasis on the initial 'general' part of college instruction. At the same time, the *citizenly* curriculum was supposed to compensate for the narrowness of professional routines – thus enabling a complementary perspective of history and culture to socialise those in the learned professions. Understandably, this training into 'culture' was precisely also the postcolonial antidote for a newly independent nation-state's claim to intellectual enlightenment. This is where a sense of continuity of Indian traditions of knowledge, as well as their amenability to change in the light of contemporary societies, could be infused into the formal structures of higher learning. The Commission notes, in a subsequent section:

> Education, according to the Indian tradition, is not merely a means to earning a living; nor is it only a nursery of thought or a school for citizenship. It is initiation into the life of spirit, a training of human souls in the pursuit of truth and the practice of virtue. It is a second birth, *dvitiyam janma.* (38)

The fact that general education in the cause of 'national welfare' has to seek legitimation and look for exemplary precedent in the figurative foregrounding of a *varnashrama*-ideal – the 'second birth' (*dvitiyam janma*) of education as potentially producing the *dvij* (twice-born) upper castes – is self-explanatory. This follows from an intrinsically caste-differentiated economy of intellectual rights, which I have discussed in the first chapter on brahminical education and its modes of ritual induction into a *brahmacharya* fold for non-*chandal* students alone. It is apparent that decolonisation, routed through the idea of 'welfare', can remain in relative harmony with feudal structures of caste and religious privilege. The clue to citizenship, steeped in 'Indian tradition' and abetted by the Radhakrishnan Commission here, rarifies hierarchies of intellectual attainment as a matter of historical entitlement instead of subjecting them to the scrutiny of a nascent constitutional consensus.

Framing Rural Development: A *Workerly* Education

The second significant direction in post-independence university planning came from the Radhakrishnan Commission's decided thrust on professional education in tandem with regional priorities and possibilities for employment. To this effect, the Report vociferously advocated the opening of adequate institutional spaces for agricultural, technical, engineering, medical, legal and rural education. In a bid to connect higher intellectual training with the life of the community, this was part of the Commission's effort at renegotiating the university's relationship with both the local and the vocational. The Report goes to the extent of suggesting a careful distribution of educated personnel in these professional disciplines across rural geographies, and often as part of course routines, in order to imagine a practical scheme of rural development as integral to the idea of 'national welfare'. A *workerly* education was thus balanced against the potential benefits of a *citizenly* training, and an initiation into practices of building 'community' was imagined as the flip side to the making of a national 'people':

> [W]e have to increase the number of professional colleges – agricultural, medical and engineering – to produce the requisite number of graduates and set up throughout the country technical schools which will supply the much larger number of technicians needed for the purpose. For a fuller realisation of the democratic principles of justice and freedom for all, we need growth in science and technology. . . . We need heavy large-scale industries for power, mining, metallurgy, oil, machinery and machine tools, automobiles, locomotives, ship-building, aircraft, heavy chemicals, pharmaceuticals. These are to be located by the State in centres selected for the availability of raw materials and local labour conditions. Our economy must be a decentralised one supported by agriculture and village industries, supplemented by the necessary large-scale industries which are worked, not for the profit of a few industrialists but for the *general welfare*. (39–40, emphasis mine)

Even while the Radhakrishnan Commission's vision for a socialist restructuring of developmental prerogatives is a salutary effort at tearing the imported model of the Indian university away from its urban–metropolitan roots, it suffers nonetheless from a deliberate myopia. By neatly diagnosing the causes of rural underdevelopment in a failed or incomplete economic initiative, the Report underplays the historical effects of a feudal social structure. The questions of caste and religious identity, and their interactions with an economy of both educational and professional opportunity, are largely ignored in the otherwise-socialistic din around 'welfare'. In the process, *class* overrides all other markers of birth and identity as the only deterrent to academic success – and conversely, by inference, to realisation of the equality-principle. A *workerly* education must therefore be regarded as a purely economic policy-implement – evening away both ends of input and output via the introduction of a neutral register of 'formal opportunity', voided of history. The Report's discussion on 'Equality of Opportunity' provokes no wonder as a result:

> Our system must provide for every young person education to the extent that he can profit from it and of a character best designed to assure the maximum development of his nature. It must of course recognise differences of gifts and interests. . . . For the great majority of our boys and girls the kind and amount of education they may hope to get, depends not on their own abilities but on the economic status of their family or the accident of their birth. . . . There is no relation, however, between the ability to profit from a college education and the ability to pay for it. . . . In distribution of educational opportunity there should be no caprice, prejudice, favouritism, special privilege, or other arbitrary action. In general each person should have educational opportunity of the kind and to the extent that is suited to his capacity and interest and which represents his fair share of the total educational resources. Application of this principle may be adjusted to the needs of society and to humane considerations. Should society need more technicians and fewer clerical workers, educational opportunity may be shifted accordingly. Exceptional ability is socially so valuable that it may be given exceptional opportunity. (43–44)

An education calibrated by 'differences of gifts and interests' can very easily legitimate a hierarchy of social value between a *citizenly* education and a *workerly* education – something that the Commission otherwise claims to discredit. At the same time, such an education erects a social economy of 'giftedness' or 'interestedness' – both conceptual equivalents of 'merit' – as expressive of humanist will, and ends up romanticising *class* as self-sufficient grounds for heroic enterprise and exceptionality. In the guise of socialist interventionism, a theory of maximal educational opportunity for the 'gifted' is the farthest removed from the quest for social justice. It only promotes a fantasy of individual aggrandisement and serves as an apology for the assumedly liberating tendencies of capital. That the 'accident of birth', which the Commission's espousal of 'equal opportunity' references, is one emptied of structural considerations of injustice becomes apparent from its dogged insistence on economic terms of exchange (like 'profit' and 'payment'). It is therefore all too fair, in the context of the Commission's recommendations, that such 'accident' be made the basis for manpower needs and a proportional provisioning of *workerly* educational opportunity calculated to the benefit of the nation. Social mobility, aided by equal opportunity in this instance, is also an injunction against breaching social relations of production or one's own historical situation. Such is the national welfare model of educational reform, which dare not touch the refractive indices of caste and religion for a life of the intellect. The Report maintains, in that exact spirit of welfare,

> The fundamental right is the right of the individual, not of the community. Every young man must have an equal chance with others to make the most of his abilities. To curtail the chance to learn for members of particular groups is inconsistent with the Fundamental Right. It would tend to increase the stratification of our society. To insist on quotas for communities would be to assume that the nation is composed of separate and self-sufficient groups, which is a negation of our national ideal and democratic principle. Discrimination practices generate tensions and the spiritual damage caused by them is not measurable. Education should not be used for creating or deepening the very inequalities which it is designed to prevent. Progress for the nation requires that access to higher education should be determined by the *interest*, and *ability* of the student. There is much to be said for the suggestion that the information about caste and religion should not be asked for from candidates for admission to colleges and universities. (45, emphases mine)

It might seem a little cognitively jarring that the same document which calls out the 'accident of birth' also goes on to appreciate a structural indifference towards 'information about caste and religion'. But, that is – as I tried explaining thus far, and will continue to do through the rest of this chapter – the delicate irony in the ideology of 'national welfare'. Even though the Commission subsequently makes peace with reserving a proportion of seats in government colleges for only 'qualified students' from the scheduled castes and other backward communities (46), its denunciation of 'communal ratios' or quotas is justified on the grounds of their being 'unfair to the nation which is deprived of high-class professional *ability* and social *competence*' (ibid.).

Preserving the Feudal-Communal Consensus

In its striving for a national-cultural consciousness, and in keeping up the spirit of an anti-colonial training of character through higher education, the Report is careful not to lapse into a mindless and slavish glorification of the past. It insists on an openness to cultural dialogue in the building of the Indian moral character, while also seeking ways to institutionalise the study of regional languages and literatures. But, not too long after, in a section on the need for religious instruction in universities, the author-members of the Commission make an impassioned plea for spiritual apprenticeship as the true mark of disinterested secularity. They emphatically hold,

> We do not accept a purely scientific materialism as the philosophy of the State. That would be to violate our nature, our *svabhava*, our characteristic genius, our *svadharma*. Though we have no State religion, we cannot forget that a deeply religious strain has run throughout our history like a golden thread. Besides, in the preamble to our Constitution, we have the makings of a national faith, a national way of life which is essentially democratic and religious. Whenever a human being strives upward toward enlightenment, goodness and concern for others, the spirit of religion is active. If we bear in mind that the whole future of our democracy depends on freedom of conscience, freedom of inquiry, moral solidarity, our secularism is an act of supreme courage and sublime loyalty to our national faith. . . . What we need is not formal religious education, but spiritual training. (257)

Here we find a restatement of the cult of the nation as a form of *faith* – easily demanding obeisance to rituals of belonging, coded as '*svabhava*' (natural disposition) or '*svadharma*' (natural duty). The Commission's curious interpretation of the Constitution's preambular commitment to secularity as 'a way of life which is essentially democratic and religious' merges quickly into a redefinition of secularism: as 'sublime loyalty to our national faith'. It is not fortuitous that one hears in this Report on postcolonial India's higher educational futures an echo from the *swadeshi* past of Hindu revivalism – that I have chronicled in the previous chapter. In trying to bridge the chasm between higher intellectual pursuits within the university and the masses that lie outside of its institutional purview, religion becomes the opportune ruse. Not surprisingly, the 'deeply religious strain [that] has run throughout our history' is laden with the symbolic overtones of a Hindu nationalism, and works by making a historical consciousness incumbent on a pietistic form of subjectivity. The result is a demand for *surrender* – a sacrificial self-giving to the nation in the spirit of *seva*. What else is religion, framed as a striving 'toward enlightenment, goodness and concern for others'? The Report's simultaneous rejection of what it calls a 'scientific materialism' of the state is why a *workerly* education must be tempered through spiritual passage into citizenship. Alternatively put, the *citizenly* is but an excuse for the moral elevation of the 'mass' within *workerly* training, and all it needs is a direct recourse to the language of devotion. The idea of welfare, which is the teleological end of this period of university reform, is in the process made amenable to a national religion of 'loyalty' without having to adopt a state religion. The Report's tedious exhortation on the need for religious instruction continues thus:

> In a sense religion is the most secular of all pursuits. It starts where man is, with the facts and problems of his concrete life and goes with him wherever he is and whatever he does. No real religion will submit to separation from life. All life must be infused with the life of spirit. . . . If we exclude spiritual training in our institutions we would

> be untrue to our whole historical development. India has believed that when one has done his duties as a *grhastha*, a householder, has been a good father or mother, a good provider for the family, a good citizen, there is still the beauty and mystery of the universe, the meaning of life and death, the aspirations of the inner soul, that sad feeling of the wistful-minded that beyond the world of positive knowledge there is a realm of forces unseen which we can feel but never know completely. . . . Each one is at liberty to approach the Unseen as it suits his capacity and inclination. If this is the basis of our Secular State, to be secular is not to be religiously illiterate. It is to be deeply spiritual and not narrowly religious. (259–61)

Once again, the rhetorical resignification of religion as the 'most secular of all pursuits' performs two shrewd moves: first, it makes 'spiritual' education the worthiest of the secular liberal university's prerogatives; and second, it implies that religion is the only chance at the university's self-exceeding into the 'mass' that it excludes. The *swadeshi* manifesto for a national education, as integrally feeding into a technique of mass mobilisation via the commonality of faith, bears heavy on Radhakrishnan's script – not in a literal but as a prophetic possibility for history's repetition. Furthermore, in making 'concrete life' the precondition for 'real' religion (as perhaps opposed to a metaphysical cult of 'after-life' transcendence), the university's attentiveness to immediate material agendas of welfare is granted a *sacral* legitimacy. Though the theory of the 'Unseen', following immediately after, appears as a contradiction in terms vis-à-vis concrete life, I believe it does something different. The 'unseen' is the *citizenly* dividend that the state reaps, in moral character and national(ist) loyalty, from the honing of material skills in the university. Through such an intangible economy of spiritual gain, what is reinstated is the university's preparatory ideal of *brahmacharya* subjectifying the citizen-worker into subsequent *varnashrama*-codes of both *grhastha* (householding) as well as *vanaprastha* (retiring from worldliness). Religious education, as the practical method for initiation into secular life, becomes at heart the reification of caste-*dharma*.

Gender and Politics: The Limits to Welfare State Socialism

As must be already apparent from the passages excerpted above, the prototypical student-subject inhabiting Radhakrishnan's university-imagination is the male citizen-worker. But in Chapter XII of the Report, titled 'Women's Education', Radhakrishnan and his colleagues begin by statistically ruing the negligible access for women to higher stages of schooling and collegiate education. It is recounted from data released by the Ministry of Education in 1945–46 that the contemporary gender ratio for enrolment had been as low as one woman for every six and a half men. Taking it upon themselves to remedy this skewed proportion of gendered access, the members contend at the very outset that uneducated girls make poor mothers and therefore retard the nation's welfare through incompetent child-raising. So, the education of women is first and foremost a question of preparing the nation's children for schooling. Unpaid domestic labour – which includes child-rearing – is dubbed as inefficient and unskilled in the absence of formal educational opportunities. Thus consecrating the woman to both the reproduction of skilled labour and the conjoined cause of national development, a case is made for her entry into the university – but only as long as she is skilled into the art of efficient unpaid (or at best, underpaid) work. The ideal of *workerly* education for the woman-citizen is tethered to a spiritual custodianship of the home and the family, and therefore shunning the inadequate *form* of wage-compensation. Women can claim their right to the post-independence Indian university, only insofar as they agree to not use their education for material gain or in competing with men. Here is how the Report puts it:

> For many women who crave to achieve standards of excellence, the home provides an excellent setting. For a woman to give the home design, beauty, order and character, without being herself a slave to home-keeping and without imposing onerous prohibitions and restrictions on the freedom of movement of children, is a high art. It will not be acquired by chance, and for many women its acquisition will be impossible, except through education. . . . Wise education for

> a woman will not leave her preparation for home and family to the bitter and wasteful school of experience. Her education as a woman should include practical 'laboratory' experience in the care of a home and family. . . . A woman should learn something, of problems that are certain to come up in all marriages, and in the relations of parents and children, and how they may be met. Her education should make her familiar with problems of home management and skilled in meeting them, so that she may take her place in a home with the same interest and the same sense of competence that a well trained man has in working at his calling. . . . There is need that the theory of equality of opportunity, but not necessarily identity of opportunity, shall find increasing expression in practice. (344–45)

For women, equal opportunity in the field of higher education demanded courses in home economics, nursing, teaching and fine arts. The assumed 'natural' propensity of women for care-work and their 'cultural' attentiveness to beauty and orderliness – as opposed to high intellect and technical intelligence – are, in the exact terms of the Report, grounds for their enlisting within agendas of national welfare as unpaid mothers and wives or underpaid teachers and nurses. The post-independence university, co-opted as it was into the task of 'welfare', could only serve as a surrogate laboratory for the woman's initiation into housework and care-giving – while at the same time maintaining her distinctness from the 'manly' prerogatives of a productive national economy:

> Probably there would be no quicker way to raise the general standard of economy and efficiency in Indian life than to make women interested and competent in the efficient, economical and convenient planning and management of their homes. . . . [I]t is the foundation of the orderly state, and the teaching of good home management is the first lesson in good government, as Confucius said. (ibid. 346–47)

Just as the 'social' dividends of welfare required a careful division of gendered labour even within the university – as well as its preservation of the caste and religious orders of passage into intellectual rights – the dangers of an outwardly 'political' independence had to be guarded against. To that extent, the University Education Commission's Report is acutely suspicious of the memory of an anti-imperialist politics that made the very fact of freedom possible. In a gesture of guarded acknowledgment of how university students participated in the immediately preceding decades of anti-colonial ferment, the authors caution that a strictly merit-based admission and scholarship programme can effectively weed out the 'unfortunate effects of communalism, the system of quotas, and discriminatory practices . . .' (302). Merit, yet again, becomes the dividing line between *social* and *political* uses of history. And, in the guise of the former, long-preserved hierarchies of intellectual 'ability' are effectively protected against the incursion of 'politics'. This was the scheme of *socialist* reconstruction that the Nehruvian university was attached to. Within such a scheme, 'scholarships are not intended to compensate poverty but to help real ability' (303), just as student unions were to become instruments of self-government for student populations. That is how the 'political effects' of independence could be neutralised into a haloed ideal of national welfare. The Indian university was to thus transform itself into a mimic-nation of self-governing citizens and spiritually-edified workers. University life became, in essence, *national service* – both through and after one's period of attachment to it. The Report recollects:

> The life of these University Unions has been a chequered one for they functioned at the period of political struggle and formed a forum, for the political activities of the students. Instead of holding debates of their own, the students generally preferred to invite political leaders and listen to their orations. When the political struggle grew intense the Unions were looked upon with great disfavour by the authorities and in some cases they were even suspended. Now that the political troubles are over the Unions can occupy their rightful place as the centres of social and corporate life in the universities. . . . [W]itnesses cited the period of the struggle for national independence in which students and staffs [sic.] were called upon by political leaders to engage in agitation, as a general cause of indiscipline carried over to the present. Such action may have served a patriotic purpose in an all-out drive for national freedom, but such practices now have a reverse effect, they promote confusion and become a serious impediment to national solidarity and integration. (330–31)

That the *social* functions of the university may run aground by its *political* misapplication is a fear that 'welfare' constantly conjures and urges against. The 'political activities' of students for national freedom are thus counterposed against the 'social and corporate life in the universities' in the cause of 'national solidarity and integration'. Following the turns of argument here, 'politics' – especially when engaged in by students and not 'political leaders' by themselves – is the nemesis of the university's pact with the nation. What served a 'patriotic purpose' during times of political trouble can now only spell trouble in times of the university's patriotic surrender. The oracular wisdom of the Commission therefore recommends a return of the 'free' university to its strictly *social* contract with a 'free' nation-state.

From Radhakrishnan to Kothari: Interpreting Social Mobility as Social Justice

It is true that the 1948–49 Report needs to be examined in its own context as well as the still-fresh legacy of a nationalist sentiment, but it did demonstrate tremendous foresight on certain counts. For example, the Commission's proposal for a formal separation between the political administration of the state and the work of financial provisioning for universities – through a clear structural autonomy of the University Grants Commission (UGC) – would go a long way in entrenching the principle of institutional self-governance (ibid. 222, 352–60). The insistence on ensuring that universities can continue to do their work needed not just their silent acquiescence to national-developmental agendas (as we have gleaned so far in the discussion), but more importantly their freedom from being beholden to political will. Alongside this, the Commission's spirited abetment of the Naliniranjan Sarkar Committee's plan of building institutions for higher technical education in the IITs – on the lines of the Massachusetts Institute of Technology (MIT) – also ensured prompt and timely action on the front. These Institutes, as Radhakrishnan and his fellow members argued, were to be imagined as engines for the country's industrial resource-training and manpower (ibid. 210–12). The wishful prophecy did in fact mature with time, the contradictions of which I will explore further on in the chapter. However, it is interesting that the Commission's desire to live past a colonial legacy of industrial modernity – while also insisting on a unique trajectory of national(ist) welfare – had to repeatedly rely on adulatory comparisons with the United States (ibid. 62, 65–66, 68–69, 83, 84, 140, 160–68, 191, 193, 199, 208, 213, 217, 222, 274, 279, 296, 301, 597–614, 685). In its discussion on every aspect of university reform, the American context became the most opportune reference as well as uncritical example for comparatively scaling the trajectories of national 'growth' in India. The post-War geopolitical balance of power must of course have been a running thread for policy-thinking in contemporary India, but doesn't this referential archive also pre-empt the outcomes of a Nehruvian idea of socialist 'welfare'?

One and a half decades later, the Government of India commissioned yet another team of 15 educationists – headed by Professor D.S. Kothari – to submit a Report on the state of Indian education and its necessary transformations. The Education Commission of 1964–66, as it was called, published its findings and recommendations under the title *Education and National Development*, and sought to envision a policy framework for the next twenty years. While being significantly more perceptive of the differential economies of educational access and attainment as well as their structural causes, the Kothari Commission – a name by which it has been subsequently memorialised – made no fuss about the *citizenly* charter of the university. On the contrary, it unapologetically saw the post-independence university as staggering under the weight of its own grand illusions about a *general* education in the arts and the sciences – none of which could deliver the promises it made in terms of social-economic mobility. The corrective was thus sought in bifurcating the purpose of foundational schooling – including the primary and lower secondary – from the distinct charge of higher education in colleges and universities. While the former could effectively invest its energies in moulding citizens fit for either a life of work or further study, the latter was to be unswervingly committed to the *workerly* needs of national development. Citizenship-building rubrics received a backseat within agendas of higher educational planning, and the theory of national welfare was now reconfigured with a double emphasis on national-economic priorities.

That said, despite the shift of focus within university reform from what I have called the *citizenly* to the *workerly* needs of the nation, the idea of 'welfare' still reigned supreme with its existing cognitive apparatuses yet unchallenged. The Kothari Commission's impressive understanding of how educational opportunities are appropriated by social privilege did not however translate into a critical tryst with the operations of caste or religion. In fact, the same socialistic aspiration for 'welfare' was used to understate, and even under-account for the structural imbalances within higher education. As a consequence, the search for policy methods of addressing 'class' seamlessly assumed a wiping out of the historical effects of differentiation, performed by caste and religious stratifications of a rights-framework.

To cite an inaugural example, the Commission insisted on an eventual abolition of tuition fees at all levels of education – for the simple purpose of maximising the benefits of public instruction for those who are historically disprivileged. But, in the same breath, it went on to cite the excuse of resource-scarcity to privilege the universal provisioning of free schooling *over* the demand for free colleges. Quickly again, in prioritising the need for tuition-free colleges over expansion of access to college education, the Report mandated a 'selective' admission-policy in the case of higher education – of course, benchmarked on the basis of 'merit'. Finally, the number of available seats in colleges as well as the opening of academic programmes in universities were to be calculated on the basis of manpower forecasts for an immediate future. Simply put, tuition-free higher education was – in the view of the Commission – an investment of the national economy in successive generations of the meritorious, without accounting for the more complex adjustments of social justice. Degrees, now churned at a rate proportional to the likelihood of employment, only end up reinstating an ahistorical fetish of national development as public debt – repayable by the meritorious poor:

> In order to restrict unplanned and uncontrolled expansion of secondary and higher education, it is necessary to restrict the provision for places in accordance with manpower estimates and wherever the applicants for admission exceed the places, to make the admissions on a selective basis. . . . This idea is gaining much wider support but is still opposed on certain socio-economic grounds. It is argued, for instance, that this policy would adversely affect access to higher education of the backward classes, the rural areas and under-privileged groups now entering higher education for the first time. These fears have some justification. But the remedy is not to be sought in the continuance of the present policy of open-door access. The under-privileged sections have a very small and disproportionate share in existing facilities in spite of the unrestricted admissions. . . . Much of the opposition to a policy of selective admissions would disappear if good methods of selection were evolved. . . . [E]xamination marks are an undependable measure of native talent or of potential growth. They are also socially unjust, being heavily weighted in favour of urban students and children from well-to-do homes and good schools. What is needed is a reliable method of selection which will take account of past performances, native talent and the principles of social justice. (*Education and National Development* 97–98)

The Commission's nuanced approach towards the evolution of a policy of admissions, which can both offset the incremental effects of prior socialisation as well as account for 'native talent and the principles of social justice', is a laudable move. Also, its forceful denouncing of the phenomenon of educated unemployment within labour-surplus societies – promoted by an expansion of low-quality higher educational infrastructures – sounds like a timely call for rethinking trajectories of development. But after making such an inspired pitch for reform, the eventual co-optation of the Indian university's futures within contingencies of economic *growth*-potential only ends up swallowing all transformative dreams. That the right to higher education must, in the last analysis, be determined by macroeconomic development targets makes the structural pretence of social justice succumb to the historical law of repetition. In a speculative future of occupational opportunities, the life of the mind is finally sledged to routines of labour; and the recognition of 'native talent' devolves into a caste-based inheritance of non-formal *know-how*. Higher education, despite its emancipatory undertones in the Kothari Commission's report, congeals professional divisions of labour as a ritualistic call to *national service*. The idea and ideology of 'welfare' are thus secured by Kothari, against a policy timeline of the next twenty years (1966–86).

'Majoring' Universities, Benchmarking Merit

By transfiguring all 'output' from the country's college sector as potential 'input resource' for the national economy, the manpower-factory model of the Indian university is more than a productivity-fetish. Its token commitment to 'principles of social justice' – by insisting on 'a suitable system of reservation of seats' (ibid. 97) and 'a reliable method of selection' (98) – does little apart from reproducing subaltern labour (now strategically certified and made concessions for as 'native talent') in the cause of national speculations of 'growth'. Ironically, Kothari's is the classic cognitive sleight that passes social mobility for social justice, by making caste or religion dissolvable in the larger spiritual totality of the nation. This is a re-packaging of the Radhakrishnan blueprint, albeit with an occasional depth of vision and a greater malleability of rhetoric – but, in the process, already beginning to use identity as both investable capital for as well as the imminent dividend of *welfare*. In other words, this is the point where socialism meets national capitalism in the guise of welfare. But, is that all that the Commission forecasts for the next couple of decades? Not really.

There is one conceptual exception to the manpower-industry of higher education, the Report of 1966 exclaims. It is termed as the 'major university' – an institutional marvel that could truly approximate to the 'idea' of the university and not the 'practice' of welfare, and therefore deserving of the highest forms of intellectual exhilaration. This most feted proposal for university reform derives, as the Commission notes, from 'experience [which] has shown that the best results follow where a goodly number of persons of high potentialities come together . . .' (ibid. 279). That a concentration of the 'best', 'goodly' and 'high' can be managed in an experimental sample of five or six universities (including an IIT and an agricultural university) is what gets set up as a goal for the next decade and striven towards. The 'major universities', we are told, will prevent a scattering of intellectual resources in an economy of scarcity while also foster a climate of intense academic exchange in the absence of the infecting touch of 'mediocrity'. Protected against the immediate demands of the economy, these universities would at the same time produce a corporative consciousness of 'community' as well as ensure a future supply of these best minds for the improvement of other non-major universities. Their work therefore consisted in the making of a 'true' university subject and its 'disinterested' intellectual vocation.

> There would be several advantages in creating such universities. In the first place, they would make their existence felt by their research and by the high standards of training which they would provide for their students. They would also supply a goodly portion of the outstanding personnel needed for the staffs [sic.] of universities, colleges and other institutions of higher education. In this way, their graduates may be expected to infuse into them the standards acquired in their own universities and to spread the ethos of genuine intellectual activity and devotion into the institutions where they are employed. (280)

There are two implications borne out by this policy rationale for the establishment of 'major universities'. Preliminarily, they are projected as the nation's bid at global competition in the field of knowledge production. To that extent, the 'major universities' almost resonate with the ideological overtones of the 'world class' – a much later turn-of-the-century phenomenon that remodels the university into an auctioneering contest for excellence or eminence. Quality, fetishised as a goal in itself and voided of considerations of equity or justice, calls forth the incarnation of the 'major university'. But, of course, as is the case with transnational capital, it is imagined that merit too can trickle down and work as an equalising force when left to itself. Alarmingly enough, the Kothari Commission had already prepared the groundwork for *welfare* to become the legitimating language of a market that was yet to rear its ugly head. Liberalism and its avowal of the unfettered exercise of talent, although regulated by the state, were indeed portents for times to come. Secondly, this section of the Report finally proposes an alternative vision of the 'university' as one governed by the 'ethos of genuine intellectual activity'. But, wasn't this the normative 'idea' of the university? In Kothari's pitch for a manpower-workshop in the university, it seems that the 'truth' of the university was itself inverted into an *exception*. And the cunning in an exception lies in that it can escape all conditionalities. It is a prohibition against social audit, and by the same logic it must be allowed to be unjust without apology.

> A possible objection to these proposals may be that what is proposed here is not quite democratic, that it seeks to institute a system of elite education by favouring certain institutions and impoverishing others. We recognize that our approach does involve at this stage a certain differentiation between the universities. *This is, however, not only inevitable in an economy of scarcity but is also the only sure and practicable way to benefit all ultimately in the shortest time possible.* Moreover, we must recognize that *pursuit of excellence implies and requires a discriminatory approach; and that to provide equal resources to all irrespective of the quality of their performance and potentiality for growth merely promotes mediocrity.* We are trying to establish a democratic social order in our country and obviously a democracy cannot flourish unless it has at its disposal the services of a highly trained and powerfully motivated educated class. Unless a system can be devised which will produce such persons in much larger numbers than is being done at present, every aspect of the country's development will be prejudicially affected. In fact, we may go further and say that there is always need for elite institutions in every academic system. (ibid. 281, emphases mine)

Social justice is finally thrown to the wind – but, amusingly again, in the name of the 'country's development'. The sovereign theory of national welfare, as the *raison d'etre* of higher educational reform, can now serve both ends of the policy: social mobility for the subaltern-as-manpower as well as entrenchment of historical privilege for the intellectual elite. But, in the very servicing of these ends, they are declared as mutually exclusive. The subaltern should not have a place within the 'ethos of genuine intellectual activity', if not on economic grounds and thus remediable through a liberal provisioning of merit-based scholarships. In reality, the *subaltern-as-mind* remains untouched as anathema to higher education – while the *subaltern-as-body* (and labour power) could be converted to the national(ist) cause through proportionate reservations in the non-major university structure. The Kothari Commission's blithe but knowing disregard for the caste and religious effects reproduced by centuries of Indian higher education, however, does not stop here.

Academic Freedom: Whose Prerogative?

The Report urges the setting up of 'centres of advanced study' across the country, in order to recognise the will to 'major university' status within colleges (ibid. 283–85). Academic departments are encouraged to shun mediocrity as the route to exceptionality. And as a ploy to enable the clamour for such 'centres', the Commission proposes a quality-classification between colleges – with the most elite and 'advanced' among them being entitled to special grants-in-aid from the government. The ground-plan for what has now come to be called 'graded autonomy' – the tiering of institutions on the basis of performance and consequent claims to finances, which I will take up in the final chapter – is in fact a legacy of Kothari vintage.

> Affiliated colleges should be classified in terms of the level of their performance. . . . This classification should be used to provide special 'merit' grants to deserving colleges. *For example, colleges which rank high on the list and continue to improve their programmes and teaching should be given certain advantages such as salary bonuses for their teachers, grants for libraries, laboratories and necessary amenities for staff and students, etc.* . . . We, therefore, recommend that the UGC, in consultation with the universities and State Governments, should

> *examine this question of classification of colleges in terms of level of achievement and make use of it in the allocation of grants to colleges* under the fourth five year plan. (286, emphases mine)

What is strikingly prophetic about the Commission's suggestion for linking state funding to criteria of institutional achievement is the insertion of a general 'will to excellence' as the will to be free from the public charge of equity. The privileged entitlement of a few – structured as 'bonus' on 'merit' – is generalised as an aspirational quest within all institutions of higher education. And, as Kothari and his colleagues already justified, a 'discriminatory approach' towards ahistorical atoms of 'excellence' is fully compatible with a 'democratic social order'.

Chapter XIII of the Education Commission's Report launches a spirited defence of academic freedom and university autonomy. The bulwarks for protecting the interests of the academy as well as securing public confidence in its pursuit of truth are sought in a more adequate representation of both teachers and students in the governance structures of the university. Kothari's is perhaps the *only* clear code of academic freedom that has ever been formulated in the history of Indian university-planning. But, when seen in light of a preceding bifurcation of the university into either a production-unit for manpower or a competition of the intellect, it is not difficult to foresee which side of the spectrum the charge of academic freedom must rest on. And insofar as the protections of freedom may imminently become the prize of the few elite 'major universities' and 'advanced centres' and high-ranking colleges, even the most useful of the Commission's statements remains far from being the norm of public education. For the overwhelming *majority* of the rest – ironically, the many absented from the 'major' – academic freedom may be legitimately eclipsed by concerns of developmental needs and labour forecasts. Not too far into the bold declaration, the Report sounds a sly cop-out:

> While universities must have this autonomy, it should be interpreted in the larger context of their obligation and responsibility to the nation and to mankind as a whole. For instance, the national needs for trained manpower have implications for the teaching functions

> of the universities; and similarly *decisions about research which, in a way, must be taken primarily by the universities, cannot be taken in isolation from the economic and social needs of the country which must influence them in a large measure*. . . . It is apparent that the conduct of university affairs cannot be left *solely* to the academics; their *relationship to social needs requires the admission of non-academic persons within the machinery of their government*. The universities have thus to share their decisions with lay agencies or authorities outside the system. . . . In matters relating to the national needs for trained manpower and research, an individual university should have the freedom to decide whether it will or will not participate and also to determine the extent of its participation, consistent with its other basic objectives. (328–29, emphases mine)

It does not require too wild a guess to foretell the differential fortunes of freedom for 'individual universities' – and which of these fall into the competing types that 'will or will not participate' in meeting developmental targets. The 'national needs for trained manpower and research' are squarely distributed one against the other, and it is only the latter that might therefore claim the *meaning* of academic freedom. The vast expanse of higher education will continue to deferentially bow to 'non-academic persons' or 'lay agencies or authorities outside the system'.

The Kothari Commission's bargaining away of social justice at the altar of 'national needs' continues into its discussion on 'science education and research' (ibid. 389–421). With an exuberant enthusiasm for the ever-expanding horizons of scientific discovery and an almost uncritical championing of a 'science-based' contemporary age, Kothari's plan for rejuvenating higher education is simultaneously a manifesto for science geared towards national reconstruction. Given the excessive euphoria around how the applied sciences can limitlessly expand frontiers of possibility, it is not a little surprising that much of what Kothari's generation expected from the field in the 'next decade or two' has remained as much a dream until now (391–92). Despite the general strain of overdetermination in this context, the Report's unravelling of a science policy consisted in giving 'special attention to gifted students' (390) for entering the field, while at the same time concentrating human and material resources to 'build centres or peaks of excellence' (391). We have already indicated what a culture of 'giftedness', as condition for excellence, does to the question of historical disadvantage. Who gets consecrated for national welfare, in the teaching and learning of science, has continued to be a vexed question until now.

Science, Culture and a *National* Policy on Education

But, how does this consecration of science unto the nation get performed? The Report reminds us very soon, that the nation cannot but command a pietistic mode of surrender even if the offering is scientific:

> If science is to be pursued with full vigour and zest and is to become a mighty force in the Indian renaissance, it must derive its 'nourishment' from our cultural and spiritual heritage and not bypass it. Science must become an integral part of our cultural fabric. It is possible that when science takes root in the native soil, and is no longer an exotic plant, its growth pattern may be visibly influenced by those features which have been characteristic of Indian philosophic thought and civilization. Part of the science 'fashion' may be set by us reflecting Indian ethos and value judgements. (396)

The obvious questions are: which 'Indian renaissance', which 'spiritual heritage', which 'cultural fabric', which 'Indian philosophic thought and civilization' – or, which 'Indian ethos and value judgements' – is Kothari's team referencing? Even if the answers are left to the reader's imagination, it is not exactly in muffled undertones that these terms appeal to a Hindu nationalist conscience. Scientific reformism, of the familiar nineteenth-century 'Indian renaissance' variety, had worked out a delicate balance of interests between the Hindu upper-caste, English-educated elite and a staunchly brahminical patriarchy. Moral good will rested on the shoulders (and hearts) of the enlightened scientific man, even though he was never required to mark a decisive break with religion. We have laid out these historical concatenations of caste privilege and secular-reformist scientificity in the second chapter, and will take it up again in the story of the IITs. Clearly, the

Commission's tempering of science with native tradition is replete with the cultural memory of Anglophilic Hindu nationalism. The university scholar's lack of reverence for nationalist wisdom, coded as an irreligious rootlessness, had already occasioned the Commission's anxiety: '[T]he Indian universities must foster national consciousness. They should ensure that every student who passes out of an Indian university takes with him some understanding of India's cultural heritage, its past achievements and triumphs in the field of art, philosophy, science and so on. He should, in other words, know what he is *heir* to' (277, emphasis mine). Both the accent on cultural triumphalism and the staking of an ancestral right to tradition end up transforming 'national consciousness' into a property claim. And it is in such passages that a communal common sense seeps into the text of the Report, by making the nation stand in for a compulsory religion of sorts. This reverberates with Radhakrishnan's call for religious instruction within universities, which the 1966 document wholeheartedly vindicates at the very start (19–20). The sovereign currency of faith, propagated via the university, rests in the nation; that is the secret truth of *welfare*. And, part of the vocation of the university is to train the student into a renunciatory gesture vis-à-vis the nation. What I mean by communal common sense is quite this: the readying for an ascetic self-effacement at the university. The *brahmacharya*-ideal is still not too far away from the modern Indian university, and a religious disposition is only the subterranean harvest of secular-welfarist higher education.

The only place in the 682-page-long Education Commission Report where this hierarchical subsumption of the university within the nation – giving short shrift to caste and religion – is challenged is a 'Supplementary Note on University Autonomy', extracted from the minutes of an Inter University Board (IUB) meeting in February 1966. Understandably, this is not part of the text authored by the Commission – but is only appendixed for corroborative purposes: 'The Board is of the opinion that a statutorily established university is practically in the same position as a statutorily established political government and the mere fact that the legislatures of such governments have certain powers of legislation should not be utilised to lower the reputation of Indian universities and to make their efficient working impossible' (346). This is an unabashedly radical statement of equality, between a university and a political government – to the extent that it allows the former to even secede from the province of legislative control once it is 'established' by law. The law of the state is named as irrelevant to the running of the university beyond its moment of founding, even while the legitimacy of state action might constantly be under scrutiny by/at the university. *Academic freedom, in the IUB's instantiation of it, exceeds the will of the people – and conversely, the project of welfare.* The nation then is only another object of inquiry for the university. And, within such an amplitude of academic freedom, both political governments and the political effects that make governmentality possible – viz. caste, class, religion or gender – are subject to the university's critical gaze. Needless to say, the Kothari Commission's conception of socialist welfare is too weak in the knees to bear the weight of this announcement, and instead leaves it as simply a curated relic.

It is in heeding the urgent impatience of the Education Commission of 1964–66, and its painstaking argument for a structural overhaul, that the Government of India tabled the first-ever *National Policy on Education (NPE)* in 1968. Extracting the bare bones of the voluminous Report drafted by Kothari and his colleagues, the NPE began by shouting from the rooftops:

> The Government of India is convinced that a radical reconstruction of education on the broad lines recommended by the education commission is essential for economic and cultural development of the country, for national integration and for realising the ideal of a socialistic pattern of society. . . . The educational system must produce young men and women of character and ability committed to national service and development. . . . This is necessary if the country is to attain its rightful place in the comity of nations in conformity with its great cultural heritage and its unique potentialities. (Section 3, 38)

It is clear that the 'ideal of a socialistic pattern', spelt out by the NPE 1968, formalises the model of *national welfare* that I have tried elaborating through policy-precedents. Higher education is wedded to the primordial penchant for economic mobility, while at the same time ensuring that 'ability' and 'cultural heritage' – euphemisms for *caste* and *religion* respectively – are not compromised in the process. The outcome is a festering of the political dissonances and differentiating effects produced by caste and religion within the university, in the cause of an outwardly social(ist) consensus. The latter ticked away, waiting to explode in moments of revolutionary fervour through the subsequent decades of the Kothari timeline.

'Ability' as Caste Privilege: The Case of Engineering Education

Let me now use two specific institutional sagas from the field of higher education to demonstrate these policy footprints of a *national welfare* model in post-independence India. They both reflect the relationship between a Congress-led welfare state at the centre and the historical concatenations of 'ascription and achievement' (Subramanian 21) among different social groups. The first of these sagas follows on a colonial legacy of reorienting technical education for the upper-castes, away from the *varna*-circumscription of manual/artisanal labour within shudra (low-caste) constituencies. As Ajantha Subramanian notes in *The Caste of Merit*, it was the gradual wearing away of the promise of colonial employment as assured returns on an Anglophonic college education (which I have already maintained in the second and third chapters) that called for an opening up of *workerly* training for caste-Hindu populations. The higher-educated but disaffected upper-caste youth were increasingly joining the ranks of nationalist rebels; and a safety-valve for such disenchantment lay in creating alternative options for absorption within civil-mechanical careers of colonial administration (TIIC 46–71; Swaminathan). Consequently, from the late nineteenth century onwards, there was a distinct trend towards establishing technical and engineering colleges as potential workshops for training upper-caste labour into an urban life of practical professions. This of course unsettled the feudal economy of hands-on work, while pushing out the caste-marked untouchable body from sectors of professional skill inheritance which were often its only claim to relative mobility. What Subramanian calls a 'racialization of caste' (96), under the cognitive conditions imposed by colonial rule, implied that caste privilege was no longer a barrier to entry into the erstwhile 'lower' muscular-nervous professions. The resignification of an engineering curriculum, as integrally suited to the class-interests of upper-caste populations under colonial bureaucracy, made the technical college into a relic of brahminical dominance.

No wonder this continued after independence, in Nehru's insistence on scientific expertise as the key to nation-building and hence 'disconnected from the rough and tumble of the political process' (Roy 120). To this extent, training in the sciences and technology called for a disinterested vocationalism akin to the 'Brahminic spirit of service' – to use Nehru's own words on the occasion of the inauguration of the National Chemical Laboratory in Pune in 1950 (ibid. 121). The Sarkar Committee's Report on *Development of Higher Technical Institutions in India* (1948) argued for a similar approach to the relationship between scientific knowledge production and democratic claims-processes.[4] That the best of merit need not be encumbered (or even tempered) by considerations of democracy was championed as the policy roadmap for national development goals, and abetted by the Radhakrishnan Commission soon after. The First and Second Five Year Plans (1951–61), proposing major state initiatives in civil and mechanical sectors of industrial engineering, coincided with the fruition of the Sarkar Committee's recommendation for setting up four IITs along the entire geographical spread of the country.

[4] See 'Note' to Para 19 (Section X) of the Sarkar Committee's Report, which – while mandating admissions 'purely on merit and no provincial quotas' – makes a recommendation for reserving 'some proportion of seats . . . for the educationally backward classes' as 'only a tentative view not unanimously subscribed to by the members of the Committee' and therefore open for 'further consideration' (6).

These IITs were to be experiments in foreign collaboration, with the first of such in the eastern division of Kharagpur (1951) receiving generous assistance and intellectual resources from 'the United States, the United Kingdom, the Soviet Union, and UNESCO' (Subramanian 71). The founding condition for foreign collaboration, in terms of both knowledge transfer and exchange of manpower, was that the 'Institutes' had to be kept free from political control and bureaucratic structures of everyday audit – even while the government committed to a far greater amplitude of public finances for their 'autonomous' functioning. In sum, techno-scientific higher education was a postcolonial nation-state's bid at honing exceptional intellects at exceptional costs in the cause of 'engineering' mass futures towards industrial development.

> In science too, a similar process had produced the Indian Institute of Science (IIS) as the most esteemed of scientific institutions. Both the IITs and the IIS were founded to distinguish effort from expertise. Indeed, this was quite explicitly stated in the government's review committee report on scientific institutions, which defined scientific expertise as the work of a "few men of high calibre" and emphasized the constitutive link between excellence and selectivity. . . . [E]xcellence "required the judicious investment of resources in 'the development of fewer establishments for advanced training and research,' since a more expansive approach would mean that 'the general level of technical education and research would be lowered.'" In other words, democratizing access to training would be antithetical to excellence. Nehru concurred. . . . Scientific and technological expertise was thus set apart from "the manpower mandate" through the development of a parallel institutional structure of higher education in techno-scientific fields with separate budgetary allocations, entrance examinations, fee structures, and curricular frameworks. (ibid. 73–74)

Pursuing the 'constitutive link between excellence and selectivity' implied two corollary moves at the level of admissions policy: the exemption of IITs – as institutions of 'national importance – from the constitutional mandate for caste-based reservation until 1973, and the provision of an exceedingly competitive mass entrance examination as eliminationist strategy starting from 1961.

While regional technical colleges, funded by state governments and affiliated to public universities, had reservation quotas that sought to address inequalities of achievement resulting from caste discrimination, the IITs were promoted as arbiters of 'casteless' meritocracy in national interest. In the process, Subramanian argues, forms of caste capital and their benchmarking of social potential for success were rendered invisible under the liberal-democratic ruses of universalistic access and meritocratic modernity (ibid. 204–57). The IITs became upper-caste bastions of conceptual-professional scientific competence, first at the behest of national development and then private corporate initiative and finally diasporic entrepreneurialism. This flight of 'merit' from the public sector to private capital (in the 1970s and 1980s) and eventually to Silicon Valley (from the late 1980s onwards) may be accurately plotted out against a policy timeline for implementation of lower-caste reservations in the IITs – with the introduction of 22.5 per cent of reservations for SCs and STs in 1973, and the reserving of jobs in central government services for other backward classes (OBCs) in 1990. The role of these elite technical 'Institutes' in cementing the aura of 'ability'[5] – normativised as the 'castelessness' of merit (Deshpande) – around histories of upper-caste subjectification in India is one of the surest vindications of what I have called the 'caste' myopia of welfare ideology.

'Heritage' as Minority Character: The Case of the 'Muslim' Universities

The second development in post-independence higher education, which sealed the pact between national progress and differential

[5] The most tragic fallout of the IITs' meritocratic ecosystem has only recently come to be documented as a sustained trend in suicides committed by students from marginalised and lower-caste backgrounds over the years. For reports on such instances, see Sukanya Shantha, "Dalit Student's Suicide" and "In Findings of IIT Delhi"; Sumedha Mittal, "Stress, dropouts, suicides"; Sophie Landrin, "India's elite schools"; *The Indian Express*, "33 IIT students"; D. Karthikeyan, "Suicide by Dalit students".

metrics of educational attainment, lies in the story of the evolution of 'Muslim' universities between 1951 and 1986. In the same year as when the first IIT was established in the cause of promoting a caste-marked scientific temper – that is, 1951 – elaborate discussions in parliament resulted in a legislative muting of the 'Muslim' character of Aligarh Muslim University (AMU) through grant of 'central university' status. The Aligarh Muslim University (Amendment) Act 1951 sought to underwrite the history of religious 'community'-formation, incipient within the founding of the institution, by subsuming it as a creature of the secular state – under the sovereign authority of the President of India (as Visitor) and a University Court that opened its doors to non-Muslim nominees of the President. As Mushirul Hasan and Laurence Gautier suggest, this change in the statutory character and structural governance of AMU was considered a political necessity, and had already been recommended by none other than Radhakrishnan's policy tome ("Report" 409–10, 412). Alongside the Benares Hindu University (BHU), AMU's reinvention as one of the first three 'central universities' in the country sent out a clear message: religion had to forsake its discursive legitimacy as the determining ground for educational provisioning, in order to participate in agenda-setting exercises for national citizenship (Gautier 90–124). This was again antithetical to a constitutional consensus, first enshrined in Article 23(3A) of the Draft Constitution of 1948 and subsequently incorporated in Article 30 in 1950, which granted religious minorities 'the right to establish and administer educational institutions'. The assumption behind the 1951 AMU Act was that a one-time conscription of minority identities into a composite 'central' law of the land would automatically offset claims-making processes that stemmed from decades of structural neglect of religious minorities in the making of Hindu nationalism. But, this was not the only rationale.

The long history of AMU, initially named as the Mohammedan Anglo-Oriental (MAO) College, coincided with Sayyid Ahmad Khan's attempts at forging a sense of a Muslim '*qaum*' (community) through the active enlistment of elite North Indian (mostly *ashraf*) representative members within a colonial 'university'-idea (Lelyveld 300–20; Tariq Hasan). According to Khan, not only would such a collaborative endeavour give Muslims of rank and privilege access to literacies suited for modern urban employment, but also leverage their status in the process as effective spokespersons on behalf of an aggregated 'Muslim' community interest. The AMU's mission was thus directed at both making way for Muslim social-professional mobility within the imperial administration as well as asserting the separateness of Muslim cultural/political demands in contradistinction to Hindu nationalism (Lelyveld 204–99). In this respect, it was not surprising that many of AMU's faculty and students were ardent votaries of the Muslim League and supported the two-nation theory at the root of the administrative designs of Partition. At the moment of India's independence, therefore, AMU was largely perceived as a 'hotbed of Muslim separatism' (Gautier 142) – and it was a singular instance of Nehru's political astuteness which sought to co-opt AMU's 'community' character in a 'national' legislative consensus around the 'central university'.

Needless to say, the 1951 Act did not go down well with many among the homegrown Aligarhites – who saw in this move, aided by a secular liberal intelligentsia at the administrative helm of the university, a portent for times to come. Through the 1950s and 60s, as Gautier painstakingly recounts, the rise of different strands of identity politics in India made AMU's Muslim students see through the majoritarian biases of secular developmentalist statecraft (140–41). The dwindling opportunities for Muslim employment within state bureaucracies and public sector jobs compounded the injustices underlying AMU's 'national university' status. There was an increasing fear of being discriminated against at national-level competitions, on communal identitarian grounds, among students of AMU. This climate of anxiety fuelled demands for an enhancement of internal quotas for employment within the engineering and medical schools of the university – which, being implemented in 1964, was withdrawn under advice from the central government in the following year (ibid. 142–48). This intensified AMU's movement for 'minority status', and became the immediate cause for a violent repressive campaign unleashed by Nehru's then-education-minister in M.C. Chagla. For Chagla and the resolutely 'secular' welfarist fold within the Indian National Congress, the spectre of minority politics on a university campus signalled the reigniting of communal passions (long identified with AMU's historical heritage) and called for an iron-fisted approach (Gautier 148–50; Graff). The Supreme Court intervened in 1967 on the matter, only to further delegitimise the university's struggle – until it was the post-Emergency electoral debacles of an Indira Gandhi-led Congress which necessitated consolidation of the Muslim minority vote in the late 1970s (Graff 1771). It was finally in 1981 that the Aligarh Muslim University Act was again amended to reconstitute its executive bodies and concede 'minority status'. The Hindu right-wing, gaining momentum with the merging of the erstwhile Jana Sangh and Janata Party in the Bharatiya Janata Party (BJP) of 1980, saw in the AMU chronicle a case of the 'secular' government's 'Muslim-appeasement politics' (Gautier 267) and took it up as a rallying point for forging a majoritarian-communal consensus.

A seemingly divergent tale emerges from the historical predicament and evolution of Jamia Millia Islamia (JMI), another 'Muslim' institution which broke out of the AMU mould to question its conciliatory attitudes with respect to colonial patronage. Situating itself against the backdrop of Gandhi's non-cooperation movement and the Khilafat demands, the coming into being of JMI in 1920 and its subsequent relocation to a rural setting in Delhi materialised the imagination of what Gautier calls a 'composite nationalism' (70) – where Muslims were as much part of a *citizenly* charter through constructive community effort. Even at the peak of the Partition debates, JMI's faculty and student populations insisted on reaching out to the Muslim middle classes and poor such that they become fit subjects for a project of secular liberal nation-building (Gautier 43–53; Hasan and Jalil 177–78). To such ends, Jamia's curricular interventions in basic and adult education in the Urdu language aimed at training democratic literacies among the non-English-speaking Muslims of India, largely alienated into an idiom of 'minority' self-identification by histories of social and educational 'backwardness'. Zakir Husain, one of the founding figures behind this experiment in Indian Muslim citizenship, was eventually tasked with translating Gandhi's Wardha scheme of crafts-based education into an implementable policy instrument (Hasan and Jalil 103–09). However, despite a long past of intimate alignments with the Nehruvian model of secular nationalism, JMI failed to elicit any significant attention from successive post-independence governments headed by the Congress. Laurence Gautier departs from Hasan-Jalil's reading of Jamia's fortunes as a parable of Muslim integration into the Congress's brand of secularism, and instead sees in it a 'paradoxical attitude' reflecting 'Nehru's ambiguities, particularly on the question of Muslim representation in secular India' (37). My contention is that there was simply no paradox in the Nehruvian state's systematic neglect of JMI.

Jamia, from the outset, was too nationalistic in its orientation to require strategic co-optation by the government or a state policy for financial sponsorship of non-elite Muslim constituents. It therefore made little sense for Nehru's cabinet to endow the institution with a 'central university' status and apportion public resources to it, because Jamia was already paying routine obeisance to the state's secular ideology of national welfare. For prolonged periods, the university was running on deficit budgets with little to compensate the 'nationalistic' efforts of its faculty and staff. Even with its recognition as 'deemed university' in 1962, there was hardly any noticeable difference in terms of financial support from the national government. Yet, through the 1960s and 1970s and quite in contrast to the high-pitched battles on AMU's campus, JMI resisted attempts at being labelled a Muslim 'minority institution' (ibid. 189–228). Demands for being anointed as a 'central university' were however regularly registered both at the local and national levels, until in the mid-1980s the Shah Bano judgment on Muslim divorce and maintenance sparked off a frenzied controversy on personal law reform and a uniform civil code (UCC) capable of encompassing all minority faiths ("The Judgement" 23–34; Mustafa

111–15; S. Anand; J. Anand). The Congress-led government's hurried enactment of a Muslim Women (Protection of Rights on Divorce) Act 1986 sought to readjust the balance in favour of the All India Muslim Personal Law Board (AIMPLB), but only to invite deep distrust from its 'secular' stakeholders as well as the by-now emboldened proponents of Hindutva (Iyer; Ukil et al.; Advani). Almost as a spectacularly sudden apotheosis to the long-ranging parliamentary and extra-legislative debates on JMI's status, the government sought to pre-emptively contain self-expressions of 'minority' interest on Muslim university campuses – especially in the aftermath of country-wide ferment over the UCC – by making a 'central university' of Jamia in 1988.

The vacillations running through four decades of postcolonial India's official ideology of national welfare (which I have documented in these two sagas of institution-building) prove that both technical-engineering education and Muslim 'minority' institutions were used as policy-facades, for covering up the architectural craters of caste and religion on which was built the monument of the Indian university.

Cracks in the Mirror of the Nation: From Naxalbari to Babri

If *exemplary* institutions enclaved the 'social life' of higher education away from the 'political effects' of caste and religion – named inconsequential to the ideology of national welfare – a critique of such ideology came to be forged in the streets by students of universities.

By the time the first official 'policy' on education was adopted and discussed in the Indian parliament in 1968, the caste character of the 'socialist welfare' programme had given way along the rural edges of Bengal. A Naxal uprising had snowballed into an armed revolutionary struggle of the landless peasantry, thus throwing open questions about how both the right to land ownership and chances of learned employment had been secured by the upper-caste *bhadralok* through collaboration with a postcolonial comprador state (Bhattacharyya; Samaddar). That it was the national ideology of welfare which sought to divert the benefits of educational modernity and developmental planning to the city-bred caste-Hindu middle classes – while riding on the backs of a burgeoning rural proletariat – was the lesson uniting elite university students with the Naxalite cause in Bengal (Banerjee 52–53; Roy Choudhury). The revolutionary ferment continued through the early 1970s, when the streets of Calcutta saw young students from relatively elite urban households shunning what they perceived as the bourgeois institution of the university and desecrating statues of upper-caste Bengali reformers. The stirring initiation into an alternative methodology of historical analysis, provided by leaders like Saroj Dutta and Charu Mazumdar, had lured college-going adult populations outside of their workshops for bureaucratic training. They were now alerted that a historical consciousness of nationhood could not have been the work of collaboration with a British imperialist state and its intellectual apparatuses – as our post-independence university curricula had made it seem. Instead, it was those caste-marked bodies of peasant revolutionaries and their mobilisations of the labouring masses that needed to be commemorated, in order for knowledge and its institutions to be decolonised out of a millennial surplusage of historical privilege. The nexus between caste and its capillaries of knowledge production/dissemination being questioned, the military state had to step in and return the liberal university to 'normalcy'.

But, the cognitive breach within the ideology of *national welfare* was now too brutal a wound for healing. The memory of the unrest caught on, until the revolutionary communist fervour of the early 1970s was tamed into a crusade against the financial corruption of political classes through different parts of the country. There was widespread disaffection among college students in the state of Gujarat, which sought an immediate outlet in protests against hostel mess charges and eventually catalysed the fall of the state government (Sheth). This was the Nav Nirman movement of 1973–74, which – in the absence of a shared vocabulary for structural redress – made student reaction appear like an event of class-mobilisation (Jones and Jones 1012–33). The rubric of *class* papered over a deeper churning within social systems of production, not just as the malaise of a welfare-imagination (as I have already documented) but also in the popular response that it provoked. The accumulated angst against decades of public planning and misdirected agendas of redistribution spilled over into the Bihar movement of subsequent years (also termed as the J.P. movement or the Sampoorna Kranti *andolan*) (Shah 335–59).

But, these outward coalitions of class-action turned out to be a mere ruse for solidifying communal-religious fissures within the liberal university. The repression of the Emergency years of 1975–77 combined with the memory of direct student action in Gujarat, Bihar and other parts of northern India, to eventually grant legitimacy to a Hindu nationalist imagination of the Rashtriya Swayamsevak Sangh (RSS) and its political offshoots like Jana Sangh and Bharatiya Janata Party (BJP). The unaddressed force of religion within agendas of educational reform had used the excuse of economic disaffection with *welfare*, in order to now regiment a student mass and rally it to the call for a creation of Hindu *rashtra* (Chandra; Jaffrelot and Anil). By the end of the decade of the 1970s and the birth of the BJP in the year 1980, the country's youth – under the aegis of the RSS-backed Akhil Bharatiya Vidyarthi Parishad (ABVP) – had become a major reckoning force within a renewed imagination of national reconstruction. The training of the student subject, through decades of post-independence welfare-reform, into an ascetic donation of the self in national service (*seva*) was now complete; Radhakrishnan's dream of religious instruction finally (and unwittingly?) realised itself in the triumphalism of Hindutva.

The early 1980s hardened this spirit of communal-nationalist dedication, through the Vishwa Hindu Parishad's (VHP) intermittent sponsorship of what has come to be chronicled as the Ramjanmabhoomi movement (Jaffrelot). In 1986 – the fateful moment of culmination of the Kothari Commission's timeline, coinciding with the second *National Policy on Education*

1986 – the inner gates of the Babri masjid were finally opened for Hindu worship, under orders from Faizabad sessions court. India's universities and law courts collaborated, albeit with the force of decades of prior attempts of subjectification, to overturn socialism's pact with religion (Gould 521–24).

The script continues to play out even today, and my next two chapters will seek to enumerate the co-actors on that stage. The aftermath of national tragedy was reaped in carnivals of profit, even as the *welfare*-bubble burst its spell off fairly quickly.

REFERENCES

Advani, L.K. "The Government must not capitulate." *The Shah Bano Controversy*, edited by Asghar Ali Engineer. Orient Longman, 1987, pp. 85–88.

Anand, Javed. "Behind demands for a uniform civil code." *The Shah Bano Controversy*, edited by Asghar Ali Engineer. Orient Longman, 1987, pp. 187–94.

Anand, Som. "Why Muslims resist a common civil code." *The Shah Bano Controversy*, edited by Asghar Ali Engineer. Orient Longman, 1987, pp. 170–72.

Banerjee, Sumanta. *India's Simmering Revolution: The Naxalite Uprising*. Zed Books, 1984 [1980].

Bentham, Jeremy. *An Introduction to the Principles of Morals and Legislation*. Batoche Books, 2000 [1781].

Bhattacharyya, Amar. *Naxalbari Andoloner Pramaanya Tathya Sankalan*. Naya Istahar, 1998.

Chandra, Bipan. *In the Name of Democracy: JP Movement and the Emergency*. Penguin, 2003.

Constituent Assembly Debates (Proceedings) [9th December 1946–24th January 1950]. Manager of Publications, Government of India, https://archive.org/details/ConstituentAssemblyDebates9thDecember1946-24thJanuary1950/page/n1/mode/2up

Deshpande, Satish. "Caste and Castelessness: Towards a Biography of the 'General Category'." *Economic and Political Weekly*, vol. 48, no. 15, 2013, pp. 32–39.

Development of Higher Technical Institutions in India (Report of Sarkar Committee) 1948. Government of India Press, 1951.

Education and National Development: Report of the Education Commission 1964–66. Ministry of Education, 1966.

Gautier, Laurence. *Between Nation and 'Community': Muslim Universities and Indian Politics after Partition*. Cambridge University Press, 2024.

Gould, Harold A. "The Babri Masjid and the Secular Contract." *Contributions to Indian Sociology*, vol. 32, no. 2, 1998, pp. 507–26.

Graff, Violette. "Aligarh's Long Quest for 'Minority' Status: AMU (Amendment) Act 1981." *Economic and Political Weekly*, vol. 25, no. 32, 1990, pp. 1771–81.

Guha, Ramchandra. "The Multiple Agendas of Jawaharlal Nehru." *Makers of Modern India*. Penguin, 2010, pp. 326–69.

Habib, S. Irfan. "Legacy of the Freedom Struggle: Nehru's Scientific and Cultural Vision." *Social Scientist*, vol. 44, no. 3/4, 2016, pp. 29–40.

Hasan, Mushirul. *Legacy of a Divided Nation: Indian Muslims since Independence*. Oxford University Press, 1997.

———. "Muslim Intellectuals, Institutions and the Post-Colonial Predicament." *Economic and Political Weekly*, vol. 30, no. 47, 1995, pp. 2995–3000.

Hasan, Mushirul and Rakshanda Jalil. *Partners in Freedom: Jamia Millia Islamia*. Niyogi Books, 2006.

Hasan, Tariq. *The Aligarh Movement and the Making of the Muslim Mind, 1857–2002*. Rupa Publications, 2006.

Iyer, V.K. Krishna. "The bill is a sin against the Quran." *The Shah Bano Controversy*, edited by Asghar Ali Engineer. Orient Longman, 1987, pp. 89–92.

Jaffrelot, Christophe and Pratinav Anil. *India's First Dictatorship: The Emergency, 1975–1977*. Oxford University Press, 2020.

Jaffrelot, Christophe. "Part IV. The Convergence of Hindu Nationalist Strategies in the 1980s" and "Part V. The Early 1990s: How to Conquer and Retain Power." *The Hindu Nationalist Movement and Indian Politics, 1925 to the 1990s: Strategies of Identity-Building, Implantation and Mobilisation*. Hurst and Company, 1996, pp. 314–521.

Jones, Dawn E. and Rodney W. Jones. "Urban Upheaval in India: The 1974 Nav Nirman Riots in Gujarat." *Asian Survey*, vol. 16, no. 11, 1976, pp. 1012–33.

Karthikeyan, D. "Suicide by Dalit students in 4 years." *The Hindu*, 5 Sep. 2011, https://www.thehindu.com/news/cities/Madurai/suicide-by-dalit-students-in-4-years/article2425965.ece

Landrin, Sophie. "India's elite schools see a wave of suicides among Dalit students." *Le Monde*, 27 Sep. 2023, https://www.lemonde.fr/en/international/article/2023/09/27/india-s-elite-schools-see-a-wave-of-suicides-among-dalit-students_6140378_4.html

Lelyveld, David. *Aligarh's First Generation: Muslim Solidarity in British India.* Princeton University Press, 1978.

Mittal, Sumedha. "Stress, dropouts, suicides: Unravelling IIT's casteism problem." *Newslaundry*, 28 Mar. 2023, https://www.newslaundry.com/2023/03/28/stress-dropouts-suicides-unravelling-iits-casteism-problem

Mustafa, Seema. "Behind the Veil." *The Shah Bano Controversy*, edited by Asghar Ali Engineer. Orient Longman, 1987, pp. 111–15.

National Policy on Education [NPE] 1968. Government of India, 1968.

Noorani, A.G. "Nehru's Legacy to India." *Frontline*, 8 Oct. 2004, https://frontline.thehindu.com/other/article30224738.ece

Patnaik, Prabhat. "The Nehru development model." *Frontline* Special Issue (Nehru's Legacy). 26 Nov. 2014, https://frontline.thehindu.com/cover-story/the-development-model-of-jawaharlal-nehru-by-prabhat-patnaik/article64763343.ece

"Report of the Third Indian Industrial Conference, held at Surat on the 30th December 1907 [TIIC]." Thompson & Company, 1908.

Roy Choudhury, Profulla. *Left Experiment in West Bengal.* Patriot Publishers, 1985.

Roy, Srirupa. *Beyond Belief: India and the Politics of Postcolonial Nationalism.* Duke University Press, 2007.

Samaddar, Ranabir, ed. *From Popular Movements to Rebellion: The Naxalite Decade.* Routledge, 2019.

Shah, Ghanshyam. "Direct Action in India: A Study of Gujarat and Bihar Agitations." *Social Movements and the State*, edited by Shah. Sage Publications, 2004, pp. 335–59.

Shantha, Sukanya. "Dalit Student's Suicide Points to Well-Known – But Ignored – Caste Discrimination in IITs." *The Wire*, 15 Feb. 2023, https://thewire.in/caste/iit-bombay-darshan-solanki-suicide

———. "In Findings of IIT Delhi Survey, a Glimpse of Hostility That Bahujan Students Face." *The Wire*, 7 Oct. 2023, https://thewire.in/rights/iit-delhi-survey-glimpse-hostility-caste-discrimination

Sheth, P.N. *Nav Nirman and Political Change in India.* Vora & Company, 1977.

Subramanian, Ajantha. *The Caste of Merit: Engineering Education in India.* Harvard University Press, 2019.

Swaminathan, Padmini. "Technical Education and Industrial Development in Madras Presidency: Illusions of a Policy in the Making." *Economic and Political Weekly*, vol. 27, no. 30, 1992, pp. 1611–22, https://www.jstor.org/stable/4398695

"The Judgement: Chandrachud C.J." *The Shah Bano Controversy*, edited by Asghar Ali Engineer. Orient Longman, 1987, pp. 23–34.

"The Report of the University Education Commission (December 1948 – August 1949)." Ministry of Education, Government of India, 1962.

Ukil, Paromita, Yubaraj Ghimire, Lekha Dhar and Prashun Bhaumikh. "How do Muslims view the divorce bill?" *The Shah Bano Controversy*, edited by Asghar Ali Engineer. Orient Longman, 1987, pp. 155–59.

"33 IIT students died by suicide in last 5 years: Govt." *The Indian Express*, 7 Apr. 2023, https://indianexpress.com/article/education/33-iit-students-died-by-suicide-in-last-five-years-govt-in-parliament-8499516/

FIVE

Reaping Dividends on Discrimination: The Neoliberal 'Turn' to the Market (1986–2012)

Identity's Policy Encounters

If – as I have documented in the previous chapter – the first four decades of independent India's educational planning served to reify the differentiating effects of a communal-feudal *status quo* in the excuse of a 'welfare' regime, the second *National Policy on Education (NPE)* of 1986 performed a devious *volte face*. Coming with a historical hindsight of the university's encounter with both left-wing radicalism and right-wing Hindutva fanaticism, the furthest end of Kothari's twenty-year educational experiment was a moment of deep policy reckoning. Not surprisingly therefore, the 1986 NPE found its most opportune cause for reform in the relative degrees of attention paid to histories of social exclusion. Wedded to an explicit agenda of equalising access to education in order to address disparities across castes, religions and genders, the question of *identity* – beyond the twin registers of social mobility and social service – entered the archive of policy wisdom like never before. In fact, as I will go on to detail through the first part of this chapter, the policy paper's preoccupation with 'those who have been denied equality so far' (Para 4.1, 6) might – when taken at face value – imply an indictment of the entire course of erstwhile educational planning in India.

But did this acute awareness of structural discrimination translate into a substantive ameliorative agenda for social justice? On the contrary, the sounding of a 'discrimination' discourse in public policy was already too good to be true, especially in the context of the Indian government's financial priorities at the time. The mixed economy model of Nehruvian vintage – with its emphasis on state regulation of national assets and private initiative – had already started generating much alarm and discontent since the end of the previous decade, and the 1980s was a period of grave concern over deficit financing through international credit-seeking.[1] Within such a climate of economic conservatism, particularly around the question of public financing of non-profit sectors (like education), the reigning rationale of the new NPE's commitment to expansion of educational opportunities certainly came with a catch. If it were not an outright hoax, there must have been a hidden subtext to the script of social inclusion professed by the contemporary political class.

The subtext requires no further than a close reading of the policy text and its subsequent expansion and amendment in 1992. The caste, religious and gender imbalances within sectors of Indian education, though millennially produced, were made to seem resolvable through a simple imaginative recourse: a gradual replacement of the government by the 'people'. The onus of resource accumulation and management was to be transferred to the (local) *community* first, and then to the (global) *market*. Consequently, the NPE 1986/1992 incarnated the therapeutic force of the 'people' as an accurate antidote to millennial historical injustices, and in the process furnished ideological fodder for the slow but eventual withdrawal of the state. It was as if the logic of state funding, and the implied inadequacy of its quantity, bred the devil of social exclusion – and, therefore, the sure-shot formula for *inclusion* must rest on an attempted disengagement of the state from the question of funding altogether. In its place, the public might be made the direct arbiter of resources for its own education, implying that a paying public will know how best to correct its deficits and defaults. This public, as I said, was to range from a nauseatingly over-rehearsed category of 'community effort' to

[1] For a critical take on the build-up of governmental policy and public sentiments towards the 'deregulation' of Indian markets in 1991, see Chandrasekhar and Ghosh.

strategic collaboration with industry – which, in the final instance, will be the effective reaper of the nation's educated/skilled human resource. What is to be noticed in the policy accents of this time is the protean character of the 'people' – the most sovereign signifier of a democratic consensus – in its journey from being first made into a sign of *civil society*, and then of the *market* (POA 7, 132, 182, 188). The contortions of democracy are underwritten into this compact with capital, starting with private philanthropy and extending all the way to the global transnational market.

> The National Policy of 1968 marked a significant step in the history of education in post-Independence India. It aimed to promote national progress, a sense of common citizenship and culture, and to strengthen national integration. . . . While these achievements are impressive by themselves, the general formulations incorporated in the 1968 Policy did not, however, get translated into a detailed strategy of implementation, accompanied by the assignment of specific responsibilities and financial and organisational support. As a result, problems of access, quality, quantity, utility and financial outlay, accumulated over the years, have now assumed such massive proportions that they must be tackled with the utmost urgency. . . . To enable the people to benefit in the new environment will require new designs of human resource development. . . . *The Nation as a whole will assume the responsibility of providing resource support for implementing programmes of educational transformation, reducing disparities*, universalisation of elementary education, adult literacy, scientific and technological research, etc. (Paras 1.4–3.10, 1–5, emphasis mine)

Exclusion as/and Human Resource

The above extract from the preambular commitments of NPE 1986 begins by ruing how a 'sense of common citizenship and culture' has only exacerbated the 'problems of access, quality, quantity, utility and financial outlay' – specifically along the coordinates of caste, religion, gender and region. The incremental accrual of an exclusionary bias within educational sectors – as we have historically examined through three of the previous chapters

– is hardly challenged by the fantasies of 'national integration' forwarded by the 1968 *Policy*. The answer to such a crisis of national(ist) welfarism, the authors of the 1986 vision contend, lies in a departure from the principles of 'welfare' altogether – and towards 'new designs of human resource development'. *The cognitive reinstatement of the 'excluded' as potential 'human resource' is the moral of the story of this discursive shift from 'welfare' to 'markets'.* That the excluded must now be included in projects of national development is at heart an investment plan; the former must be remade into an asset for potential sale in the market. And because the promise of future profit lies with the markets, the latter must necessarily be invited to invest in such underused human resource. This is the historical scenario that I hope to construct through policy detours, spanning from the NPE of 1986 to the attempted introduction of a Foreign Education Providers (FEP) Bill between 2010 and 2013.

In telling the story of these two-and-a-half decades of educational planning, around the turn of the millennium, this chapter will track the conditions of India's passage into what has famously been termed as 'neoliberalism'. In other words, what follows is a saga of the disappearance of a regime of *welfare* into a rule of the *market*. But unlike how this disappearance is mourned in classic tracts of progressive resistance, I want to emphasise that the lament makes sense only if welfarism was innocent in the first place. Quite on the contrary, it was the structural myopia of the welfare-state that sounded the maiden overtures to private voluntarism. In other words and put more directly, the systemic inattention to how caste and religion manufactured the intellectual *disposition* is what was sought to be redressed by the 'equalising' tendencies of an economy of capital and resource allocation. Lest the dirge for national welfare seem too misplaced, this chapter will end with a hint of the horrors of minting exclusion.

The argument here will be divided into three parts. The first records the early lineaments of the market in the spectre of 'local community' – a euphemism for *civil society*. The strategic slippage from a 'national development' to a 'community development' model of provisioning educational services is also, at the same time, a rooting of the nation beyond the macroeconomics of policy and in the microgeographies of *identity*. To this extent, the seceding of ground by the state to the community privatises both action and relation, as much as it bails the government out of its constitutional obligations. Furthermore, since caste and religion are community-identifiers, we are made to believe that the containment of their political expression must also necessarily be entrusted to forms and resources of community-action. *In the process, social justice is already left to the unregulated and unlegislated space of private conscience and philanthropic good will.* This is the inaugural gesture of wooing the market. I will explore the layers in that gesture through a close reading of the NPE 1986, and a subsequent revision of its 'goals' in the 1992 *Programme of Action* (POA). Having traced the emergence of the *community*, as both a discursive and political trope for arbitrating the effects of exclusion, the second part of this chapter will outline the stealthy incursions of the *market* that follow close on the heels of this state-community dichotomy. In this section, I will deal with a chronology of policy fortunes of the 'Indian university' between the moment of India's liberalisation (1991) and the end of the era of state-led planning,[2] soon after the postulation of the twelfth and last Five Year Plan in 2012. How the world of international finance influenced decisions around domestic markets for educational

---

[2] Within a year of the anointing of the Modi government, a Cabinet resolution (2015) declared the abolition of Nehru's socialist instrument for state-led development in the Planning Commission and its Five Year Plans. The Twelfth Five Year Plan period (2012-17) was to be the last of the nation's planning schedules, succeeding which a merely 'advisory' body in the National Institution for Transforming India (NITI) Aayog was to take over. With a decided macroeconomic shift in policy from state-sponsored planning to outcome-based emphasis on 'growth' targets, what was delegitimised was a minimal vocabulary of 'welfare' – even though the substance of it had long been evacuated. As the Cabinet resolution from 2015 noted, the NITI Aayog's mandate was to reconceptualise the government as an 'enabler' rather than a 'provider of first and last resort' (Para 6a).

goods and services will of course remain the backdrop for such discussion. The third and final part of this chapter is a cautionary reading of the history of this period, which saw the most insidious co-implication of markets and communities right around the ceremonial turn of the Indian economy towards globalisation. The intellectual dividends of caste and religion, when sought to be redistributed via the market, could only lead to the corrosive violence of anti-Mandal agitations in 1990 or the destructive scenes atop a Babri masjid in 1992.

'Local Community' and an Absentee State

Let me begin with a portent. Months before the tabling of the second *National Policy on Education* and while discussions about its drafting were already underway, the Ministry of Education (MoE) in India was renamed as the Ministry of Human Resource Development (MHRD) in September 1985.[3] The stated reason for this rather telling name-change was that it enabled the clubbing together of some other government departments (like youth affairs and sports, etc.) with education. Needless to say, there was a far more symbolic operation at work here: the reimagining of an educated citizenry as human capital. As has been argued by thinkers like Wendy Brown, the calibration of life as human resource or capital requires an imaginative manoeuvre: the staking of the very fact of one's existence as the excuse for appreciation and extraction of value (Brown 175–200). Life measured in terms of its productive capacity is not only a negation of the dignity of life by the crude conditions of livelihood, but it is also a permanent surrender of one's own being as the means to the ends of somebody else's will. In that sense, the theoretical postulation of 'human resource' is an act of reneging on the very Kantian

---

[3] Refer to the "Cabinet Secretariat Notification" dated 25 September 1985, which brought into effect the 174th Amendment to the Government of India (Allocation of Business) Rules 1961. Para 12 of the First Schedule is amended to bring into existence the Ministry of Human Resource Development, in place of the erstwhile Ministry of Education.

promise of Enlightenment modernity (Blacker 102–08). But that was precisely the foretold premise of NPE 1986 – the *potential incorporation of all forms and stages and periods of life – whether left out or dropout – into the great cycle of capital accumulation.*

There were several measures proposed for the purpose, all geared towards making education into a 'lifelong' prospect for bolstering the value of life. It was to begin with an active encouragement of 'early childhood care and education (ECCE)', for children aged between 3 and 5 years and therefore constitutionally outside of the ambit of compulsory formal schooling. This too was earmarked for 'particularly children from sections of the population in which first generation learners predominate' (NPE 1986, Para 5.1, 10) – with a caveat that the 'local community will be fully involved in these programmes' (Para 5.3, 10). The grand idea of 'welfare' was already foisted for a dismantling, in that it had only aggravated the accident of social origins and its uneven economies of access to learning. Embedding questions of provision and infrastructure within the 'local community' not only saved the state from the burden of welfarist commitment, but also routed the fantasy of democracy in a 'bottom-up' symbology of the *grassroots.* But then again, the age of 'welfare' had also erred in tying education to formal processes of institutional attainment. And therefore, the apparent freeing up of education's democratic energies called for a vigorous championing of non-formal instruction, adult and continuing education as well as vocational training. All of these became the discernible parameters of 'change' indicated by the NPE 1986 – sometimes in a spirited note of campaigning for the 'universalization of elementary education', or in the suggestion of a 'phased drive', symbolically called Operation Blackboard at others (Para 5.7, 11). There is a refrain however that lingers on:

> Talented and dedicated young men and women from the local community will be chosen to serve as instructors, and particular attention paid to their training. Steps will be taken to facilitate their entry into the formal system in deserving cases. All necessary measures will be taken to ensure that the quality of non-formal education is comparable with formal education. (Para 5.9, 11–12)

Community effort being valorised as 'comparable' and complementary to state initiative, the charge of equality and social justice is squarely counterposed to histories of governmental will. The NPE elaborates developments in the fields of education of women, scheduled castes and tribes, minorities, other educationally backward classes and the disabled as woefully incongruous with the relative attainments of those privileged by gender, caste, religion and physical ability. It reiterates its resistance to the ideology of welfare which has congealed these structures of privilege, and promises that the 'new Policy will lay special emphasis on the removal of disparities and to equalise educational opportunity by attending to the specific needs of those who have been denied equality so far' (Para 4.1). In doing so, the task of policy-planning is seemingly consecrated to a politics of identity – which, by the evident look of it, was responding to the contemporary ferment of Dalit-Bahujan articulations in mainstream Indian politics (Kothari 1589–94; Satyanarayana; Pai).

But, a little further on, in Part XI of the document – titled "Resources and Review" – the truth of this social transformative claim is laid threadbare:

> Resources, to the extent possible, will be raised by mobilising donations, asking the beneficiary communities to maintain school buildings and supplies of some consumables, raising fees at the higher levels of education and effecting some savings by the efficient use of facilities. Institutions involved with research and the development of technical and scientific manpower should also mobilize some funds by levying a cess or charge on the user agencies, including Government departments, and entrepreneurs. All these measures will be taken not only to reduce the burden on State resources but also for creating a greater sense of responsibility within the educational system. However, such measures will contribute only marginally to the total funding. The Government and the community in general will find funds for such programmes as: the universalisation of elementary education; liquidating illiteracy; equality of access to educational opportunities to all sections throughout the country; enhancing the social relevance, quality and functional effectiveness of educational programmes; generating knowledge and developing

> technologies in scientific fields crucial to self-sustaining economic development; and creating a critical consciousness of the values and imperatives of national survival. (Para 11.2, 28)

The 'imperatives of national survival', pitted against the historical oversights of national welfarism, perform a few particularly cunning gestures. First, it exposes the scandal of democracy and *pits social justice as achievable through a mere combination of the will of the state and resources of the market.* The method of 'mobilising donations' as resource-generation technique makes it appear that the government needs to do no more than simply *will* a transformation – and then leave it to non-state actors to implement such a will. In this, the theoretical neatness of democratic governance – as manifestation of the 'general will of the people' – is given both practical legitimacy and sovereign agency. Second, the spontaneity of this partnership between public will and private monies is assumed to issue from 'a greater sense of responsibility within the educational system'. When freedom from oppression becomes the responsibility of the oppressed – by going as far as 'asking the beneficiary communities to maintain school buildings and supplies of some consumables' – the calculus of historical guilt is left untouched. Exalting the local community as patron and provider of development demonstrates the redundancy of a policy of affirmative action, by making redressal a cause of self-improvement.

Third, and perhaps most importantly, the NPE's fundamentals of resource generation are explicitly modelled as an art of *making adjustments.* The imminent option of 'raising fees at the higher levels of education', in order to compensate for unequal rights of entry at the lowest levels, creates a hierarchy of moral imperatives as integral to a developmentalist imagination. This is exactly where the involvement of community at the grassroots works hand-in-hand with a push for the deregulation of stakes higher up in the structure. The pawning off of higher education to the market, in the cause of 'equalising' educational opportunities for the structurally excluded communities, is a policy plan that will only gain more and more traction in the coming years. That community participation is structural adjustment demanded by a free market is also portended here, slightly before the shadow of the 'Washington Consensus' descended on the Indian economy[4] (Tabb; Williamson). Fourth, and finally, the NPE 1986 urges attempts at 'effecting some savings by the efficient use of facilities'. This too is a far-reaching imaginative move, in terms of the groundwork for a neoliberal rationality. By turning forms of historical disadvantage into a question of imprudent financing – or, more succinctly, a fallout of resource wastage – the call for 'savings' establishes a causal connection between the abundance of welfare-spending and the scarcity that thus resulted. The supplication to non-state sources becomes a crisis-resort, and the market but a benign disburser of charity. In the process, there is a degree of public suspicion that is invited towards every instance of public spending, as disproportionate to questions of *need* and calculations of *benefit*. An ideology of austerity is postulated as common sense, and a permanent check on the prodigality of the welfare state.

Against State Welfare: From a *Policy* (1986) to a *Programme* (1992)

It appears that, in the space of a single paragraph, the NPE 1986 propounded a theory of neoliberal reason – as both moral antidote to 'national welfare' as well as economic remedy to its social exclusions. How this theory was to be implemented, and the exact areas for its application, had to wait until after India's transition into the free-market economy was announced in mid-1991. A Programme of Action (POA) on the NPE was publicly

---

[4] The 'Washington Consensus' of 1989 argued for a slackening of state controls in the social sector (including education and health) within 'Third World' or developing economies – famously termed as a regime of 'structural adjustment programs' – for assured credit streams from the World Bank and International Monetary Fund (IMF). These internal policy adjustments were made into a precondition for easing the massive debts incurred by South Asian, African and Latin American nations in the 1980s, as well as for opening up these economies as 'emerging markets' for multilateral foreign trade.

launched in 1992, in a bid to contextualise the reform-directions in education with specific reference to the country's newly hailed economic priorities. I will spend some time now, surveying these directions circumscribed by the POA 1992 and how the pulls of social and educational reform were balanced through alternating invocations to the market and the community. The "Introduction" to the POA starts off in an oracular fashion:

> If implemented with sensitivity, vigour and persistence, the proposals contained in the Programme of Action regarding reorientation of the whole system to promote women's equality, special provisions for the Scheduled Castes, Scheduled Tribes, other educationally disadvantaged sections, minorities, the physically and mentally handicapped, and for the areas which need special attention will enable the educational system to move towards the democratic and socialist ideals enshrined in the Constitution. . . . [E]very institution, every centre of non-formal education and of adult education, every teacher and student and every member of the society must examine what they can do. Some retired teachers can help out as substitute teachers, some housewives can impart literacy to their illiterate sisters, some institutions can extend their facilities to neighbouring institutions, some newspapers can start for their readers a weekly column on everyday science, and so on. While the Central and State Governments will fully shoulder their responsibilities and will give an account of it to State legislatures and Parliament, *it is peoples' involvement in the educational reconstruction which will make the real difference.* (6–7, emphasis mine)

Much like the spirit of the NPE 1986, the POA recycles the overarching intention of reform planning but with a more concrete catalogue of possible recourses: the enlisting of 'peoples' involvement' as the singular means to realising 'the democratic and socialist ideals enshrined in the Constitution'. Notwithstanding the re-codification of terms like 'democracy' and 'socialism' with deference to the palliative force of 'civil society', we are in fact forced to recognise that what passed for state socialism thus far – in the ideology of national welfare – was utterly undemocratic and made little 'real difference' in people's lives. At the heart of this sickness of the polity's soul is diagnosed an over-reliance on the 'Central and State Governments' as the only resort for 'action'. The will to social justice in education is instead projected as devolving into the sporadic efforts of 'retired teachers', 'housewives', 'neighbouring institutions' and 'weekly columns' in newspapers – which, when cumulatively harnessed, translate into the fullest measure of 'peoples' involvement'. The policy proposal that comes out of this workshop of local initiative is a vigorous insistence on the expansion of non-formal education (NFE) and adult and continuing education (ACE). In the same breath, it is maintained:

> Wherever possible the administrative and supervisory structure for NFE and adult education will be amalgamated – including the programmes to be taken up through *panchayati raj* bodies and voluntary agencies (VAs). . . . Several voluntary agencies have, in the past successfully organised NFE programmes. Very often voluntary agencies have bands of committed workers who have the capability to establish rapport with the local community and they can also function with flexibility and dynamism. . . . It is also proposed to improve the existing administrative arrangements for support to VAs. (24)

The 'bands of committed workers', which supposedly embody an ethic of selfless voluntarism, are also to be selected 'preferably from the weaker sections of society' (23). What is thus insidiously reworked into systems of non-formal instruction for the marginalised is a careful immunitary safeguard against risks of contact with the outcaste or the minority. The coteries of caste/religious/gender privilege that the NPE-POA seek to unsettle are in fact emboldened by the segregationism of 'local community'. In other words, the resolute localisation of exclusion, even when acknowledged in policy, does not dare breach the injunctions on touch and sociality. It also assumes that the experience of exclusion can itself be a self-sufficient impetus for the *exceptional* and the *exemplary* – which is further reinforced by the POA's emphasis on vocational education as the instrument of economic mobility. The bifurcation of the 'vocation' from a 'general' education, or non-formal adult literacy programmes from formal training in the liberal arts, is constitutive of what I have already discerned as an investment-economy around the socially excluded as 'human resource'. A statistical indexing of this comes soon after:

> [I]t is the unorganised sector which absorbs the bulk of workforce. Consequently one sees the phenomenon of mounting unemployment among the educated at one end and shortage of plumbers, car mechanics, electricians, carpenters and manpower in numerous other trades at the other end.
>
> It is estimated that about 80% of the student population do not go beyond class 10. The drop outs upto and inclusive of class 8 are over 120 lakhs per year. Roughly 20 lakhs of boys and girls cross class 8 but do not go beyond class 10. All of them form a large pool of unskilled labour force. They need opportunities for training in some skills either in their traditional occupations or in new areas to enable them to take up skilled and gainful occupations. (34–35)

Social justice, seen this way, does not consist in questioning the basis of social relations of production; instead, it reproduces these relations as the only possible ground for social mobility. By such sleight, the historical situation of the marginalised is what makes them particularly amenable to resource-extraction, and therefore hardly merits any socially transformative labour. The same POA that argues for a delinking of jobs from degrees (77) here succumbs to a demand for manpower-skilling for informal employment as the destiny of the socially excluded. The 'unorganised sector which absorbs the bulk of workforce' is neither subjected to scrutiny for its shadowy extortionism of work-contracts, nor is its principles of minimum pay and workday routine questioned by any means.[5] In stark contrast, it is this haven of exploitation with no structures of collective bargaining that is made into a means of deliverance for the millennially disprivileged. Vocational education, as it were,

[5] In India, it has been severally calculated that nearly 94 per cent of work contracts are informal in nature, without regularised or fixed conditions of payment, social security or leave entitlements. This includes a substantial proportion of employment within the organised sectors of economic activity. (NSSO, *Employment-Unemployment Situation in India*; NSSO, *Informal Sector in India*; Unni, Table 3; GoI, *Economic Survey 2007–2008*).

could redeem the injustice of unequal access through the indignity of informal work.

Addressing Gender, Caste, Religion, Disability

Analysing gender disparities in the provisioning of education, the POA dwells on the magnitude of the problem by noting that '57 percent of the illiterate population and 70 percent of the non-enrolled children of school stage' (100) are women. There are two effective measures advocated with a view to remedying this state of affairs. The first proposes the introduction of women's studies as a component in the core curriculum of a national system of education, as well as in teacher's training programmes. The ideological impetus behind the institutionalisation of women's studies, as a discipline and later as independent departments under the aegis of the Eighth Five Year Plan, is something I will discuss in detail a little later in this chapter. The second pathway to women's development, in the POA, is sought through a proportionate expansion of educational opportunities in the non-formal, adult and professional or vocational sectors – all of which was again tied to the generous voluntarism of community-based and corporate philanthropy:

> The present programme of non-formal centres for girls on 90:10 pattern will be extended to all educationally backward pockets of the country. *NFE Centres should be community based. Responsibility of planning, selection of instructors and monitoring should be with the community including parents. Increased assistance to voluntary agencies to run non formal education centres for girls should be given.* . . . The skill development given by the Continuing Education Centres will be supported by other programmes of non formal, vocational training and skill development to be administered by a variety of organisations and institutions, such as Polytechnics, Community Polytechnics, ITIs, Shramik Vidyapeeths, Central Social Welfare Board, State Social Welfare Advisory Boards, Voluntary agencies, Krishi Vigyan Kendras, Women's Centres in Agricultural and Home Science Colleges as part of their extension activities. Besides, Industries which employ women should themselves run non formal vocational training courses. (104, emphasis mine)

The strategic relegation of equity goals within education, from being the mainstay of the NPE 1986, to the 'extension activities' of voluntary agencies and industries continues well into the POA's delineation of strategic targets for the education of scheduled castes, scheduled tribes and other backward sections. Maintaining that the SC/ST enrolment ratios cannot compare with their census proportions, and that their drop-out rates are exceedingly high at all stages of education, the POA prescribes a by now well-rehearsed panacea as systematic redress:

> [E]xtension approach at the village level [will help] to persuade parents to send the children to school, with the involvement of teachers, parents, local leaders, social workers, etc., and provision of remedial coaching at all stages and special remedial coaching for classes IX-XII for preparing SC/ST children for professional courses. . . . In addition to an in-built, mechanism for continuous evaluation of programmes, evaluation of important schemes like scholarships, hostels and the proposed incentive scheme may be undertaken by external agencies. (108–09)

The stealthy outsourcing of constitutional obligations – with respect to both consciousness-raising campaigns as well as the stock-taking of infrastructural and resource availability – to 'external agencies' only serves to make equity a non-institutional/non-governmental stake in the provisioning of education. Caste-based discrimination at all levels of formal instruction, and the structural eliminationism resulting of it as one moves higher up the ladder, is given a length of policy attention that welfare planning never quite conceded. But, does this increased visibility of caste do something by way of substantive equality of opportunity? The answer is astutely made *external* to state agendas of reform – and, much like in the case of women's participation in education, left at the mercy of 'teachers, parents, local leaders, social workers, etc.'

In the case of educational provisioning for religious minorities, the discourse of policy intervention curiously changes its registers though not its intention. The POA reports matter-of-factly in the relevant section:

> According to 1981 Census, the religious minorities constitute about 17.4% of the population of which Muslims are 11.4%, Christians 2.4%, Sikhs 2%, Buddhists 0.7% and Jains 0.5%. Ministry of Home Affairs have identified Muslims and Neo-Buddhists as educationally backward at national level. It was agreed that the State Governments may also identify other groups which are educationally backward at the State level. Special efforts need to be taken to bring these educationally backward minorities on par with the rest of the society and to make them participate fully in the national developmental activities. (110)

Through the rest of this section, several of such 'special efforts' are named and targeted for delivery through 'community polytechnics' (111) or 'voluntary societies of all India repute' (114). The work of implementation is specifically delivered unto the charge of 'state governments', and resolutely detached from national-level planning effort. The implication is that, despite the prefatory perspective provided by national census data, the question of religious community-identification and minority development is not a national imperative. The figural status of the 'minority', reduced to a numerical aggregate, is passed off as a local administrative issue and therefore unworthy of inherence within a politics of social justice. The overseer role of state governments, as a result, comes with a readymade script – where minority participation in 'national developmental activities', monitored at the state level, could only mean a successive abdication of responsibility on to the 'local' beneficiary community itself (110). The reference to religion as a vector of structural discrimination is indeed a belated confession in policy, but it does little more than erecting a logic of self-help as the only attenuating recourse. Minorities are admitted to the status of a repressed unconscious in the imagining of national development, but only to the extent that they represent yet another aggregation of untapped 'human resource'.

The 'education of the handicapped' which comes next (116–23) in this sequence of the POA's priority-areas is consigned to a similar fate. Repeated concerns about 'economic viability criteria'

(120) and the 'very costly' (117) character of education in special schools blend into the confession that the 'voluntary sector' may continue as the best provider.

Moving On: The Passage from Community to Markets

After having painstakingly routed all claims to structural redress to a morally redemptive imagination of the 'community' – more familiarly termed 'civil society' – the POA's recommendations end with a decisive conjuring of the market as the final condition for the NPE's felicity. The civil society, Gramsci had alerted us, is the space for a slow garnering of consent in favour of existing or emergent systems of production (12). The NPE/POA archive of policy-referencing, coming at the exact moment of a macroeconomic transition, was extraordinarily clear-sighted about this Gramscian subtext of securing hegemony. Hence, it did not take a chance, and simply grounded the rhetoric of reform in the localism of community life-worlds at the outset. That the voiding of state welfarism by the prerogatives of the market must seek ideological legitimation in the middle ground of community – *first as historical casualty and then as therapeutic democratisation* – is the story told thus far. In this, the egregious scenes of deprivation underlying education's relationship with *caste* or *religion* were merely an opportune instrument. By highlighting the elisions of specific communities from the national(ist) narrative of intellectual progress, it was suggested that social justice has been failed by constitutional state-motive. Instead, community disaffection required a return to the healing propensities of community-based networks of care. This was already half the road charted towards a systematic disavowal of public bursaries in and through the state. But, if redistribution is guilty of purposeful erasures and must therefore be shunned, where will the resources for reconstruction come from? The answer is two-fold and mutually self-supporting: the deprived as uncirculated capital is itself the market's social investment. In one of the conclusive sub-sections on the 'management of education', the POA comes into its own and unassumingly registers the rule of the market:

> Educational planning will need to be linked to manpower planning by setting up mechanisms for assessing the needs of the industry, commerce, professional services, agriculture in the context of the technological trends and growth strategies. Based on different assumptions indicating the level and structure of income and income distribution, nature of technologies likely to be used in different capital-labour coefficients, structure of employment and job/skill profiles required, alternative scenarios of development for the next 15-20 years and the task for education derived from such scenarios will require to be formulated. At present no agency has either the capacity or the responsibility to undertake the kind of exercise required even in quantitative terms, to link long term planning of education to match developmental and manpower needs in the country. This capacity of manpower demand forecasting will have to be provided for in the overall structure for the management of the educational system. (181)

The purposive orbit within which the Policy reinscribes itself at this point is hard to miss: connecting 'long term planning of education' with questions of 'developmental and manpower needs'. Needless to reiterate, 'development' and 'manpower' are the operative terms at work here, thus *setting up histories of deprivation (as developmental deficit) against prospects of mobility (as potential manpower resource).* The social backyards of educational planning are thus staged as the launchpad for meeting economic targets of productivity. But, in the guise of this interplay of social and economic registers in educational planning-discourse, there is a significant restructuring of the institutional logic of governance that takes place. To provide for 'manpower demand forecasting' within the 'overall structure for the management of the educational system' is the real writing on the wall; it needs to be read carefully and with thoughtful consideration of its full resonance. To allow forces of manpower requisitioning a necessary stake in the *management* of education, when seen in its real aspect, translates thus: the market must be a structural determinant of the governance of institutions. In other words, the time for the state to fund and regulate education is over! The POA's policy-parable on 'management' resumes on that very strain:

> [T]he implementation process will require special measures to be taken to ensure that the groups who are left out of the ambit of education namely the weaker sections of the society including SC/ST and women and, adult illiterates in the age-group 15-35, are enabled to participate effectively as beneficiaries of the relevant educational programmes so that achievement of national goals and objectives could be ensured. This would call for a planning model which would have the flexibility to cater to the immense diversities encountered in the context of universalisation of elementary education, equalisation of educational opportunities especially in respect of disadvantaged sections and reorienting the content and process of education. *Decentralisation of the planning and management process within a multilevel framework appears to be inescapable for the implementation of educational programmes.*
>
> Decentralisation, as far as education at higher levels, namely at under-graduate/postgraduate or at the level of polytechnics, technical colleges etc. is concerned, would be required essentially to allow the exercise of initiatives and making of innovations by teachers, students and management with a view to enhancing the relevance and improving the quality of education. (181, emphasis mine)

Once again, the need for a market-oriented reform of educational management is linked to the best interests of 'groups who are left out of the ambit of education, namely the weaker sections of the society'. Social justice parades as the outward justification for a spectacular red-carpet ushering-in of markets. The new 'planning and management process' – presciently called 'decentralisation' – is a euphemistic rhetorical substitute for deregulation. The coinage 'decentralisation', consisting of a dethroning of the centrality of the centre, sounds too lucratively similar to a deconstructive politics of/at the margins. A policy vision trained into attending to marginality is therefore its preferred site. But alas! *decentralisation is not de-centring; in fact, it is quite the obverse.* It resurrects an invisible centre in the diffusive totality of global markets. Even more prophetically, this extract from the POA ordains 'education at higher levels, namely at under-graduate/postgraduate or the level of polytechnics, technical colleges etc.' as the *starting-point for decentralisation*. Put more pointedly, the university – the NPE and POA convergently argue! – must be the first to be deregulated. There is a fanciness to the rationalisation provided: the markets 'allow the exercise of initiatives and making of innovations'. The full chain of substitutions makes for a delicious (and by now all too familiar) recipe: democracy requires the dispersion of the state in the community; the community mobilises consent for the incursion of markets; the efficiency of markets requires an evacuation of the regulatory powers of the state; deregulation favours autonomy, and therefore returns us to the democratising agendas of education. We are back to the foundational premise and promise of the NPE 1986, redrawn by the POA in its closing accents:

> The *National Policy on Education* gives pre-eminence to people's involvement, including association of non-governmental agencies and voluntary effort. People's involvement should, even more than non-governmental agencies and voluntary associations, mean involvement of parents, developmental agencies, employers, professionally competent teachers and representatives of financing bodies with educational processes at all levels. People's involvement should lead to establishment of closer linkages between educational institutions and the community, improvement in relevance and quality of education, reduction of absenteeism and irresponsibility, greater access to community resources and better discipline in the management of educational institutions. At the same time, *it should eschew importation of local politics and power play into educational institutions*. (182, emphasis mine)

That 'people's involvement', even when it foregrounds the local community, must still 'eschew importation of local politics and power play' is a telling feature of the NPE/POA model of planning. The latter's acute awareness of caste and communal apartheid in education is however emptied of any willingness to address the *political economy of access*. For the NPE 1986/1992, *caste* and *religion* are exhumed not as the calculated political effects of a history of policy-engineering around education, but are instead mere economic justifications for the market. In this, *the idea of discrimination is itself depoliticised – and in fact regarded as the greenfield condition for capital's regeneration*. The hope of maximal returns is pegged on the investee's erstwhile exclusion from processes of social production; the constant hope of pulling in more and more human resource at the behest of capital is the apotheosis of market efficiency. As long as there is a reserve army of labour, there is the promise of surplus in production. The NPE is unambiguous about its courting of the market, when it defines 'people's involvement' as *more than* 'non-governmental agencies and voluntary associations'. It goes on to qualify that the fetishization of democracy in education is about using the community to forge ties with 'financing bodies'. What comes of it is an economic virtue of 'better discipline', and not a political imagination of 'power play'.

The Political Economy Behind Policy

For the precise reason that a shift from welfarism to marketism works by abnegating the political basis of democracy, I must now take the reader through a brief outline of the political economy of a neoliberal 'turn' in India. This outline will insist on seeing the *politics of policy*, as I set out a broad-stroke parallelism between national-economic priorities and higher educational fortunes.

It was already by the 1970s and early 1980s that Nehru's model of 'national capitalism' – supplementing state regulation of private initiative with import substitutions – started gathering detractors, who were arguing for means of overriding a general slowdown in real economic activity (Patnaik, "Market Question"; "A Critique"; "Capitalism and India's Democratic Revolution"; *Quarter Century*; Chandrasekhar and Ghosh). Added to this were fears of defaulting international loans, and the need for controlling fiscal deficits through cost-cutting measures. Trade and financial liberalisation seemed like *fait accompli*, in tiding over both the debt-crisis and the repeatedly drummed-up anxiety of deficit-financing. While the Indian economy was finally opened up to world markets in 1991, the state's preparedness for structural adjustment programmes was already in evidence by way of its withdrawal from capital formation

– through cutbacks on social spending and critical infrastructural provisioning. The blocking of the government's implementation of constitutional safeguards for socially and educationally backward communities – indexed by the Mandal Commission as 'Other Backward Classes (OBCs)' – by means of violent public agitations in 1990, only helped in reinforcing governmental attitudes towards any possible increase in public expenditure on higher education (Balagopal). Alternatively, it meant that the educational and professional 'benefits' of globalisation were, by a plebiscitory consensus, to be securely channelled to the Hindu upper castes alone. The ideological implications of such a move will be taken up for closer analysis in a later section.

The state's continued reluctance to make up for revenue shortfalls through direct corporate taxation performed an ironic inversion. It allowed domestic capital to function freely in a market already heavily tilted towards foreign investors, in that there was little corroborative support in terms of capital assets or supplies of power or transport. The lifting of import controls and access to international finance did not quite create a conducive climate for competitive investments among national private players. Neither were there conditions enough for massive productivity boosts in the cause of export production, nor did foreign investments exceed the speculative returns on short-term portfolio bubbles. In fact, the immediate aftermath of liberalisation only ended up making the 'real' basis of economic exchange and production even more uncertain as well as susceptible to speculative plunges. Foreign markets were sceptical of the risks of volatility in a newly deregulated economy, while homegrown industrialists felt largely betrayed by the state's non-participation in easing conditions of doing business. This was the general mood of the 1990s – in keeping with which, the Indian government drafted a Private Universities (Establishment and Regulation) Bill in 1995 and tabled it in Parliament. With a declared policy target of stemming the commercialisation of higher education, what this Bill effectively sought to do was just its opposite: legalise a framework of guidelines for the 'incorporation' of private investment in the science and technology disciplines which promised a proportionate 'commercial application' (GoI, *The Private Universities (Establishment and Regulation) Bill* 1). Though the Draft Bill was stayed in the Rajya Sabha and kept lying there till 2007, at least six or seven state legislatures extracted an operative framework of the policy and got it passed at the regional levels. As a result, without the occasion of a national policy fanfare, the corporate financing of higher education was already an offsetting adjustment to the state's withdrawal from public expenditures in the sector.

The situation began to change by around the turn of the millennium, owing largely to developments in transnational market behaviours. The gradual setting in of a recessionary trend in Western markets – from the time of the Enron and dotcom crises (2001–04) – generated a sense of alarm that sought the safety of investment havens in the global South. The 'emerging market economies', with their structural adjustments in place, served as a ready escape for the threatened fortunes of globalised finance capital. After nearly a decade of lukewarm confidence from investors in the developed world markets, the financial 'decoupling' of the globe finally reaffirmed the globality of capital flows through a strategic diversion of attention to countries like India – primarily in the archives of World Bank, International Monetary Fund (IMF) and the Organization for Economic Cooperation and Development (OECD). Concurrent with the shift in global financial priorities, Indian politics witnessed electoral gains in favour of the Hindu right-wing – forging an umbrella coalition to occupy the nation's centre-stage between 1998 and 2004. Understandably, the latter reaped its political dividends out of the economic discontents that immediately followed the liberalisation regime, and its aborted reform-promises at the level of both domestic investors and citizens.

What followed was a frenzied attempt at making good on these unrealised promises, aided by the fortuitous coincidence of international interest in the potential of Indian markets. Import protections were dramatically lifted, public sector enterprises were remodelled through indiscriminate sell-out of equity stakes, and legislative frameworks like the Fiscal Responsibility and Budget Management Act 2003 allowed for notional deficit-financing through aggravated slashes in social sector funds. The government's foreign exchange reserves ballooned as a result, alongside the inundation of India's manufacturing industry by foreign-made capital goods and a mortgaging of key public sector enterprises to international investors. The services industry boom, made possible by an export-oriented production paradigm in the West and its outsourcing of key IT functions, also heralded a period of exponential 'growth' prospects hardly ever seen before (Upadhya; Ganguly-Scrase and Scrase). India's strategic placement in this 'growth'-story owed to its population statistics – now suddenly celebrated as a 'demographic dividend', waiting to be skilled and readied through education as cheap flexible labour. The entry of the formerly excluded into routines of higher skill-training or 'lifelong' instruction or vocational education was all that was needed of this new moment of investment euphoria.

From Craze to Crisis: Universities, Jobs and a 'Growth'-Story

Sensing such a turn of events, a 'special subject group on policy framework for private investment in education' – headed by Indian industrialists Mukesh Ambani and Kumar Mangalam Birla – submitted a report in April 2000 to the Prime Minister's Council on Trade and Industry. In it, they recommended a complete slackening of state regulations for higher education and a compensatory channelling of thus-freed state funds into the sectors of primary and secondary education (Ambani and Birla 840–45). The readjustment of national priorities in favour of the lower levels of schooling as opposed to college/tertiary education would, they argued, be a more prudent means of rationing limited resources towards the largest cross-section of Indian masses. Higher education, with its fabled assurance of higher private lifetime incomes for incumbents, might in its turn be handed over to private financiers looking to enter the market and reconfigure knowledge services within a commodity logic. What the Programme of Action for NPE 1986 had envisioned, in the terms of a 'decentralisation' project for the management of higher educational institutions, was now on its course to being abetted and adopted by a right-wing nationalist government at the Centre. Scurrying along the path, the 2001 Doha conference of the World Trade Organization (WTO) – of which India was a member state since its founding in 1995 – saw the pledging of the country's higher education sector to multilateral corporate capital, in the form of an 'offer' pending 'commitment' (AIFRTE). This move called on the government to enable a 'level playing field' for competitive bids through an effective rollback of national subsidies and allied mechanisms of state support (Manuel; *Sanhati*; Prasad). The spirit of the WTO's General Agreement on Trade in Services (GATS) was subsequently honoured through the central regulator's (UGC) notification of a Model Universities Act in 2004. This Act demarcated the policy contours of a 'model university' as one which is capable of generating its own revenue through profitable alliances with philanthropy and industry.[6] Once again, the community routing of the market's fantasy for institutional take-over was now unequivocal common sense.

Mounting opposition to such a mandate for remodelling universities in the country led to the next United Progressive Alliance (UPA – I) government's prompt retraction on the front. The UGC's 'model'-missive was withdrawn, but not without a quick compensatory call for rethinking the futures of higher education: in the setting up of a National Knowledge Commission (NKC) in 2005, under the tutelage of a corporate telecommunications entrepreneur. The NKC went into a visible overdrive of churning out policy prescriptions, through periodic reports published between 2006 and 2009 – all of which concurred on the single most important need for reaping India's 'demographic

[6] Refer to "Commercialisation of Education"; "Protest against UGC Act continues".

dividend' (NKC 3) through a restructuring of Indian society into a 'knowledge economy' (ibid. 15). This meant 'diversifying the sources of financing' among potential private entrants, ranging between the oft-repeated polarities of 'philanthropic contributions' and 'industry linkages' (ibid. 14). It hardly astonishes us anymore to note that the Commission, in its new-found evangelical impatience for converting India's university sector into a self-regulating market, predicted the steepest-ever massification of the desire for higher learning at the exact historical conjuncture of a 'great recession' in Western economies. Across the Global North, while colleges and universities were in the grip of a punitive drive towards austerity-disciplining and untold closures, the Indian demand for educational goods and services soared to such heights that the NKC urged for 'need-blind admissions' and removal of all 'current barriers to entry'.

The enthusiasm peaked and wore out in less than a decade, insofar as the mass credentialling of India's human resource as employable labour power held out a set of obvious corollaries. With more and more people entering the job market with identically honed skill-sets, work contracts and wage rates were increasingly precaritised. Finding jobs adequate to one's qualifications and skill-sets became scarce, and a wholesale informalisation of work arrangements swallowed nearly 90 to 94 per cent of a 'growing' India's employment capacity. Even as the numbers of rural/semi-urban youth seeking an escape from agricultural modes of labour and livelihood kept swelling through this period, the optics of such 'economic mobility' were undergirded in the final instance by a steadily dwindling rate of public expenditure on social infrastructures. If rural developmental initiatives came to be tied to interests of private profiteering, job creation in the public sector too was by now an outrageous improbability. Fiscal consolidation was the name given to a wilful neglect for public utilities and asset ownership by the taxing state. I have etched out this historical moment in India's growth-narrative elsewhere, in the following terms:

> The developmental dream [was] a paradox: as increasing numbers of higher-educated laborers wanted to migrate away from their rural fortunes, cities crowded them out through steadily deteriorating conditions of informal work and itinerant livelihood. The combination of unregulated private initiative and the sadistic absenteeism of the state—in terms of either employment generation or rent control and regulation of living costs—only created structures for systemic precarity. The much-hailed IT 'transformation', by virtue of its necessary circumscription within urban geographies of desire and circulation, dug deep into these cycles of expropriation by making the bulk of India's technology-dependent service industries double up as self-sustaining pools of underpaid underemployment. (Bhattacharya, 'They Paint Sedition on the Walls' 158)

As the Indian economy transitioned through what Kannan and Raveendran called a trajectory of 'jobless to job-loss growth' from around 2012 onwards, the scale of demand in domestic markets obviously suffered. Consumption patterns stagnated first and then showed sharp declining trends – which were sinister enough for foreign capital to go hunting for more opportune investment climes already. Structures of debt bondage held entire masses of India's exponential 'growth'-beneficiaries hostage to private and informal credit agencies – until the National Sample Survey (NSS) data on employment-unemployment statistics (EUS) betrayed an absolute fall in the size of India's workforce for the first time in the history of post-independence state planning (Kannan and Raveendran; Himanshu; Nath and Basole). A net job loss of more than six million was registered between 2012 and 2017–18, which – when compared against rates of population growth for the period under analysis – assumed an even darker aspect of foreboding (Raveendran and Kannan; Abraham). Aside from an unheard-of condition of employable masses withdrawing from the market, the rate of 'usual status unemployment' on an annual basis shot up to a forty-five-year high of 6.1 per cent (Patnaik, "The Dramatic Increase"). The data of course demonstrated stark differences in work participation rates between social groups, gender categories and regional demographies. But, by way of pre-empting our discussion in the next and final section of this chapter, the 68th round of NSS-EUS samples revealed that the worst affected among the country's economic precariat were but the Muslims and OBCs (NSSO, *Periodic Labour Force Survey* 72–78).[7]

The 'education for equality' refrain – running and reigning through the aftermath of the 1986 NPE and its slew of recommended reform imperatives in the next two-and-a-half decades – was dissolved into a calculated anticlimax. Neither *caste* nor *religion*, in its encounters with the 'freedom' of the market, emerged any freer of the burden of history. But, as I have explained previously, it is yet the community through which the market's appellate tribunal must necessarily seek legitimation as the substitute for state welfare. I will now move to demonstrating the symbiotics of this 'market–community' relationship in the story of India's higher education.

Playing Caste against Religion: A Hindu Nation *Redux*

Let me flag this section with an interrogative gesture: how has the fact of structural discrimination within India's universities created grounds for a tactical solidarity between the community and the market, in the cause of giving short shrift to the state? We have exhumed the policy blueprint for this in the NPE 1986/1992, but how did history respond to it?

The first case in point is the timing of the attempted implementation of the Mandal Commission's recommendations in 1990 – by when the Indian economy's free-market plunge was but ineluctable destiny. The Commission, established in 1979 under the chairmanship of B.P. Mandal, had submitted its recommendations the very next year on the basis of available caste-census data. Arguing for the structurally embedded nature of 'backwardness' in terms of caste identity, the report pegged the proportion of OBCs in India's population at a chilling 52 per cent. Consequently, it called for a 27 per cent reservation of educational and job opportunities for such 'classes', maintaining

[7] See also Kannan and Raveendran.

the total quantum of affirmative action within the public sector at less than 50 per cent still. For a decade after this, successive governments allowed the commission's recommendation for a revised reservation policy to gather dust – until the spectre of financial liberalisation and structural adjustment programmes renewed the din. It was imagined that the expansionist tendencies of transnational capital might be better appeased by making potential consumers of the erstwhile 'backward' constituencies through access to skills and jobs.

But of course, all hell broke loose! How can the market reap the historical dividends of caste oppression without prior recourse to community consensus? Masses of Hindu upper-caste students from elite public institutions of higher education marched out into the streets, in uncontained scenes of violence and vandalism, to reclaim the gift of the market as a meritocratic entitlement (Bharti). They asked, almost with murderous vengeance: must the 'freedom' of the market be sacrificed without competition, at the altar of the undeserving unmeritorious? The latter may better be left to the philanthropic good will of a caste Hindu India, actively working through its *seva*-organisations to impart education to those left out of the state's developmental radar. In one-teacher schools run by the RSS and its network of frontal offshoots, it was an education for realising Hindu 'unity' that could effectively work past the millennial stigma of 'inequality' (Iwanek). To have the state look after the bulk of India's marginalised populations through forms of affirmative action would not only re-erect the transformative illusions of a welfare state, but also wean the vulnerable away from the everyday conquests of the dominant community.

Had the Mandal report not been blocked by mob-action, sponsored for the most part by right-wing Hindutva, the outliers within India's developmental project could not have been enlisted into a communal common sense against the Muslim 'outsider'. Given that the Mandal Commission had regarded 90 per cent of Indian Muslims – and more than 80 different communities among Muslims – as belonging to 'backward classes' and therefore falling within the purview of reservations, there were two rallying points for populist mobilisations among the upper-castes. First, fears were let loose that a setting aside of educational and professional opportunities for Muslim OBCs would further endanger the rightful jobs and lands of the Hindu poor – who were anyway reeling under the decades-long neglect of the state. Second, the Hindu (and non-Muslim) OBCs were instead exhorted to secure their interests by forging a larger Hindu solidarity in the cause of reclaiming the nation's resources from Muslim 'infiltrators'. The steadily rising chorus of a Ramjanmabhoomi movement, spearheaded by the Vishwa Hindu Parishad (VHP) since the 1980s – and accurately coinciding with growing economic discontents – served to whip up the anti-Mandal sentiment into a communal crescendo. The ceremony of India's 'turn' to globalisation had hardly worn its initial charms off, when in December 1992 the sham of a *secular* constitutional consensus collapsed under the chariot-wheels of a Hindutva mob taking over the Babri mosque in the heart of mainland India (Noorani).

The effects of this spectacular transition into a 'communal' will, working at the behest of a free-market India, continued until the Hindu right won elections and occupied state power in 1998. As I recounted above, this also started a brief recovery spell for the initially-thwarted dreams of a liberalised economy. Between 1998 and 2004, even as the nationalist BJP went on a mass disinvestment programme within public sectors, educational curricula across schools and colleges fell prey to the aggressive proselytising intention of Hindutva – often popularly referenced as the 'saffronisation of textbooks' debate.

Going further, it is definitely no coincidence that the eventual implementation of OBC reservations in Indian higher educational institutions had to wait until the squalling of a crisis in international finance – and the prompt redirecting of transnational capital towards Indian markets. The Central Educational Institutions (Reservation in Admission) Act 2006 paved the way for Mandal's mandate to be put to action, but not before being challenged in and cleared by the Supreme Court only in 2008 (*EPW*; Babu). By then, the National Knowledge Commission (2005–09) had already made its pitch for 'need-blind admissions' in India's university sector, seemingly attending to the massive domestic demand for higher educational goods and services. The corresponding large-scale withdrawal of the state from social sector spending meant that the fanfare of democratic access and an undoing of caste apartheid within higher education was to be largely self-financed. Affirmative action, as state legislation, would be no more than a mere policy carcass, if not for the merciful generosity of the market. Also, the subaltern's rite of passage through the workshop of communal hate was nearly complete, and so s/he could be ushered into the marketplace of labour as *human resource*.

Funding Discrimination 'Studies': A Cautionary Tale

For an ending to this chapter, let me use an anecdotal reference to how discrimination discourse is sponsored by the strides of the market. It was between the Eighth and the Tenth Five Year Plans – spanning from 1992 to 2007, which were the precise limits of India's rise to neoliberal adventurism – that proposals for setting up university centres in the interdisciplinary social sciences were mooted.[8] The first such spurt of a suggestion was made by the NPE 1986, by way of stressing on the need for women's studies as a curricular component in courses of higher instruction (6). Following up on that policy prescription, and even bettering it, more than a hundred and fifty centres for women's studies and 32 'centres for the study of social exclusion and inclusive policy' were opened across the country's universities by 2007. Through the Twelfth Plan period (2012–17), they were even going to be supported by public funds on a recurring basis to offset faculty recruitments and research expenses.[9] It was as if the state was responsible for easing its structural disappearance into finance capitalism, by allowing (only within the university!)

[8] Refer to Section 1.1 of *Guidelines for Development of Women's Studies in Indian Universities and Colleges During Eleventh Plan (2007–2012)*, p. 4.
[9] See Section 5 of "XII Plan Guidelines For Establishment of Centres in Universities for Study of Social Exclusion and Inclusive Policy", p. 3.

a compensatory intellectual preoccupation with the 'outsides' to a market-society (Bhattacharya, "The Dangerous Ground for Democracy" 168–70). Roderick Ferguson has brilliantly examined the fortunes of similar interdisciplinary intellectual preoccupations – like critical race studies or gender studies – within the post-1968 American university, as a means to curate a range of 'instructed minorities' as part of diversity activism (180–208).

But, there was danger lurking by. Intellectual preoccupations do not go by a plan (five-year or otherwise). Many of these centres set up on Indian institutional campuses transgressed their mandate of manufacturing a hegemonic consensus for neoliberal capital. The undersides of caste, religion and gender came to be examined not just as structural adjustments to the market's benign propensity for democratisation, but as the very condition of possibility of a society premised on undervalued (and unwaged) labour.

Before long, by 2013, the UGC started hounding these centres with notices for targeted defunding and imminent closures (Mukul). Threats to the existence of these departments continued well into 2017, when the abolition of the Planning Commission was itself made into a cause for the lapsing of these 'special' interdisciplinary pursuits (Chari; Qazi; Dasgupta, "Notice to JNU's social exclusion centre forged"; Dasgupta, "JU School of Women's Studies staffers brace for uncertain future"; Ramakrishnan; Ara; "Jamia Reverses Decision"). Tellingly, India's flirtations with transnational markets had stopped blowing in bubbles of a 'lifelong' profit by then. And, the chequered histories of caste and religion within Indian higher education had turned the university into a site of its own critique.

References

Abraham, Vinoj. "Stagnant Employment Growth: Last Three Years May Have Been the Worst." *Economic and Political Weekly*, vol. 52, no. 38, 2017. https://www.epw.in/journal/2017/38/commentary/stagnant-employment-growth.html

All India Forum for Right to Education (AIFRTE). "Fight against inclusion of higher education in WTO." *The Companion*, 5 Apr. 2015.

Ambani, Mukesh, and Kumar Mangalam Birla. "Report on a Policy Framework for Reforms in Education." *Journal of Indian School of Political Economy*, vol. 15, no. 4, 2003, pp. 840–45.

Ara, Ismat. "As Students and Teachers Panic, Jamia Withdraws Notice Disbanding Two Departments." *The Wire*, 7 Apr. 2020. https://thewire.in/education/as-students-and-teachers-panic-jamia-withdraws-noticedisbanding-two-departments.

Babu M. T., Hany. "The Curious Case of OBC Reservations." *Economic and Political Weekly*, vol. 45, no. 47, 2010. https://www.epw.in/journal/2010/47/commentary/curious-case-obc- reservations.html.

Balagopal, K. "This Anti-Mandal Mania." *Economic and Political Weekly*, vol. 25, no. 40, 1990. https://www.epw.in/journal/1990/40/roots-specials/anti-mandal-mania.html.

Bharti, Indu. "Politics of Anti-Reservation Stir." *Economic and Political Weekly*, vol. 25, no. 6, 10 Feb. 1990. www.epw.in/journal/1990/6/roots-specials/bihar-politics-anti-reservation-stir.html.

Bhattacharya, Debaditya. "'They Paint Sedition on the Walls': Toward a University of Immigrants." *Critical Times: Interventions in Global Critical Theory (Special Section: Global Higher Education in 2050)*, vol. 5, no. 1, Apr. 2022, pp. 150–82.

———. "The Dangerous Ground for Democracy: Doing Interdisciplinary Social Sciences in the Public University." *Inclusive Pedagogies: Teaching and Learning Practices in Higher Education in India*, edited by Kanika Singh. Primus Books, 2024, pp. 157–86.

Blacker, David. *The Falling Rate of Learning and the Neoliberal Endgame*. Zero Books, 2013.

Brown, Wendy. "Educating Human Capital." *Undoing the Demos: Neoliberalism's Stealth Revolution*. Zone Books, 2015, pp. 175–200.

"Cabinet Secretariat Notification - Government of India (Allocation of Business) (One hundred and Seventy-fourth Amendment) Rules, 1985." *The Gazette of India: Extraordinary, Part II, Section 3 (ii)*. Government of India Press, 25 Sep. 1985, https://cabsec.gov.in/writereaddata/allocationbusinessrule/amendment/english/1_Upload_212.pdf.

"Cabinet Secretariat Resolution No. 511/2/1/2015-Cab". *The Gazette of India*. Government of India, 1 Jan. 2015, pp. 6–9. http://niti.gov.in/content/cabinet-resolution.

Chandrasekhar, C. P. and Jayati Ghosh. *The Market That Failed: Neoliberal Economic Reforms in India*. LeftWord, 2002.

Chari, Mridula. "35 staff at Mumbai's TISS are fired because of UGC funding ambiguity." *Scroll*, 26 Mar. 2017. https://scroll.in/article/832881/35staff atmumbaistissarefiredbecauseofugcfundingambiguity.

"Commercialisation of Education – Teachers Protest Against UGC Model Act." *Labour File* vol. 2, no. 1, Jan.–Feb. 2004.

Dasgupta, KumKum. "Notice to JNU's social exclusion centre forged, says UGC. Is there more to it?" *Hindustan Times*, 21 Mar. 2017. https://www.hindustantimes.com/opinion/notice-to-jnu-s-social-exclusion-centre-forged-saysugc-is-there-more-to-it/story-wwehHzK1DYcWZtLeRUtuVO.html.

Dasgupta, Priyanka. "JU School of Women's Studies staffers brace for uncertain future." *The Times of India*, 31 Mar. 2017. http://timesofindia.indiatimes.com/city/kolkata/juschoolofwomensstudiesstaffersbraceforuncertainfuture/articleshow/57926340.cms.

Economic and Political Weekly (*EPW*). "Editorial: Caste, Courts and Reservations." vol. 42, no. 14, 2007. https://www.epw.in/journal/2007/14/editorials/caste-courts-and-reservations.html.

Ferguson, Roderick. "The Golden Era of Instructed Minorities." *The Reorder of Things: The University and Its Pedagogies of Minority Difference.* University of Minnesota Press, 2012, pp. 180–208.

Ganguly-Scrase, Ruchira, and Timothy J. Scrase. *Globalisation and the Middle Classes in India: The Social and Cultural Impact of Neoliberal Reforms.* Routledge, 2009.

Government of India. *The Private Universities (Establishment and Regulation) Bill.* Ministry of Human Resource Development, 1995.

———. *Economic Survey 2007–2008: Social Sectors.* Ministry of Finance, 2008.

Gramsci, Antonio. "The Formation of the Intellectuals." *Selections from the Prison Notebooks*, edited and translated by Quintin Hoare and Geoffrey Nowell Smith. International Publishers, 1971, pp. 5–14.

Guidelines for Development of Women's Studies in Indian Universities and Colleges During Eleventh Plan (2007–2012). University Grants Commission, 2007.

Himanshu. "The Seriousness of the Problem of Unemployment in India." *Live Mint*, 1 Aug. 2019. https://www.livemint.com/opinion/columns/opinion-the-seriousness-of-the-problem-of-unemployment-in-india-1564679281965.html.

Iwanek, Krzysztof. *Endless Siege: Education and Nationalism in Vidya Bharati Schools.* Oxford University Press, 2022.

"Jamia Reverses Decision to Discontinue Centres After Outrage." *Newsclick*, 7 Apr. 2020. https://www.newsclick.in/jamia-reversesdecision-discontinue-entres-outrage.

Kannan, K. P., and G. Raveendran. "From Jobless to Job-loss Growth: Gainers and Losers during 2012–18." *Economic and Political Weekly*, vol. 54, no. 44, 2019. https://www.epw.in/journal/2019/44/insight/jobless-job-loss-growth.html

Kothari, Rajni. "Rise of the Dalits and the Renewed Debate on Caste." *Economic and Political Weekly*, vol. 29, no. 26, 25 Jun. 1994, pp. 1589–94.

Manuel, Thomas. "It's Not Wise to Trade in Higher Education." *The Wire*, 14 Dec. 2015. https://thewire.in/education/its-not-wise-to-trade-in-higher-education.

Mukul, Akshaya. "UGC Faces Flak for Withdrawing Scheme for 32 Centres for Study of Social Exclusion and Inclusive Policies." *The Times of India*, 2013. http://timesofindia.indiatimes.com/home/education/news/UGCfacesflakforwithdrawingschemefor32CentresforStudyofSocialExclusion.

Nath, Paaritosh, and Amit Basole. "Did Employment Rise or Fall in India between 2011 and 2017? Estimating Absolute Changes in the Workforce." *Economic and Political Weekly*, vol. 56, no. 34, 2021. https://www.epw.in/journal/2021/34/special-articles/did-employment-rise-or-fall-india-between-2011-and.html.

National Knowledge Commission (NKC). *Report to the Nation, 2006–2009*. Government of India Press, 2009.

National Policy on Education [NPE] 1968. Government of India.

National Policy on Education [NPE] 1986. Ministry of Human Resource Development, Government of India.

National Sample Survey Organisation (NSSO). *Employment-Unemployment Situation in India, 1999–2000*, Part I, 55th Round. Government of India, 2001a.

———. *Informal Sector in India, 1999–2000*, 55th Round. Government of India, 2001b.

———. *Employment and Unemployment Situation among Social Groups in India: NSS 68th Round, July 2011–June 2012*. Government of India Press, 2015.

———. *Periodic Labour Force Survey: Employment and Unemployment Survey, 2017–2018*. Government of India Press, 2019.

Noorani, A.G., ed. *The Babri Masjid Question, 1528–2003: 'A Matter of National Honour'*, Volume II. Tulika Books, 2003.

Pai, Sudha. *Dalit Assertion and the Unfinished Democratic Revolution: The Bahujan Samaj Party in Uttar Pradesh*. Sage Publications, 2002.

Patnaik, Prabhat. "Market Question and Capitalist Development in India." *Economic and Political Weekly (Annual Number: Focus on Industry)*, vol. 19, no. 31/33, Aug. 1984, pp. 1251–60.

———. "A Critique of the Welfare-Theoretic Basis of the Measurement of Poverty." *Economic and Political Weekly*, vol. 48, no. 14, 6 Apr. 2013, pp. 16–19.

———. "Capitalism and India's Democratic Revolution." *Social Scientist*, vol. 44, no. 1/2, Jan.–Feb. 2016, pp. 3–15.

———. "The Dramatic Increase in the Unemployment Rate." *People's Democracy*, vol. 43, no. 24, 16 Jun. 2019, https://peoplesdemocracy.in/2019/0616_pd/dramatic-increase-unemployment-rate.

Prasad, Madhu. "Why Higher Education in India Must Not Bow to the Market." *Sabrang*, 14 Dec. 2015. https://www.sabrangindia.in/indepth/why-higher-education-india-must-not-bow-market.

Programme of Action [POA] *for National Policy on Education 1986*. Ministry of Human Resource Development, Government of India, 1992.

"Protest against UGC Act continues." *The Times of India*, 22 Jan. 2004.

Qazi, Musab. "TISS Announces Closure of 3 Centres: Students Demand Answers." *Hindustan Times*, 28 Mar. 2017. http://www.hindustantimes.com/mumbainews/studentsaskforclarityaftertissannouncesclosureofthreecentres/story.

Quarter Century of Liberalisation in India: Essays from Economic and Political Weekly. Oxford University Press, 2018.

Ramakrishnan, Sushmitha. "All for a name? JNU centre on UGC fund exclusion list." *The New Indian Express*, 17 Mar. 2017. https://www.newindianexpress.com/states/tamil-nadu/2017/mar/17/all-for-a-name-jnu-centreon-ugc-fund-exclusion-list-1582297.html.

Raveendran, G., and K. P. Kannan. "Growth sans Employment: A Quarter Century of Jobless Growth in India's Organised Manufacturing." *Economic and Political Weekly*, vol. 44, no. 10, 2009. https://www.epw.in/journal/2009/10/special-articles/growth-sans-employment-quarter-century-jobless-growth-indias

Report of the Backward Classes Commission (Mandal Commission Report), Volumes I–VII. Government of India, 1980.

Sanhati. "Fight against Committing Higher Education to WTO." 4 Dec. 2015. https://sanhati.com/articles/15637/.

Satyanarayana, K. "Dalit Reconfiguration of Caste: Representation, Identity and Politics." *Critical Quarterly*, vol. 56, 2014.

Tabb, William K. "The World Trade Organization? Stop World Take Over." *Monthly Review*, vol. 51, no. 10, 2000, pp. 1–18.

The Foreign Educational Institutions (Regulation of Entry and Operations) Bill. Ministry of Human Resource Development, 2010/2013.

Twelfth Plan Guidelines (2012–2017): Development of Women's Studies in Indian Universities and Colleges & Capacity Building of Women Managers in Higher Education. University Grants Commission, 2012.

Unni, Jeemol. "Size, Contribution and Characteristics of Informal Employment in India." *Country Case Study*. International Labour Organization, 2002.

Upadhya, Carol. *Reengineering India: Work, Capital, and Class in an Offshore Economy*. Oxford University Press, 2016.

Williamson, John. *Latin American Adjustment: How Much Has Happened?* Institute for International Economics, 1990.

XII Plan Guidelines for Establishment of Centres in Universities for Study of Social Exclusion and Inclusive Policy. University Grants Commission, 2012.

Six

Towards NEP 2020: The Age of the Platform University?

(Un)free or Unwilling to Work?

While outlining the political economy of India's educational planning around the turn of the twenty-first century, and in the shadow of the market, a curious tale emerged. The market – as a place for the sale and purchase of *free* labour – had itself entered a crisis of meaning by 2017–18, as references to the latest NSS-EUS data bore out. Even though the NPE 1986/1992 proposed a graded secession of the state from the market, via the middle ground of community, the next thirty years had exhausted the conditions for continuing with such a plan. Of course, there were rich dividends reaped in the interim – whether through a depoliticisation of historical injustice as immediate grounds for an appeal to capital or through an effective pawning of educational governance to 'manpower demand forecasts' (POA 1992, 181). The cunning patchwork of a discourse around the socially excluded as 'human resource' had, unsurprisingly, tethered the priorities of higher education to questions of employability and employment. This was the classic textbook *turn* to neoliberal policy-making in India's educational sectors, and it made felicitous use of global sentiments and fears regarding the volatility of markets.

But, by 2017 – when the 'news' around India's universities had dramatically and exclusively been yarned into an ideological plot, through charges of 'anti-nationalism' or 'sedition' or 'urban Naxalism'[1] – there was some anxious flutter going on behind the

[1] For a quick overview of the kind of public discourse that swallowed the 'best' of India's universities and the frivolous nature of charges brought against them by a massive section of the country's mainstream news media, ever since the coming to power of a Hindu right-wing government under

scenes. As I pointed out in the previous chapter, the workforce participation rate (WPR) in a five-year period of economic activity had slumped in absolute numbers for the first time in the history of postcolonial India's 'growth' story, and by an alarming margin of 5.8 per cent. Successive Labour Bureau Surveys from preceding years (2014 to 2016) had already demonstrated that the proportion of formally-trained skills in the market outpaced the availability of jobs by a multiple of three.[2] By now, *working-age populations were definitively withdrawing from India's labour markets.* In other words, there were fewer 'willing' workers – an analogue for Marx's *free* labour – in the national economy, and India's long-celebrated demographic dividend had stopped translating into the fabled abundance of labour power. Education underwent a crisis of legitimacy, insofar as its preparatory-disciplinary routines neither bolstered the prospect of landing jobs nor the desire for seeking employment. Was the formally skilled worker finally on her way to being disenchanted of the ideological effects of the educational apparatus, and thus about to prove Gramsci and Althusser wrong?[3] Or, did she now see through the sham of *freedom* conjured around the auctioning of *labour as commodity* – in the marketplace? What had been foregrounded, since Adam Smith to Karl Marx, as the very subjective *condition* of capitalism was seemingly on its way to being demystified. In the Indian worker's decided retraction from the job market, was the worker claiming her long-confiscated agency at last, or was the market demonstrating its redundancy as the privileged site for exchange of skills and wages?

Narendra Modi, see Yamunan; "Rohith Vemula"; "My Birth Is My Fatal Accident"; "Police Crack Down"; Pandey, "JNU Student"; Sethi; Hebbar; "After National Flag"; DC; "Who is an urban naxal"; Verma.

[2] For data comparisons over this three-year period, refer to *Report on Education, Skill Development and Labour Force, Volume III, 2013–14*; *Economic Survey 2014–15* and *Report on Education, Skill Development and Labour Force, Volume III, 2015–16*; see also Varma.

[3] Understandably, I refer here to Antonio Gramsci's concept of 'hegemony' and Louis Althusser's account of ideological 'interpellation' of individuals as 'subjects'.

Looking Beyond Economy: A New *National* Education Policy

The answers to this set of questions, each promising deep theoretical reflection, would require of us a persistent detour into moments of history against the context of contemporary developments. The period 2012 to 2017 – which indexically records a state of alarm in the Indian economy – is significant for a number of reasons. First, this was an electoral turning point, which, riding on the economic discontents of a citizenry at large, wrought in a personality-cult in the 'strongman' and populist '*wave*' narratives around Narendra Modi. The latter, being sworn into a sovereign optics of 'supreme' leadership in mid-2014, was working precisely on promises of turning domestic 'deprivation' into global 'recognition'. Alongside such peddling of respite from the mundane in the grandeur of an international 'resurgence' – a rhetoric that sought to make India a 'superpower'! – the ready antidote lay in a nauseating insistence on the superiority of a *Hindu way of life* over everything foreign, and most prominently the *Muslim immigrant*. The polemical overtones of this body of 'international relations' discourse consisted in proclaiming the cause of India's greatness in a belated scene of national self-realisation. It was implied that the state of the economy could revive only if we were to look past our economy altogether, and look into our millennia-old religious-cultural wealth.

Second, consonant with this shift in rhetorical emphasis, the thrust of economic policy too had to be reoriented. Therefore, in August 2014, the newly anointed Prime Minister Modi announced from the site of his Independence Day address (televisually streamed to the entire nation) that the originally 'socialist' legacy of state regulation in the Planning Commission was to be abolished ("PM Narendra Modi scraps Planning Commission"). The Commission was a Nehruvian structure, imported from socialist experiments with developmental agendas in Stalin's Russia[4] – and against which the early advocate of neoliberal 'free

[4] Refer to Note 1 to Chapter 4.

markets' in Friedrich von Hayek had ferociously cautioned (Hayek, "Economics and Knowledge"; *The Road to Serfdom*; "The Use of Knowledge in Society"). Modi chose to replace the extant arbiter of state planning with a dummy titled National Institution for Transforming India (acronymically, NITI Aayog). Even while urging his electorate to turn away from the economy and inwards into the soul of Hindu richness, the supreme ruler's declaration of doing away with a legacy of national planning sent out the right feelers to transnational capital. But, if the name-change is anything to go by, the replacement of a 'planning' regime with the register of 'transforming' cannot be innocuous! A deep structural need is responded to in this gesture, almost prophesising that the time had come for a radically different approach towards the relationship between the state and markets. One was no longer a supporting rampart for the other, but instead the state itself called for a total 'transformation' with no reference to markets at all. The rationality of 'planning' assumes a continuity with past performance and future targets; it is an enunciation of economic activity as dialogically framed along the coordinates of time. In simpler terms, planning is for a mid-term future and with regard to the short-term past. The act of 'transforming', on the other hand, assumes a break with time and heralds an ushering into newness as the only viable long-term relation with a future. The move from the Planning Commission to the National Institution for Transforming India (NITI) is potentially an acknowledgment of the absolute disposability of old market structures, and a portent for some striking novelty in its place.

Third, with the lapsing of the Planning Commission and its then-current Twelfth Five Year Plan (2012–17), all educational schemes and initiatives provisioned by Plan outlays in successive annual budgets were to become defunct. As I have discussed in the fifth chapter, this immediately spelt doom for the 'special' university/college centres for studying social and gender discrimination. Even though such 'discrimination' scholarship was historically promoted as the reason and redress for a market economy, the willing non-participation of caste and religious minorities in Indian markets (as evidenced in declining OBC and Muslim WPRs in the NSS data) meant that exclusion could no longer be neatly theorised as 'human capital'. On the contrary, this 'exclusion discourse' had to be forcefully throttled, in order for an alternative reality of the wealth of national-cultural 'oneness' to be 'Modi-fied' as *common sense.* If caste-religious-gender differentiations were accentuated in the cause of capital, this changed conjuncture in Indian economic history demanded a selective naturalisation of these differentiations as integral to India's cultural body-politic. Consequently, all castes and genders had to be re-incorporated into a Hindu India's crusade against the Muslim *outsider* – and the numerical accretion of divided communities into a unified nationalistic imagination was itself conceived as the guarantor of a surplus. Colleges and universities had to be put to a radically different *use* – stitching together an alternative semiotics of citizenship.

Fourth, and following from this, the period under question – culminating in 2017 – is simultaneously the timeline for the newly elected government's search for a *new* education policy. Between 2015 and 2017, two committees were set up to frame a draft national education policy (NEP) – the first of which submitted a report (namely, the Subramanian Committee Report [2016]), only to be eventually dumped and superseded by the Kasturirangan Committee.[5] The latter worked with a consciousness of the incompatibility of the 1986/1992 NPE with current market situations, and finally submitted a draft NEP in late 2018 after over a year of apparent 'consultations'. The BJP government was by then readying for a plebiscite on the renewability of its reform-promises in the general elections of early 2019, and therefore decided to shelve the Report without any ado. Within a week of the re-election of Modi, the 484-page-long Report was unveiled as containing the imminent possibilities for educational reform in India. There was one point on which this Kasturirangan

[5] See "9-Member Panel"; Sharma.

Committee Report – also called the *Draft National Education Policy (DNEP) 2019* – was absolutely clear, when it came to the field of higher education: *employment was no longer the governing rationale for college/university instruction.* The terms of reference for a 'new and forward looking vision for India's higher education system' were thus set out: 'The purpose of quality higher education is . . . more than simply the creation of greater opportunities for individual employment; it represents the key to more vibrant, socially engaged, and cooperative communities and a more happy, cohesive, cultured, productive, innovative, and prosperous nation' (DNEP, 202). In stark contrast to the logic of manpower-provisioning that both welfarist and market economies had enjoined national policy to, the DNEP 2019 aimed at a training into routines of *citizenship* through higher education. In a vehemently forceful pitch continuing throughout the document, the structural overhaul was rooted in the hailing of a 'liberal arts education, as so beautifully described and practiced in India's past' (224). Needless to say therefore, this idea of *citizenship* that the university was to become a workshop for, consisted in a return to the 'golden age' of Vedic Hindu lore. It simultaneously worked by marking difference from the spectre of the Muslim 'illegal migrant', which the Citizenship Amendment Act (CAA) 2019 was soon to proscribe as the outermost limit to national security and identity[6] (Bhattacharya, "A Liberal Poetics of Policy" 50–51).

[6] An amendment to India's citizenship laws in December 2019, which has occasioned the most heartening scenes of resistance across the country, consisted in making religion the determinant for grant of citizenship to 'illegal migrants'. The CAA 2019, as the draconian legislation has been called, mandated that only non-Muslim refugees from the three neighbouring countries of Pakistan, Afghanistan and Bangladesh are entitled to Indian citizenship, subject to their fulfilling certain other documentary requirements. Coupled with the government's declared intentions of bringing about a National Register of Citizens (NRC), the CAA 2019 was designed as a means for selectively eliminating the Muslim poor from civil and political rights-claims in India. See, for example, Shankar; Dutt; Naqvi; Kumar; Dalmia; De and Ranganathan; "CAA+NRC".

Education in (Times of) 'Crisis'

But, if the market had really receded as the condition for higher skilling, did the period under analysis contain a critique of the employment scenario that I opened with a vignette of? Or, was the debate about building civic sensibilities – as the ideological touchstone for nationalism in a Hindu *rashtra* – a smokescreen for deeper structural re-adjustments that the recessionary tendencies of the job market rendered inevitable? If the mainstream media's narrativisation of India's university sector, as oscillating between the polarities of 'seditious' knowledge-production and 'citizenly' patriotism, was only a script for deflecting attention from the underlying economic malaise, what was the new national education policy consecrated to?

The argument for this final chapter of the volume will revolve around this missing register within debates on India's third national education policy (NEP) – which, taking off from the Kasturirangan committee's recommendations, was finally approved by the Cabinet without recourse to parliamentary processes and released at the height of the pandemic in July 2020 (Prasad; Menon; "National Education Policy 2020: Why Bypass Parliament"). A growing chorus of critical voices spilled over into the public media after the policy was 'unveiled' through a set of dissimulating official press releases,[7] with no trace of

[7] The moment of public 'launch' of the National Education Policy 2020 was shrouded in a maze of classic diversionary tactics. While on the evening of 29 July 2020, a press conference presided over by the HRD Minister came to be touted as the spectacular site of 'release' of the final Cabinet-approved policy document, what was actually disseminated for public consumption was a misleading summary of reforms (in PPT slides) and a list of "Highlights" published on the Press Information Bureau (PIB) website [see https://pib.gov.in/PressReleasePage.aspx?PRID=1642061]. Both these releases contained references from an earlier pre-approved draft of the NEP, which went into circulation among mainstream media reportedly through government sources. For nearly thirty hours after this official 'announcement' of the Policy, the actual text was nowhere to be found and a spate of public debates was sparked off on national television and print channels on the basis of a former draft version of the document. When this was finally reported by

consultation with either elected members of opposition parties or state governments. Most of these voices converged in their estimate of the reform-routes suggested by the NEP, as poised between an uncritical ideological hailing of Hindutva and a stealthy neoliberal push for commercialisation (Chaudhuri; Patnaik; Mohanty; Devy; Roy; Sadgopal; Trivedi; Nawani; Agarwal; Deshpande; Pathak; John; Kidwai). While continuing to be in conversation with such critiques, this chapter hopes to extrapolate from the policy framework a *political economy* of its exact terms of reference, as against the historical conditions of their emergence. In the course of it, I will contend that the NEP 2020 contains a clear move *away* from the 'neoliberal' market economy, and that its smattering of 'liberal' rhetoric is only a decoy. In fact, it is neither the labour market nor simply national citizenship that the proposed curricular reforms seem to be directed towards. Contrarily, the market's infirmity in terms of employment generation is worked into successive policy instantiations, towards the making of the final NEP 2020, as the very basis for flights of potential labour recorded in the falling WPR. The resulting lineaments of a financial 'crisis', discernible within the Indian economy from before the 'Modi wave' to after the pandemic, called for a re-articulation of the *ends* of higher education.

The NEP 2020 carved out its mandate from this need for envisioning an education suited to the visible (mal)contents of a *crisis*-ridden market economy. When the institutional benchmarking of labour could no longer hold value as commodity for exchange, education ceases to cater to the production imperatives of the market. This is the moment when the Marxian definition of labour *as* commodity falters, because neither employment nor exchange as the basis for trade in goods and services suffices. Since employment is no longer the desired outcome of education, *what matters is not so much participation in*

newspapers like *The Hindu* ("National Education Policy 2020: Document still not available") the following day, and became a cause of widespread alarm, the final 66-page-long NEP 2020 was stealthily uploaded on the MHRD's website during the late night hours of 30 July.

productive processes in the present as the acquisition and ownership of assets for an indeterminate future. Knowledge, within such a *crisis*-conjuncture, is geared towards the amassing of *skills as assets for claiming credit capital.* The NEP 2020 works with a similar consciousness of the failed market condition, where productive employment is not as full of economic promise as the mere ownership of multiple skill-sets as asset-equivalents for hedging against future risk. *This is definitively the university's ushering into a platform ecosystem, as opposed to a market economy* – inasmuch as every asset (or skill) owned by a student-investor may now be diversified and traded as derivatives on the platform. The Draft Policy of 2019 spelt out the advent of an 'asset economy' in higher education, where the university system must in the final instance function as a *platform* for the trading of credit-values assigned to assets:

> It should be emphasised that higher education must build *expertise that society will need over the next 25 years and beyond. Simply tailoring people into jobs that exist today, but that are likely to change or disappear after some years, is suboptimal and even counterproductive.* The future workplace will demand critical thinking, communication, problem solving, creativity, and multidisciplinary capability. Single-skill and single-discipline jobs are likely to become automated over time. Therefore, there will be a great need to focus on multidisciplinary and 21st century competencies for future work roles – these are indeed the capabilities that will separate humans from robots. In particular, *education must empower workers of the future to become enterprising and creative innovators.* By focusing on such broad based, flexible, individualised, innovative, and multidisciplinary learning, *higher education must aim to prepare its students not just for their first jobs – but also for their second, third, and all future jobs over their lifetimes.* In particular, the higher education system must aim to form the hub for the next industrial revolution. (DNEP 2019, 202–03, emphases mine)

The 'next industrial revolution' – elsewhere named as Industry 4.0, and borrowed from the World Economic Forum's prophecy for an age of informational/data capitalism (Schwab) – is concurrently a confession about the destructibility of a market for 'jobs that exist today'. That employment *in the present* is not only shorn of the security of social benefits and formal return-guarantees, but might also be vulnerable to the risks of 'change or disappear[ance]' of value relative to time is what the university system must forewarn its apparent beneficiaries about. To really benefit from the system would therefore require a diversification of investment in the form of *assets*, each of which may increase the credit-score of the owner-investor for future loans in a climate of absolute uncertainty. The creditworthiness of students, calculated in terms of the multiplicity of their skills and their diverse potential for application, is the true value of their insurability against future risk. 'Multidisciplinary education' – as the hallmark of education's empowerment of 'workers of the future' – is essentially a euphemism for risk management through innovative skill-combinations that might survive price fluctuations and regimes of heightened informality. It urges the asset owner to shun the immediate realisation of value through exchange of labour in the market, and instead trade the abstract qualities of each of these assets as claims for more and more credit – pending repayment in an indefinite future (Feher; Streeck). This is the *exact financial underprint of derivatives-trading*, where the 'underlying' primary asset of knowledge is only rendered evermore irrelevant to the realisation of future profits.

The 'workers of the future' are no longer translatable as cheap, semi-skilled, informal labour for global markets – because, the Policy-text argues, 'single-skill and single-discipline jobs are likely to get automated over time'. Does the answer to this lie in creating a multi-tasking workforce, again long evidenced in the informalisation of employment through multiple shifts and workday changes? Is multidisciplinary education a fancy theorem for the familiar neoliberal script of 'multi-tasking literacies'?[8] But, in that case, the falling WPR would remain an unsolvable

[8] In some of my earlier critiques of the NEP 2020, I did make such an argument – see, for example, Bhattacharya, "A Liberal Poetics of Policy"; and Jain. However, this chapter hopes to nuance such a reading beyond a classic 'neoliberal paradigm'-approach.

mystery. It is here that the NEP, in its planning stages, proposes a resignification of institutional charters as consisting not in skill-training but in *credit-rating students as the future indebted*.

Before we proceed further, it needs to be unequivocally maintained that the pedagogic rationale of multidisciplinary education is grossly opposed to that of the interdisciplinary 'studies' departments. Why else would a policy primer that unreservedly extols the virtues of moving past disciplinary *silos* not spare a single mention of the actually existing departments of interdisciplinary inquiry in colleges/universities – namely, women's studies, studies in social exclusion and inclusive policy, human rights studies, comparative literature or social and economic planning? As discussed in the previous chapter, all these 'studies' centres had been reeling under threats of defunding and discontinuation – through stalled recruitments, non-disbursal of faculty and staff salaries, periodic annual audit mandates and curtailment of teaching functions – since 2017.[9] And yet, they are definitively kept out of the NEP planners' epistemic forecast for the 'Multidisciplinary Education and Research University (MERU)' (NEP 2020, 221).

The reasons are not difficult to guess. The interdisciplinary social sciences contain the risk of an insurrection against accepted truth-procedures (Sitze 597), which account for the authority of disciplinary 'method'. For example, a women's studies curriculum potentially stages the methodological aporias that indict the institutional pursuit of political science, sociology, history, literature, philosophy, economics – and even commerce and the sciences – for propounding truth as gendered prerogative. These 'studies' departments, despite the trappings of historical circumstance which underwrote their coming into being at the moment of India's embrace of economic/trade liberalisation, had thus far exceeded the output-expectations of commissioned survey research. They ended up questioning potted summaries

[9] See, for example, "Future of Women's Studies Centres"; and Bhattacharya, "The Dangerous Ground for Democracy."

of 'empowerment' and 'development' discourse, by precisely intervening at the interstices of self-separated disciplines. This alchemy of 'undisciplinable' knowledge at the limits of a discipline is the danger of counterfactual thinking; it overturns the university against its own history of collaboration with capital (Bhattacharya, "Between Disciplines and Interdisciplines" 199–202). Multidisciplinary education, on the other hand, is about *neutralising the danger of such knowledge with a technology of credit-scoring which privileges non-knowledge as the basis of price volatility in the future.* I will explain what that means in the subsequent sections.

Skills, Assets, Derivatives

As Lisa Adkins, M. Konings and Melinda Cooper maintain in their wonderfully prescient analysis of the rise of an 'asset economy', the privileging of asset ownership over productive employment is the triumphal footprint of a culture of indebtedness (12–32). The value of the owned or inherited asset does not lie in its monetisability in the present, but in its benchmarking of the credit-score of the owner as security against risk. In accounting terms, the asset – as opposed to the commodity – is immune to the rule or logics of exchange. It is a promissory note for a future of which no knowledge is reliable. To that extent, the 'asset economy' signals the irrelevance of the market for labour and goods (Graeber; Lazzarato, *The Making of the Indebted Man*; *Governing by Debt*), and is a beckoning unto what Randy Martin calls the 'social logic of the derivative'. Assets cannot foist value for an industry of credit-ratings without the permutations of its derivative properties; and such permutations of promised value cannot be made available for investment in the absence of a *platform* that brings owners and independent contractors together. If, in the NEP's imagining of an asset economy, multidisciplinary skills are but derivatives – owned by 'enterprising and creative innovators' – the 'underlying' asset of knowledge becomes irrelevant to the business of the university as a platform ecosystem.

It is this subtext that animates the shaping of policy prerogatives behind the NEP – evinced in the repeated and unguarded enthusiasm of the 2019 Draft for bringing together 'all branches of creative human endeavour (including mathematics and science)', exploring 'the numerous remarkable relationships that exist among the sciences and the humanities, mathematics and art, medicine and physics, etc.', developing 'all capacities of human beings' and 'all aspects of being human' (DNEP 2019, 223–24). This totalistic insistence on an encompassing whole, any part of which may be abstracted for use or sale for an anticipated profit and at a rate of payment yet undecided, makes the ontological core of an 'asset'. The latter contains the guarantee of a surplus value, but the moment of its realisation is necessarily belated beyond the immediate present – so that it may serve as a securitising instrument against the unknown and the unknowable. What is crucial in this definition of the asset is a devaluation of knowledge: in other words, an asset promises the thrill of a surplus only as long as the mathematical calculus for its conversion into price at a given point of time resists prediction in the present. The appropriate stage for an appearance of the asset economy is not so much the 'knowledge society', which markets for human resource tried moulding the economy into, but a 'world risk society' as Ulrich Beck would have it ("Living in the World Risk Society"; *World At Risk*). There are enough glimpses of the uncertainty of a future world, against which the DNEP's recommendations promote the benefits of liberal education:

> [O]ne never actually knows what one's job is going to be in the long term, or what work it will entail! . . . With the coming fourth industrial revolution, and the rapidly changing employment landscape, a liberal arts education is more important and useful for one's employment than ever before. . . . [E]ven if one somehow knows in advance what job one will have forever, one still never knows when certain ideas and concepts from other disciplines might make an appearance, in a way that could improve or even completely transform the work that one is doing. For example, many of the world's greatest innovations and breakthroughs have occurred due to such cross-fertilisation of ideas across seemingly different fields. X-rays, CAT scans, MRIs,

> and lasers in medicine all originally came about due to physicists and space scientists thinking about these concepts for completely different reasons. In most cases, the immediate purpose was pure curiosity in that field! Radiocarbon dating, as used in archaeology, anthropology, and history, is another example of where ideas from – in this case – physics and chemistry resulted in a revolution in completely different fields. Music is another subject that has had incredibly interesting influences on and has in turn been influenced by many areas: psychology, physiology, sociology, engineering, physics, and mathematics. (224–25)

The way in which liberal education is championed as a prophecy for 'the coming fourth industrial revolution, and the rapidly changing employment landscape' is thoroughly instructive. The policy framework's ruminations proceed from the premise that knowledge is a woefully inadequate bulwark against the unforeseen-ness of the future. Because there is something resolutely vertiginous about the 'long term'; one can only stake one's best bet by allowing 'pure curiosity' precedence over *knowledge*. The default breadth of interests and cross-disciplinary abandon that 'curiosity' carries as the very mark of its exercise is hence most suited to an education policy for these times. That there is no value to specialised higher education, if not compounded with a token liberality of academic pursuits, is the most frequently rehearsed among the committee's recommendations. But, hidden beneath this compulsory eclecticism within the proposed structure of Indian university curricula, lies an admission of how this too might change. That the current situation – more 'than ever before' – makes this baggy incarnation of liberal education worth the present, does not mean that it will hold for ever after. And, in attending to this unpredictability of 'manpower demands', no forecast about the *value* of knowledge is possible.

Neutralising Risk: Education as Managing Non-Knowledge

The DNEP 2019 transforms the work of policy into an art of prophesying – where the only thing known is that there is no knowing what/which knowledge will pay off. And therefore, all practice of knowing must be turned into a matter of 'curiosity' – a chance encounter with truths that might or might not hold. In such a predicament as this, the potential holds more value than the actual; and the performative promise of materialisation converts every skill into an asset capable of abstract diversification. It is hardly jarring that a national policy, claiming to pronounce on the future course of knowledge production and professions in the country, instead *ends up sounding the death-knell of knowledge as an ontological value*. A more damning indictment of the 'limits' of knowledge and knowing could not have been imagined, if not as the ground on which the NEP 2020 must be brought into being. But, isn't this the exact parallel to Beck's postulation of a 'world risk society' and the grounds of its coming to being?

> World risk society is a *non*-knowledge society in a very precise sense. In contrast to the premodern era, it cannot be overcome by more and better knowledge, more and better science; rather precisely the opposite holds: it is the *product* of more and better science. Non-knowledge rules in the world risk society. Hence, living in the milieu of manufactured non-knowing means seeking unknown answers to questions that nobody can clearly formulate. (Beck, *World At Risk* 115)

The idea of a self-regulating economy, as propounded by champions of the 'free market', is however hinged on a hope that knowledge is everybody's forte and is achievable in proportion to their interests (Hayek, "The Use of Knowledge in Society"). The formulation of a 'rational choice' theory and capital's price-determination processes are all harnessed to the belief that human beings are capable of knowing their own good – and left to the forces of the market and the stability promised by a monetarist regime, they realise the maximal returns on their investment (Friedman; Becker). The very logic of competition, driving the axiom of 'freedom' immanent to the market economy, insists that an equilibrium between costs and benefits may not only be attempted but insistently achieved by human actors and agents within the economy. Knowledge, in a word, is the sovereign territory of neoliberalism's self-demonstration as both reason and common sense. Randy Martin captures this constitutive pact between the economy and knowledge – later parasitically merging into each other as the 'knowledge economy' – very succinctly:

> The market frees knowledge from the minds of experts to our common expertise. The economy, then, would be . . . the common sense of purpose that comes when all act as if their calculative agency would indeed redound to their benefit. . . . If all possessed knowledge, could wield it to their benefit or detriment under conditions free of force and coercion or distraction from external consequences or complications, that happy state neoliberals like to refer to as freedom might just be achieved.
>
> Hence, if the matter of economy is knowledge, its antimatter would be nonknowledge. If knowledge cannot fix the economy, nonknowledge would have its moment to come rushing in. (44)

That 'knowledge cannot fix the economy' is the dystopic truth that we set out on our reflections with, and subsequently arrived at as the grand announcement that necessitated a new national education policy. According to Martin, the consciousness that knowledge cannot hold – whether in the 'minds of experts' or in 'our common expertise' – is what gives birth to the 'social logic of the derivative'. In a titular flourish characteristic of Martin's oeuvre of scholarship, he calls this a 'knowledge LTD' society – a space of human negotiations around price and profit that is not just reconciled to the *limits* of knowledge, but invests the unknown as 'limited' capital for a limitless play of derivatives. This is an extreme outcome of financialisation, where assets are traded in the market not for their knowable margins of returns, but are disassembled and distributed as bundles of associated risk which can guarantee returns precisely because of their unknowability (Bryan and Rafferty). The incapacity for knowledge is the only capital worth risking, and the only risk self-assuredly generative of capital. The best and most profitable state of being, within a 'knowledge LTD' society, is the state of non-knowledge. Ignorance indeed is bliss, *and more* – it is a bounty for futures, however uncertain.

In a society that purposively delegitimises knowledge, there is an ironic wisdom that nonetheless lies at the heart of its operations of risk management. This wisdom concerns the secret substance of the 'crisis', as a *permanent plague* on the history of capital. From the manufacturing crisis of the 1970s to the oil/energy crisis and 'stagflation' soon after, the 'dotcom' and Enron scandals of the early 2000s to the subprime mortgage crisis and the terrible recession of 2007–08, the crisis in Indian markets from mid-2010s to the aftermath of the pandemic – how did neoliberal capital delude itself with a pretence of expertise if none of its crises was ever portended or prevented? The event of the 'crisis' is a singularity, in that its advent puts all operations of knowledge in abeyance even if there were signs or warnings in its coming. And insofar as the story of capital has been integrally folded into a cautionary tale of crises and their overcoming, non-knowledge is never signposted as an end/outside to knowledge but the internal limit to it. A shift of cognitive accent from the apocalyptic moment of 'crisis' to the ubiquitous malleability of 'risk' performs a double trick. First, it orients the accumulative engines of capital towards the future, and therefore past the fetishisation of knowledge as commodity. There is no point anymore in erecting apparatuses of diagnosis or running institutions of expertise, if not in the cause of a future that is anyway beyond the pale of the knowable. *Non-knowledge, precisely, has to be made into the fuel of education – not knowledge.* In Beck's 'risk society' or Martin's 'knowledge LTD', colleges and universities are better transformed into instruments not of controlling the present, but of speculatively trading futures. Second, and more importantly, the passage from 'crisis' to 'risk' is at the same time a pre-emptive capitalisation of 'loss', by imaginatively multiplying bailouts as investment devices. As a result, the censure and moral downturn that an event of financial loss calls forth in the world of symbolic representations – that is, the world of knowledge – is steered clear of. Phrased simply, the moral economy of affect surrounding the fortunes of capital is made redundant within a social order of derivatives. *Education, when tied to an industry of managing non-knowledge without seeking to know it, can similarly be rendered immune to the scourge of the moral.*

Understanding 'Multidisciplinary Education': The Promise of NEP 2020

One might, on closer attention, discern the same movement from a society on the brink of a 'crisis' (of employment) to one hedging against 'risks' (of asset ownership) within the rhetorical manoeuvres of the DNEP 2019 and NEP 2020. Identical effects are achieved in the process: a preoccupation with non-knowledge as the basis of policy, and the shedding of moral compunction otherwise associated with the knowledge project. Both of these bear out in the policy's privileging of derivative contracts as the substance of higher educational routines – fancifully termed as 'multidisciplinary education'. But, what is the exact extent and content of this much-vaunted principle of *multidisciplinarity* – and how does it compare with what Martin famously names as the 'social logic of the derivative'?

The NEP 2020 begins by identifying the 'major problems' of the Indian college sector as consisting in a 'severely fragmented . . . ecosystem' and a 'rigid separation of disciplines, with early specialisation and streaming of students into narrow areas of study' (33). The remedy is suggested in a section titled "Towards a More Holistic and Multidisciplinary Education". I had set out by critically examining parts of such remedial vision in the first chapter of this volume, but let me reproduce the puzzle here in all its pieces:

> The very idea that all branches of creative human endeavour, including mathematics, science, vocational subjects, professional subjects, and soft skills should be considered 'arts', has distinctly Indian origins. This notion of a 'knowledge of many arts' or what in modern times is often called the 'liberal arts' (i.e., a liberal notion of the arts) must be brought back to Indian education, as it is exactly the kind of education that will be required for the 21st century. . . . Such a holistic education shall be, in the long term,

> the approach of all undergraduate programmes, including those in professional, technical, and vocational disciplines. . . . Students of arts and humanities will aim to learn more science and all will make an effort to incorporate more vocational subjects and soft skills. . . . Departments in Languages, Literature, Music, Philosophy, Indology, Art, Dance, Theatre, Education, Mathematics, Statistics, Pure and Applied Sciences, Sociology, Economics, Sports, Translation and Interpretation, and other such subjects needed for a multidisciplinary, stimulating Indian education and environment will be established and strengthened at all HEIs (higher educational institutions). . . . [L]essons in *seva*/service and participation in community service programmes will be considered an integral part of a holistic education. (36–37)

In the first of such examples of multidisciplinary curricula rolled out in the country, the University of Delhi implemented the NEP's proposal from the session 2022–23 by instituting a bunch of special undergraduate courses available to students of all departments and subject-streams. Supplementing a slew of already existing cross-disciplinary electives – titled 'Skill Enhancement' (SEC) and 'Ability Enhancement' courses (AEC) – the NEP's gift of multidisciplinary offerings, now newly introduced into the 77 affiliated colleges of the university, were resonantly named as 'Value Addition Courses' (VAC). But, the irony in this philosophy of 'value addition' – mirroring the logic of derivative-trading as incrementing the value of 'underlying' assets – was reserved for the exact titles of papers floated under the scheme: namely, "The Art of Being Happy", "Swachh Bharat", "Panchkosha: Holistic Development of Personality", "Vedic Mathematics", "Ethics and Values in Ancient Indian Traditions" and "Fit India".[10] At the other end, a bouquet of 'skill enhancement courses' approved by the Executive Council of the University for its NEP-model undergraduate programmes included paper-offerings like "Political Leadership and Communication", "Negotiation and Leadership", "Finance for Everyone", "Harmonium", "CAD for Fashion",

[10] See University of Delhi's "Notification: Amendment to Ordinance V (Value Addition Courses [VACs] under UGCF-2022)", dated 14.09.2022, p. 2.

"Digital Marketing" and "Cyber Sphere and Security: Global Concerns"[11] – again thrown open for enrolment across streams and subjects, irrespective of the 'major'/'minor' disciplinary choices of the student concerned.

'Production is Inside Circulation': Knowledge, Propaganda and Price

To return to a question I posed above, how do the disassembling, reassembling and bundling effects of the NEP's multidisciplinary curriculum relate to techniques of *risk management*, as manifest in an economy of dealing in derivatives? Let me simply use Randy Martin's careful annotation of the 'social logic' contained in the *form* of the derivative, *ad verbatim*, to make this parallelism stick:

> First, . . . a derivative logic speaks to what is otherwise balefully named fragmentation, dispersion, or isolation by allowing us to recognize ways in which the concrete particularities . . . might be interconnected without first or ultimately needing to appear as a single whole or unity of practice or perspective. Second, derivatives articulate what is made in motion, how production is inside circulation. . . . Third, derivatives work through the agency of arbitrage, of small interventions that make significant difference, of a generative risk in the face of generalized failure . . . [a] wreckage of the economic where its conventional meanings are interred. . . . Shifts in scale from concrete to abstract or local to global are no longer external yardsticks of equivalence. (52, 60)

A 'more fully elaborated social logic of the derivative', as Martin goes on to propound, requires its disembedding from the 'wreckage of the economic' – which, in the Indian case, translates into the visible countenance of an employment 'crisis' that a new education policy must respond to, on emergency basis. This calls for an opportune conjuring and strategic use of a 'crisis' discourse about the 'generalized failure' of higher education, which

[11] Refer to University of Delhi's "Notification: Amendment to Ordinance V (Skill Enhancement Courses [SECs] under UGCF-2022)", dated 06.09.2022, pp. 1–2.

the NEP 2020 adopts as its inaugural bid at self-justification: the 'otherwise balefully named fragmentation, dispersion, or isolation' of institutions, disciplines and students.[12] The answer is sought in an apparent force of 'integration' – a 'commoning' of all disciplines as it were, through a 'knowledge of many arts' – which slyly performs just the opposite of what it proclaims on the surface.[13] Far from 'needing to appear as a single whole or unity of practice or perspective', the logic of the derivative – reflected against the sheen of *multidisciplinarity* – only fractures the object of knowledge into fields of inquiry that have nothing to do with either methods or practices of knowing. The playful nebulousness that 'multidisciplinary' offerings, like "The Art of Being Happy" or "Swachh Bharat" or "Digital Marketing", embody as their very raison d'*être* makes a lie of the *value* or *virtue* of knowledge altogether. Instead, the 'balefully'-lamented fragmentation of knowledge or knowers is taken to its cognitive extreme, while grounding the amorphousness of its institutional pursuit in a fiction of 'interconnectedness' (alternatively, 'multidisciplinary education').

It is especially significant to note that the myth of a 'common' ground of intellectual inquiry, which becomes the legitimating ruse for multidisciplinary education, is as far removed from a politics of intellectual 'commons' as may be conceivable. The

[12] In a near-literal analogue to the scene of 'wreckage' that Martin alludes to as the ground for derivatives' emergence, the NEP 2020 opens its recommendations on 'higher education' by listing a set of 'major problems' which include – 'a severely fragmented higher educational ecosystem'; 'less emphasis on the development of cognitive skills and learning outcomes'; 'a rigid separation of disciplines, with early specialisation and streaming of students into narrow areas of study'; 'an ineffective regulatory system' and 'large affiliating universities resulting in low standards of undergraduate education' (Section 9.2, 33).

[13] The NEP 2020 displays a perverse fascination with the word 'common' – which, in stark opposition to a politics of 'commoning' as breaking free of logics and technologies of 'enclosure', insists on a top-down one-size-fits-all uniformity of models as common structure, common examination, common curriculum, etc.

former is a hold-all rubric intended to implode the distinctiveness of disciplinary traditions, till each is cloned into the other and all are packaged under an amateurish disposition of 'curiosity'. This 'common thread' narrative, striving to forward the instance of the 'multidisciplinary' as both rehearsal and realisation of 'oneness'[14] – albeit masked in a rhetorical flirtation with the *many* – is the manual for projecting every 'risk' as a security-threat. The 'risks' of knowing, as manifest in questioning, are foreclosed in the staging of the derivative as an intense preoccupation with non-knowledge; 'risk', in the process, is not only neutralised but also made 'generative' by being made collateral to the 'generalized failure' of knowledge. The making of a 'commons', on the contrary, is about shunning the 'common ground' theory of knowledge. It consists in foregrounding the operations of power that make 'commonness' apprehensible as the 'property' (or asset) of a tradition, community, national heritage or culture. In this respect, the idea of the 'commons' is radically counterposed to a unification narrative – parading as *common* sense, and dispersible in a multiplicity of derivative forms. Multidisciplinarity, by such a stretch of reasoning, is anything but an attempt at recovering the 'commons' of knowledge.

Martin attunes us to the second enunciation of the derivative, as pointing towards 'what is made in motion, how production is inside circulation'. This is the exact analogue to what I have earlier identified as a passage from the commodity to the asset. That production lies *inside* circulation makes living labour redundant, if not as owners of assets amenable to multiplication and diversification. The 'multidisciplinary' course curriculum of NEP-vintage, a sample of which exists for our reference, assures no skill-sets that may be immediately relevant to productive

[14] The policy's declared preoccupation with 'oneness' is routinely betrayed in its attempts at harnessing education to a factory of nationalistic (and patriotic) sentiment. To this extent, the repeated references to a spectre of 'Ek Bharat, Shrestha Bharat' (One India, Best India) as the governing rationale for educational reform is not to be missed.

exchange. Instead, it flaunts a deep chasm within the substance of formalised learning as potentially capable of spawning tangential multiplicities of 'non-knowledge' – each of which, by virtue of the circulation guaranteed by being named after state schemes or the latter's ideological priorities, is full of the promise of hedging against the risks of volatile markets. Governmental initiatives like "Swachh Bharat" or "Fit India", in being turned into curricular derivatives, not only ensure the reverberative effects of propaganda (as weaponisation of non-knowledge), but are also liable to be treated as investable securities against a failed economy and unknowable future.

The third aspect which, in Martin's estimate, accounts for the success of derivative contracts is their resort to the 'agency of arbitrage, of small interventions that make significant difference'. Going by the glossary of current-day financial capitalism, arbitrage refers to a practice of simultaneous trading of an asset across different markets, so that price variations may be effectively set off against an 'underlying' value and taken advantage of. This is a form of risk management that disperses the asset in space in order to minimise fluctuations (in prices and payments) across time. The NEP 2020's evangelical thrust for a multidisciplinary model of higher educational services adapts the risk-bundling technique of 'arbitrage' for use in India's university sector. The lateral opening of VAC or SEC course-bouquets across streams and disciplines enables a classic weighing in of all kinds of differentials in the price-determinations of these courses for widely divergent constituencies of students – enrolled, for example, in nearly 80 colleges of one university alone. The true import of the 'multiple' in the 'multidisciplinary' lies here: the same course will hold different values for different student-owners of the asset, first separated by departments and then by colleges, histories and social aspirations. Most recently, the same University of Delhi has announced a further expansion of enrolments within its multidisciplinary curriculum by opening a slew of 'skill courses' (from the Centre for Innovative Skill Based Courses) to *non*-university publics as well[15] (Pandey, "Delhi University's SOL Offering Courses"). The logical next step consists in a mass-digitisation of VACs, redesigned as Massive Open Online Courses (MOOCs) – making available an experience of the NEP-era university to a theoretically infinite globality of consumer-investors.[16] As preparatory ritual in the direction, another central university in Delhi – Jamia Millia Islamia – issued a notice in January 2025, making it mandatory for all undergraduate students of all streams to opt for an online SWAYAM (Study Webs of Active-Learning for Young Aspiring Minds) course in their second semester as VAC equivalent.[17] This pitch for an 'anybody anywhere' model of the university's self-distribution, while mustering the aspect of a democratic exhilaration, is also at the same time the surest compounding of the 'social logic' of the derivative. This is the point at which, as Martin says, '[s]hifts in scale from concrete to abstract or local to global are no longer external yardsticks of equivalence'.

The University as Platform

But, if equivalence – the nominal and symbolic principle behind exchange – becomes irrelevant to the derivatives-market and its 'shifts in scale', what subsists as the *medium* for this new order of economic activity? It is here that I would posit the 'assemblage'-structure of the *platform*, which the Indian university too is beckoned to remodel itself as. Definitionally, as Nick Srnicek lays bare in his book *Platform Capitalism*,

---

[15] See the "Centre for Innovative Skill Based Courses" website at https://sol.du.ac.in/skill_courses/index.php.

[16] The issue of transitioning 40 per cent of the university's course offerings to digital platforms had already found its place on the agenda of an Academic Council meeting in late November 2023. See Chettri; "Delhi University".

[17] SWAYAM, a free online learning platform partnered by the Ministry of Education, aims at 'extending classrooms beyond walls'. For reference, see Jamia Millia Islamia's "Notification No. C&O-4(121)/RO/2025" dated 16.01.2025 (https://jmi.ac.in/upload/advertisement/notification_SWAYAM_2025january16.pdf) and "Addendum" dated 23.01.2025 (https://jmi.ac.in/upload/advertisement/addendum_swayam_2025january23.pdf).

> At the most general level, platforms are digital infrastructures that enable two or more groups to interact. They therefore position themselves as intermediaries that bring together different users: customers, advertisers, service providers, producers, suppliers, and even physical objects. More often than not, these platforms also come with a series of tools that enable their users to build their own products, services, and marketplaces. Microsoft's Windows operating system enables software developers to create applications for it and sell them to consumers; Apple's App Store and its associated ecosystem (XCode and the iOS SDK) enable developers to build and sell new apps to users; Google's search engine provides a platform for advertisers and content providers to target people searching for information; and Uber's taxi app enables drivers and passengers to exchange rides for cash. Rather than having to build a marketplace from the ground up, a platform provides the basic infrastructure to mediate between different groups. (32)

The name that NEP 2020 attaches to the platform-reincarnation of the Indian university is, far-sightedly enough, the 'Academic Bank of Credit (ABC)'. Initially mentioned in passing in Section 11.9 of the policy blueprint, the 'ABC' of Indian higher education was to 'digitally store the academic credits earned from various recognized HEIs' by students, and thus track their respective stages of progress towards the award of degrees (NEP 2020, 37). In this nascent *avatar*, it was at worst a digital repository and at best a platform for arbitrage between markets for derivatives in higher education. In any case, the ABC was still expected to provide a *common* infrastructure – in other words, a digital interface – to 'mediate between [the] different groups' of institutions and student-users of those institutions. Within a year's time, in July 2021, a *Gazette* notification kickstarted the process of implementing the NEP by codifying 'regulations' for the 'establishment and operation' of ABCs. Understandably, the *platform* potential of the university was the first of the NEP's features to be amplified, and made into a precondition for the university's fitness to a social logic of the derivative. Though this early legislative move around the NEP was restricted, in its original version, to universities in order of their ranking/rating scores,[18] a quick amendment was brought in to subsequently induct *all* universities of the country within the ABC's ambit.[19] This is the cardinal operational principle of the platform, where the sheer numerical volume of its user-subscribers is what makes for its 'network effects'. The more the users on a platform, the more likely is it to attract even more users. The monopolistic tendencies implicit within this structural algorithm of platform-design are counterbalanced through a democratic façade of plenitude – insidiously enabled through a range of instruments from compulsory registration to lock-in and app-trial periods. Similarly, the mandatory opening of 'academic bank' accounts meant that there was no alternative to the platform-university.[20] A default 'network effect' was achieved through the leveraging of all existing 'service-providers' (HEIs), and through them the databases of all pre-subscribed 'customers' (student enrolments).

Now, how does the ABC perform its platform operations? According to the published text of the "Regulations", the Academic Bank of Credit is a 'digital or virtual or online store-house entity of academic credit data base of Higher Education Institution with students as its stakeholder [sic.]' (Section 5.1, 11). The stakeholder in the student is then invited to freely trade in the 'multidisciplinary' derivatives on offer across the nation's higher educational institutions, without care for routines of formal admission or physical attendance. The idealised form of platform-mediated mobility is called 'credit transfer' between institutions – where a student, taking a 'common university entrance test' (CUET), may choose to enrol in any institution across the country and opt for only 50 per cent of the total credit-worth of a degree from such institution of enrolment. This is the 'underlying' asset value, to be effectively topped up with multidisciplinary derivative

[18] See Section 7.1, "UGC Regulations 2021", pp. 12–13.

[19] Refer to "UGC (First Amendment) Regulations 2021".

[20] See, for example, "UGC Implementation", 2022 – cautioning all institutions to mandatorily implement the ABC scheme and open academic bank accounts for student-consumers 'on urgent basis'.

contracts as credit-claims against a risk-prone future. Because the asset owner is assured a 'flexibility of curriculum framework', allowed to 'choose [her] own learning path' and guaranteed maximal mobility on 'principle of multiple entry-multiple exit as well as any-time, any-where, and any-level learning' ("Regulations 2021" 10), it is assumed that the cumulative value of the derivatives contracted – on the basis of both reputational capital of institutions and the credit-rating of professors or courses offered – will far exceed the imminent risks of future indebtedness. Though the permissible quantum of derivatives-trading within such an arrangement is equivalent to the value of the 'underlying' asset (50 per cent), the returns on risk-management through a judicious (and diversified) combination of 'credit' and 'choice' are expected to be exponentially greater.

The "ABC Regulations" provide for institutions to be restructured as 'bank[s] for academic purposes, on the pattern of commercial banks for financial purposes, with students as academic account holders to whom, the Academic Bank of Credits shall provide a variety of services including credit verification, credit accumulation, credit transfer or redemption and authentication of academic rewards' (Sec. 5.3, 11). Tellingly, the terminology of reform is a guide to its intentions: not only is the institution urged to allocate credit capital by assessing the creditworthiness of students, the latter too are successively expected to cross-transfer (and reinvest) their credit as security against risks of eventual repayment. The cyclical self-generation of the derivatives-market is thus appropriated in the outward aspects of the Indian university, now instantiated as a *platform* where users incessantly invest and redeem credit in an effort to rate each other. The stock-market reinvention of higher education, evolving newer and newer instruments of risk-management in a multidisciplinary derivatives-trade, is proverbially completed in the ABC.

David Theo Goldberg had etched out a portrait of the *platform university* – in his words, the "Uber U" or uber-varsity – which bears a chilling resemblance to what I described above:

> Just as the Uber platform makes getting a ride easier, often less expensive, easily shareable and cashless, so the *Uber U platform potentially simplifies getting credentialed and is supposed to drive down costs and render higher learning more accessible*. . . . Just as one can follow in real time on the platform, map the progress of the Uber car approaching the pickup point, so one can map out and monitor the timeline of the student working through the training modules for which he or she has registered. . . .
>
> *The certification autogenerated by the platform, much like the Uber receipt on one's smartphone, is more about customer service, liability and immunity from potential litigation than it is about the acquisition of consequential knowledge.* (emphases mine)

The NEP's bid at Uberising the Indian university, through a 'super-app' like the ABC, mimes a similar set of operations. With the entire university system of the country mapping itself onto the app, it is but a matter of time for the Academic Bank's software to come pre-loaded on mobile devices or for institutions to track (and extract) student data through mobile activity on the application. This absolute abundance of data capital thus available for brokering via the 'super-app' will become the basis for a wider market of derivatives-trading. The internet footprints of student consumers on the ABC-installed device – algorithmically construed as 'data doubles' – may even converge the fortunes of the Indian university with what Kevin D. Haggerty and Richard V. Ericson portentously called the 'surveillant assemblage' (605–22).

How Do Platforms Work? Making Value out of *Not-Knowing*

Let me now turn attention to *three* distinguishing 'elements' of a platform ecosystem, and how they might be read into the NEP 2020's substantive articulations about the future of Indian higher education. I use the framework as well as theoretical justification for understanding the platform as an assemblage of 'elements' from Jane I. Guyer's fantastic collection of essays on economic anthropology, written as responses to discrete provocations over a period of fourteen years. Guyer's larger argument – if I may hazard one, despite her constant caution against an overdetermining analysis – consists in understanding the economy's self-demonstrative processes through equivocations of the everyday, manifest in both acts of living and believing. For her, the closest approximation to the current world economy – the 'reality' of which is distributed across incommensurables and therefore never quite realisable in the same way across places and peoples – lies in the platform's 'apportunities':

> An 'opportunity' presents itself at some juncture in the life and structure of the platform, and—given the mode by which it is actualized, through apps—novelty can be inserted in ways that are not reducible either to "rational choice" nor just "improvisation." This term ["apportunity"] is simply a convenient invention on my part, and it may not work in other languages. But it captures a certain terminological need. The shift from "market economy" to "platform economy" imposes committed attentiveness to very complex phenomena. (118)

The insertion of 'novelty' in the 'life and structure of the platform' that Guyer talks about is factored into the ABC's euphoric exultations over 'freedom' of choice – which, as the anthropologist maintains, is 'not reducible to either "rational choice" nor just "improvisation"'. Instead, the play with terms like 'flexibility' or 'mobility', which quickly translates into the ludic indeterminacy of 'any-time, any-where, and any-level learning', is what promises *novelty* in its 'apportunistic' sense. This is newness inexhaustible and immune to figuration in time or place; and therefore, it survives as the *permanent possibility of both surprise and risk*. The only way out of such a double-bind of 'novelty' is to resort to Martin's 'social logic' of the derivative, where crisis may be prevented through an imaginative multiplication of risk-scenarios. But, what are the exact ways in which the platform brandishes its 'apportunities', if they can neither be localised as fixed 'value' nor teleologised as 'truth'? Contextualised against our discussion around the NEP 2020, how does the Indian *platform-university* (an analogue to Goldberg's 'Uber U' or Francois Germinet's 'Airbnb of education') hedge against the non-knowledge of a *permanently novel* future?

Guyer would argue that there are roughly *three* metaphorical figures through which to understand the platform's procedures of value-approximation: namely, *ranking* sequences, vague *wholes* and *distant* horizons. This last section of the final chapter of this book will deal with each of these forms of cognitive acrobatics, in order to get to the political economy of 'uncertainty' that underwrites the nation's most recent education policy.

1. The Desire for Order: Ranking Ecosystems in Higher Education

The quality by which value-bearing elements may be placed in a sequential *order*, such that it appears like a ranking chart – where the exact place of an element is also the index of its investability or credit-worthiness – is called 'ordinality'. Against a backdrop of malignant non-knowledge and its associated risks, ordinal flowcharts feed into a nostalgic desire for *order* and *merit*. From Guyer's account, it emerges that the ordinal mechanisms of platforms are crucial to their relative pricing of assets or the potentiality for derivative contracts. There is however a specific shape that the algorithms of ordinal representation usually assume: the 'parabolic scalar' graph (Guyer 133), with a steep shooting pinnacle and an infinite tail. This graph achieves a couple of effects: the conversion of order into a measure of 'quality', and the projection of an arduous felicity at the top and default density at the bottom. The sparseness of ordinal elements at the *higher end* of the curve is accompanied by a steepness that signifies the *breadth of difference* between the first and those that come right after; while the concentrated population of 'averages' at the bottom almost makes difference negligible at the lower end of the scale. Translated into quality-metrics, the *best* is way ahead of the next while those below are all nearly of the same mettle. This is the principle of numerical expression on the platform, where credit ratings of assets are ordinally laid out for those *at risk* (at the bottom of the scale) to trade in derivatives along the sharp edges of the best-rated. Because, as Guyer perceptively explains,

> In very many domains, the 'first' is icon or idol, and often at a very wide interval from the second, third, and fourth. . . . Narrative commentaries often make clear that, at the top, it is, in fact, the intervals along the order scale, and not the absolute amounts, that are at stake in "competition." In many cases, intervals diminish radically going down the scale, both in real terms and in proportion to their next positions. (ibid.)

Pithily put, 'quality' is an extreme rarity and a lonely *exception* at the very top! By granting the 'first' a visible solitariness, there is a quasi-mythical *aura* of its heroic achievement that is also secured by numerical cartographies. It becomes the equivalent of an 'icon' or 'idol' – better still, a legend and *sovereign essence*. Plotted against the platform-analogy in Indian higher education, the ABC could only take off by bartering the promise of credit allocations from the best institutions in the country, without as much as the logistics of entering through their gates or sitting in their classrooms. The best way to do it is through multidisciplinary derivative course-contracts – say, for example, "The Art of Being Happy" – which may be touristically gleaned (and 'booked') from the drop-down lists of renowned institutions. This mass digitisation of the delivery of higher educational services propped up the DNEP 2019's magical formula, whereby it was suggested that enrolments in Indian higher education could be doubled in the next twenty years by bringing down the number of institutions to one-fourth of its then-current size.[21] The painful demystification of what sounded like 'magic' in 2019 had to only wait for the onslaught of the pandemic in less than a year's time – and its forced acceleration of the university's

[21] Section 2.3 of the *All India Survey on Higher Education Report 2018–19*, when read in conjunction with chapter 10 ("Institutional Restructuring and Consolidation") of the *Draft National Education Policy 2019*, provides the exact numerical jugglery: the Draft policy of 2019 argues that the gross enrolment ratio (GER) for Indian higher education must be doubled from a then-current 26.3 to 50 by quartering the number of colleges and universities from a then-existing 52,000 to 12,300.

'pack-up' schedule in a wholesale online transition, until the NEP 2020 sealed it all as official destiny.

But, a simple dematerialisation of the Indian university, by making the costs and routines of its material production – as physical infrastructure – unnecessary and inconsequential, was not the only mandate of the Academic Bank of Credit. The latter had to then apply the principle of ordinality to a targeted *consolidation* of the university's ecosystem (DNEP 2019, 212–15). Quartering the numerical expanse of institutions, as I said, from over 52,000 to a proposed 12,300 was hence not enough. This pooled concentration of 'college complexes' – alternatively enshrined as 'cluster hubs' or 'Multidisciplinary Education and Research Universities (MERUs)' in policy parlance (221) – was to be now 'tiered' into three 'types', each assigning a rank-status in the series of ontological priority (213–14). This was called the 'graded autonomy' model, according to which the amplitude of 'autonomous' functioning allowed to an institution was to effectively devolve into its ordinal 'place' on the parabolic tier-graph (329). With only a maximum of 300 institutions allowed into the charmed circle of 'Type 1: Research Universities' and a corresponding undergrowth of 10,000 institutions scrambling for relevance at the third rung of the ladder (that is, the 'Type 3: Autonomous degree-granting colleges'), the 'graded' pattern of ordinality only sets off a mythology of the 'great' icons at the top.

A slightly more piercing look into the policy-archive gives away the devil in the detail, but not before one compares this outline of institutional 'Type'-casting against the government's funding-commitments towards these different institutional categories. Section 4.7 in Addendum A1 of the *Draft NEP 2019* unclutters the economic calculus behind such restructuring, in that the 10,000 *merged* 'Type 3' colleges across the country are earmarked for only half the additional funding-support from the government as is promised to 300 'Type 1' universities (419). How an ordinal scale of rankings creates structural conditions for 'greatness' as *exception*, by competitively crowding out the 'mediocre' as the optimal instance of production – and therefore, leaving it to self-finance its inclusion or exclusion – is the portent borne by the platform university.

2. The Drive towards Totalisation: Of GERs and GDPs

The second feature of a platform that Guyer directs our attention to is its compulsive need to posit a *wholeness*, in the face of a general incursion of uncertainty and risk. This need, she surveys, is best answered by yet another numerical sleight of expression: the *percentage*. Though originally an 'archaic form', the proliferation of percentage expressions in the twentieth and twenty-first centuries piques Guyer's anthropological imagination and urges her to sift through widely separated archives of its current-day use.

> Percentage may be even more complex than ranking because it also necessarily contains a philosophical implication of completion, or wholeness of some kind, to the category name—the denominator—that equals the "100." The denominator equates to a category "name" that presumes stability. It seems to me that it is this implicit designation of completion that allows its ever-ramifying inventive applicability. . . . At one frontier in the present, it seems that the centum—the whole, the benchmark—has accrued aspirational, rather than simply descriptive, qualities. One hundred percent can be a benchmark for identifying how far we fall short, and how much excess is being demanded, with the insinuation that we should work at redressing it. . . . [One notices] a growing proliferation of use for the percentage form, the expanding practice of not naming the denominator in clear definitional terms, and visual sophistication for drawing attention to the numerator rather than the denominator. (Guyer 141–42)

The growing popularity of the *percentage form* in a platform age, Guyer suspects, may be related to the unknowability of the denominator itself. That there are no equations of proportionality or equivalence that might, in the event of a dispute, settle the question of value in a permanently novel future – calls for a symbolic operation of adequacy in numerical measure. It is that purpose of adequation against radically incommensurable quality-quantity fluctuations of '[non-]knowledge' – a 'craving for intelligibility', in Hayek's terms (*The Road to Serfdom* 204) – that the 'hundredness' of the percentage serves. The loss of a standard that the centum substitutes – through an arbitrary consensus on number converted into the grace and *jouissance* of 'completion' – is how the social logic of the derivative must necessarily work itself through. In an unknown and unknowable future, the trading in derivative contracts far from completes the asset's value; on the contrary, it promises to supplement value with no relation whatsoever to the 'reality' of the asset that it is abstracted from. In such a sphere of imaginary transactions that the platform makes possible, both 'completeness' and 'wholeness' are forever elusive virtues. The percentage secures the redemption of a ceaselessly unwholesome world by staging an illusion – a denominator that projects closure and might be striven towards. But, in the course of the peddling of the centum's fiction, a series of devious elisions are performed. First: the numerator in the mathematical formulation is justified beyond any reference to a context or a 'real'. In other words, the numerator of a percentage – say, for example, 26.3 per cent of populations of college-going age – has no real ground of comparison. The act of counting is immaterial, if held together by an assumption of the 'total'. That only 26 out of a hundred eligible youths can ever attend college makes hundredness immaterial, if not as a confabulated scale against which successive numerators (from changed annual contexts) record margins of increase or decrease. The percentage in this sense is an analogue of the incomparable; it cannot but be sampled randomly and enumerated as a 'part' independent of the whole. The numerator is just any other number, thriving in a referential vacuum. The second ramification from this: if the denominator is an aggregation of every instance (included or rejected) by a count of one, then there is no accounting of historical difference possible within such an exercise. The *percentage form*, by demanding an approximate figuration of instances separated by histories, can only proliferate non-knowledge as the basis of the platform.

The NEP 2020's fixation with the form of the percentage – whether in its calculation of a gross enrolment ratio (GER) or in its pitch for a desired quantum of GDP spending on education – falls into the same loops of referential vagueness that I detailed above. The GER for higher education, which it is the primary thrust of the policy to double, assumes 'hundredness' as denominator, and works by inscribing the quest of 'completion' within the Indian university's race for massification. But what misses this auditing enthusiasm is the fact that every enrolment and non-enrolment, equated by a measure of one, *goes on to legislate history by the force of arithmetic.* By considering all 'academic credit' account holders – whether in the Type 3 colleges or the Type 1 universities, and then again within every such institution or outside – as equally 'creditworthy' to trade in derivatives, the NEP's platform imagination assumes a level playing field that does *not* exist. In a similar vein, the policy's fevered pitch for budgeting 6 per cent of the Gross Domestic Product (GDP) on education – notwithstanding successive governments' shameful disregard of such a demand for more than fifty odd years! – hangs in a zone of impossible reference. At the precise moment when the NEP 2020 was announced as taking effect, the annual GDP of the country was estimated as standing at minus 23.9 per cent[22] – hit as it was by massive recessionary trends compounded by the debilitating effects of the pandemic. Against the backdrop of such a tottering economy, is the 6 per cent of GDP calculation to be denominated against an immediate annual rate in the negative, or against the providential grace of a 'fullness' in the hundred? The numerator of the percentage, existing in a space of solipsistic reference, is all that the platform-university has at its disposal to foist the myth of 'completion'.

3. The Search for Origins: Telescoping Risk through Myth

The third – and final, for my analysis here – facet of the platform ecosystem that Jane Guyer points towards is its implosion of the 'near future', going hand in hand with a search for 'ultimate

---

[22] See "Minus 23.9 per cent"; and "GDP growth".

origins and distant horizons'. She breathtakingly observes in one of her essays:

> [A] sense of foreignness in the present has come to revolve around a strange evacuation of the temporal frame of the "near future": the reach of thought and imagination, of planning and hoping, of tracing out mutual influences, of engaging in struggles for specific goals, in short, of the process of implicating oneself in the ongoing life of the social and material world that used to be encompassed under an expansively inclusive concept of "reasoning". . . . From my own vantage point in historical time, the shift in temporal framing has involved a double move, toward both very short and very long sightedness, with a symmetrical evacuation of the near past and the near future. . . . [I]t seemed that ultimate origins and distant horizons were both reinvigorated, whereas what fell between them was attenuating into airy thinness, on both "sides" (past and future) of the "reduction to the present." (89–91)

The 'shift in temporal framing' towards a future that is radically unknowable – and therefore only conceivable through a punctuated telescopy of *risk* – heightens the desire for anchorage, or the Hayekian 'craving for intelligibility', in an exhumation of the irrecoverable past. The latter is the only frame of reference to which any knowledge of the present must necessarily be submitted and surrendered for assessment. The procedures for such verification call forth the totalitarian apparatuses of the state, as the final arbiter of any truth if at all. Even the supreme leader of the state must in such an instance manifest an ethic of incarnation, from the distant past – and thus be the only hope and succour of a rudderless present, seeking with all its might to hedge against the risks of the future. Unsurprisingly, one hears the echoes of Arendt's analysis in "Ideology and Terror" at such a conjuncture, ringing even truer by the side of Guyer's anthropological dismay. The cacophony surrounding the building of a Ram temple at the site of the demolished Babri masjid – announcing the advent of a '*Ram rajya*' ruled by Narendra Modi ("Reimagining Ram") – conches away in the background as I write this, while the NEP

2020 continues to prepare ground for our universities to join in the celebrations in a gesture of total surrender (Ghosh; Vijay; "When Saffron Sparks Debates"; Jafri).

If the 'near future' is a means of implicating ourselves in 'the ongoing life of the social and material world', the 'distant horizons' framework of a platform economy consists in evacuating the *livedness* of historical time as experienced in the everyday. It is therefore perfectly consonant with distortions of history and ideological exhumations of a 'golden past' of greatness. We have effectively returned here to the spectres of the great 'ancient Indian universities' that I began this book with – and the obsession with which accurately exhausts the ironies of a platformised higher education in present-day India. The NEP 2020 chimes the chilling portrait of this platform-university in India, looking into the portals of a distant horizon of the 'fourth industrial revolution', with its gaze turned towards a myth of 'ultimate origins':

> The ancient Indian universities Takshashila, Nalanda, Vallabhi, and Vikramshila, which had thousands of students from India and the world studying in vibrant multidisciplinary environments, amply demonstrated the type of great success that large multidisciplinary research and teaching universities could bring. India urgently needs to bring back this great Indian tradition to create well-rounded and innovative individuals, and which is already transforming other countries educationally and economically. (NEP 2020, 34)

References

Adkins, Lisa, Melinda Cooper and Martijn Konings. *The Asset Economy: Property Ownership and the New Logic of Inequality*. Polity Press, 2020.

"After National Flag, Smriti Irani Ropes in Army to Teach Nationalism on Campus." *India Today*, 15 Mar. 2016. https://www.indiatoday.in/india/story/after-national-flag-smriti-irani-ropes-in-army-to-teach-nationalism-on-campus-313367-2016-03-15

Agarwal, Khushi. "Why We Must Be Critical of the New Education Policy 2020." *Feminism in India*, 6 Aug. 2020. https://feminisminindia.com/2020/08/06/new-education-policy-nep-2020-critical-analysis/#google_vignette

Althusser, Louis. "Ideology and Ideological State Apparatuses (Notes towards an Investigation)." *Lenin and Philosophy and Other Essays*, translated by Ben Brewster. Monthly Review Press, 1971, pp. 127–86.

Arendt, Hannah. "Ideology and Terror: A Novel Form of Government." *The Origins of Totalitarianism*. Harcourt Brace and Company, 1951.

Beck, Ulrich. "Living in the World Risk Society." *Economy and Society*, vol. 35, no. 3, Aug. 2006, pp. 329–45.

_______. *World At Risk*. Polity Press, 2013.

Becker, Gary S. *The Economic Approach to Human Behavior*. University of Chicago Press, 1976.

Bhattacharya, Debaditya. "Between Disciplines and Interdisciplines: The University of In-discipline." *The University Unthought: Notes for a Future*, edited by Bhattacharya. Routledge, 2019, pp. 183–208.

_______. "A Liberal Poetics of Policy: The Contemporary Fortunes of Indian Higher Education." *Radical Philosophy* 2.10, Summer 2021, pp. 44–54.

_______. "The 'Dangerous Ground' for Democracy: Doing Interdisciplinary Social Sciences in the Public University." *Inclusive Pedagogies: Teaching and Learning Practices in Higher Education in India*, edited by Kanika Singh. Primus Books, 2024, pp. 157–86.

Bryan, Dick and Mike Rafferty. *Capitalism with Derivatives: A Political Economy of Financial Derivatives, Capital, and Class*. Palgrave Macmillan, 2006.

"CAA+NRC Can Lead to 'Disenfranchisement' of Indian Muslims: US Body." *Indian Express*, 20 Feb. 2020. https://indianexpress.com/article/india/caa-nrc-india-us-trump-6277969/.

Chaudhuri, Sukanta. "A Disaster Foretold." *The Telegraph*, 2 Jun. 2021. https://www.telegraphindia.com/opinion/the-new-education-order-reinvents-the-varnashram/cid/1817422.

Chettri, Shradha. "You May Take 40% of Courses Online at Delhi University." *The Times of India*, 28 Nov. 2023. https://timesofindia.indiatimes.com/city/delhi/you-may-take-40-of-courses-online-at-delhi-university/articleshow/105545481.cms.

Dalmia, Shikha. "India Is Laying the Groundwork for a Mass Faith-cleansing." *The Week*, 12 Dec. 2019. https://theweek.com/articles/883317/india-laying-groundwork-mass-faithcleansing.

DC, Abinash. "Ramjas Can 'No Longer Be Considered a Safe Space': A Student Recounts the ABVP's Violent Attack." *The Caravan*, 22 Feb. 2017. https://caravanmagazine.in/vantage/ramjas-abvp-cultures-of-protest.

De, Rohit, and Surabhi Ranganathan. "We Are Witnessing a Rediscovery of India's Republic." *New York Times*, 27 Dec. 2019. https://www.nytimes.com/2019/12/27/opinion/india-constitution-protests.html.

"Delhi University: Soon, You May Complete Nearly Half of Your Course Online." *The Economic Times*, 28 Nov. 2023. https://economictimes.indiatimes.com/industry/services/education/delhi-university-soon-you-may-complete-nearly-half-of-your-course-online/articleshow/105552987.cms?from=mdr.

Deshpande, Satish. "As Students Gear up for University, the Devil is in the NEP's Details." *The Indian Express*, 6 Jul. 2022. https://indianexpress.com/article/opinion/columns/as-students-gear-up-for-university-the-devil-is-in-the-neps-details-8010792/.

Devy, Ganesh N. "National Education Policy Seeks to Reinvent the Wheel and Ensure a Cultural Revolution." *National Herald*, 30 Aug. 2020. https://www.nationalheraldindia.com/opinion/national-education-policy-seeks-to-reinvent-the-wheel-and-ensure-a-cultural-revolution#google_vignette.

Dutt, Barkha. "How Citizenship Act, NRC Will Alter the Idea of India." *Hindustan Times*, 14 Dec. 2019. https://www.hindustantimes.com/columns/how-the-amended-citizenship-act-and-nrc-will-alter-the-idea-of-india/story-Qti007fZz8HIsqFn8NmTKL.html.

Feher, Michel. *Rated Agency: Investee Politics in a Speculative Age*. Zone Books, 2018.

Friedman, Milton. *Essays in Positive Economics*. University of Chicago Press, 1953.

"Future of Women's Studies Centres Hanging in Balance, Yet Again." *Newsclick*, 22 Mar. 2019. https://www.newsclick.in/future-womens-studies-centres-hanging-balance-yet-again.

"GDP Growth at -23.9% in Q1; First Contraction in More than 40 Years." *The Economic Times*, 2 Sep. 2020. https://economictimes.indiatimes.com/news/economy/indicators/gdp-growth-at-23-9-in-q1-worst-economic-contraction-on-record/articleshow/77851891.cms?from=mdr.

Germinet, Francois, qtd. in Marine Miller, "The Uber-ization of Higher Education," translated by Nina Fink. *L'Etudiant*, 8 Jan. 2016. https://www.letudiant.fr/educpros/actualite/the-uber-ization-of-higher-education.html.

Ghosh, Shreya. "College Campuses Too Join in Celebrations." *The Times of India*, 21 Jan. 2024. https://timesofindia.indiatimes.com/city/delhi/college-campuses-join-in-celebrations-of-ram-mandir-consecration-in-ayodhya-new-delhi/articleshow/107021952.cms.

Goldberg, David Theo. "Coming to You Soon: Uber U." *Inside Higher Ed*, 11 Aug. 2016. https://www.insidehighered.com/views/2016/08/12/dangers-uberization-higher-education-essay.

Government of India. *Report on Education, Skill Development and Labour Force, Volume III, 2013–14*. Labour Bureau, 2014.

________. *Economic Survey 2014–15*. Ministry of Finance, 2015.

________. *Report on Education, Skill Development and Labour Force, Volume III, 2015–16*. Labour Bureau, 2016.

Graeber, David. *Debt: The First 5,000 Years*. Melville House, 2011.

Gramsci, Antonio. "The Formation of the Intellectuals." *Selections from the Prison Notebooks*, edited and translated by Quintin Hoare and Geoffrey Nowell Smith. International Publishers, 1971, pp. 5–14.

Guyer, Jane I. *Legacies, Logics, Logistics: Essays in the Anthropology of the Platform Economy*. The University of Chicago Press, 2016.

Haggerty, Kevin D. and Richard V. Ericson. "The Surveillant Assemblage." *British Journal of Sociology*, vol. 51, no. 4, Dec. 2000, pp. 605–22.

Hayek, Friedrich August. "Economics and Knowledge." *Economica*, vol. 4, Feb. 1937, pp. 33–54.

________. *The Road to Serfdom*. University of Chicago Press, 1944.

________. "The Use of Knowledge in Society." *The American Economic Review*, vol. 35, Sep. 1945, pp. 519–30.

Hebbar, Prajakta. "Haryana Professors Reprimanded for Staging Play Based on Mahasweta Devi Story." *HuffPost*, 9 Nov. 2016. https://www.huffpost.com/archive/in/entry/haryana-professors-reprimanded-for-staging-play-based-on-mahaswe_in_5c11f131e4b003d830eaec68 https://www.ugc.ac.in/pdfnews/0719410_ABC_001.pdf.

Jafri, Abdul Alim. "Ram Mandir Inauguration: All Educational Institutions in UP to Remain Closed on Jan 22." *NewsClick*, 10 Jan. 2024. https://www.newsclick.in/ram-mandir-inauguration-all-educational-institutions-remain-closed-jan-22.

Jain, Akshita. "How NEP Will Increase Cost of Good Education and Produce A Semi-skilled Workforce." *HuffPost*, 6 Aug. 2020. https://www.huffpost.com/archive/in/entry/national-education-policy-cost-heirarchy-education_in_5f2a825fc5b6e96a22abb1a0.

John, Mary E. "Analysing the New Educational Policy in the Context of Higher Education: Where is Gender?" *Sociological Bulletin*, vol. 72, no. 4, 2023, pp. 393–404. https://journals.sagepub.com/doi/full/10.1177/00380229231196459.

Kidwai, Ayesha. "Towards Inequality." *Postcolonial Studies*, vol. 24, no. 1, 2021, pp. 33–39. https://doi.org/10.1080/13688790.2021.1882080.

Kumar, Sanjay. "India's NRC and BJP's Dangerous Game of Citizenship and Religion." *Dawn*, 29 Nov. 2019. https://www.dawn.com/news/1519154.

Lazzarato, Maurizio. *The Making of the Indebted Man*. Semiotext(e), 2011.

______. *Governing by Debt*. Semiotext(e), 2015.

Martin, Randy. *Knowledge LTD. Toward a Social Logic of the Derivative*. Temple University Press, 2015.

Menon, Nivedita. "NEP 2020: Elitist and Corporatized Education under Hindu Rashtra." *Kafila*, 8 Sep. 2020. https://kafila.online/2020/09/08/nep-2020-elitist-and-corporatized-education-under-hindu-rashtra/.

Ministry of Human Resource Development. *Draft National Policy on Education (NPE) 2016: Report of the Committee for Evolution of the New Education Policy*. Government of India Press, 2016.

_______. *Draft National Education Policy 2019*. Government of India Press, 2019.

_______. *National Education Policy (NEP) 2020*. Government of India Press, 2020.

"Minus 23.9 per cent." *The Indian Express*, 1 Sep. 2020. https://indianexpress.com/article/business/economy/economy-slowdown-gdp-contraction-minus-23-9-per-cent-6578116/.

Mohanty, Basant Kumar. "Out: Secularism; In: Gita Ideal." *The Telegraph*, 2 Aug. 2020. https://www.telegraphindia.com/india/new-education-policy-secularism-in-gita-ideal/cid/1788008.

"My Birth Is My Fatal Accident: Rohith Vemula's Searing Letter Is an Indictment of Social Prejudices." *The Wire*, 17 Jan. 2019. https://thewire.in/caste/rohith-vemula-letter-a-powerful-indictment-of-social-prejudices.

Naqvi, Saba. "Citizenship Amendment Bill: A Noose Around Necks of Muslims." *Outlook*, 11 Dec. 2019. https://www.outlookindia.com/opinion/opinion-opinion-citizenship-amendment-bill-a-noose-around-necks-of-muslims-news-343986.

"National Education Policy 2020: Document Still Not Available in Public Domain." *The Hindu*, 30 Jul. 2020a. https://www.thehindu.com/education/national-education-policy-still-not-available-in-public-domain/article32232507.ece.

"National Education Policy 2020: Why Bypass Parliament, Asks Tharoor." *The Hindu*, 30 Jul. 2020b. https://www.thehindu.com/news/national/national-education-policy-why-bypass-parliament-asks-tharoor/article32233409.ece.

Nawani, Disha. "NEP 2020 Fails Those Trapped in Vicious Cycles of Disadvantage." *The Indian Express*, 25 Sep. 2020. https://indianexpress.com/article/opinion/columns/national-education-policy-2020-nep-6609564/.

Pandey, Munish Chandra. "JNU Student Najeeb Ahmed's Disappearance to Remain Mystery, CBI Ends Search." *India Today*, 16 Oct. 2018. https://www.indiatoday.in/india/story/jnu-student-najeeb-ahmed-disappearance-to-remain-mystery-cbi-ends-search-1368745-2018-10-15.

Pandey, Puniti. "Delhi University's SOL Offering Courses in Cybersecurity, Finance." *NDTV*, 17 Feb. 2024. https://www.ndtv.com/education/delhi-universitys-sol-offering-courses-in-cybersecurity-finance-check-details-5075703.

Pathak, Avijit. "NEP: Fancy Ideals or Real Concerns?" *Mainstream Weekly*, vol. 58, no. 37, 2020. https://www.mainstreamweekly.net/article9847.html.

Patnaik, Prabhat. "Against Excellence." *The Telegraph*, 9 Sep. 2020. https://www.telegraphindia.com/opinion/nep-2020-a-retrograde-paradigm-shift-in-education/cid/1791410.

"PM Narendra Modi Scraps Planning Commission." *Hindustan Times*, 15 Aug. 2014. https://www.hindustantimes.com/india/pm-narendra-modi-scraps-planning-commission/story-EJdGN4v0ETFV1SJZEeFy1J.html.

"Police Crack Down at JNU, Arrest Student Leader for Sedition." *The Hindu Business Line*, 12 Feb. 2016. https://www.thehindubusinessline.com/news/education/police-crack-down-at-jnu-arrest-student-leader-for-sedition/article64308129.ece.

Prasad, Madhu. "At the Mercy of the Market." *Frontline*, vol. 37, no. 17, 28 Aug. 2020, pp. 4–8.

"Rohith Vemula Didn't Get Fellowship for Past 7 Months, Says Letter." *The Economic Times*, 19 Jan. 2016. https://economictimes.indiatimes.com/news/politics-and-nation/rohit-vemula-didnt-get-fellowship-for-past-7-months-says-letter/articleshow/50638216.cms?from=mdr.

Roy, Kumkum. "National Education Policy Needs Close Scrutiny for What It Says, What It Doesn't." *The Indian Express*, 31 Jul. 2020. https://indianexpress.com/article/opinion/columns/national-education-policy-reservation-6531546/.

Sadgopal, Anil. "Decoding the Agenda of the New National Education Policy." *Frontline*, 10 Aug. 2020. https://frontline.thehindu.com/cover-story/decoding-the-agenda/article32306146.ece.

Schwab, Klaus. *The Fourth Industrial Revolution*. World Economic Forum, 2017.

Sethi, Aman. "Reading Foucault in Mahendragarh; or, Why We Need a Public University System." *The Wire*, 10 May 2016. https://thewire.in/education/reading-foucault-in-mahendragarh-or-why-we-need-a-public-university-system.

Shankar, Soumya. "India's Citizenship Law, in Tandem with National Registry, Could Make BJP's Discriminatory Targeting of Muslims Easier." *Intercept*, 30 Jan. 2020. https://theintercept.com/2020/01/30/india-citizenship-act-caa-nrc-assam/.

Sharma, Kritika. "4 Years On, India's Still Waiting for New Education Policy—Modi Govt's Big 2014 Promise." *Print*, 14 Sep. 2018. https://

theprint.in/india/governance/4-years-on-indias-still-waiting-for-new-education-policy-modi-govts-big-2014-promise/117022/#:~:text=Economy- ,4%20years%20on%2C%20India's%20still%20waiting%20for%20new%20education%20policy,Modi%20govt's%20big%202014%20promise&text=Committee%20formulating%20the%20new%20education,launched%20in%20this%20govt's%20tenure.

Sitze, Adam. "Academic Unfreedom, Unacademic Freedom: Part One of Two." *The Massachusetts Review*, vol. 58, no. 4, 2017, pp. 589–607.

"Special Issue: Reimagining Ram." *Frontline*, vol. 41, no. 2, 9 Feb. 2024. https://frontline.thehindu.com/magazine/issue/vol41-02.

Srnicek, Nick. *Platform Capitalism*. Polity Press, 2017.

Streeck, Wolfgang. *Buying Time: The Delayed Crisis of Democratic Capitalism*, translated by Patrick Camiller. Verso, 2014.

Trivedi, Divya. "Prof. Krishna Kumar: 'NEP 2020 Offers More of the Same Remedy.'" *Frontline*, 11 Aug. 2020. https://frontline.thehindu.com/cover-story/it-offers-more-of-the-same-remedy/article32305017.ece.

UGC. "University Grants Commission (Establishment and Operation of Academic Bank of Credits in Higher Education) Regulations, 2021." *The Gazette of India: Extraordinary*. New Delhi, 28 Jul. 2021.

______. "University Grants Commission (Establishment and Operation of Academic Bank of Credits in Higher Education) (First Amendment) Regulations, 2021." *The Gazette of India: Extraordinary*. New Delhi, 28 Dec. 2021.

______. "Implementation of Academic Bank of Credits (ABC) on Urgent Basis [Ref. D.O.F. No.1-1/2022(ABC), dated May 13, 2022]." New Delhi.

University of Delhi. "Notification: Amendment to Ordinance V (Skill Enhancement Courses [SECs] under UGCF-2022)." 6 Sep. 2022. https://www.du.ac.in/uploads/new-web/21092022_SEC.pdf.

______. "Notification: Amendment to Ordinance V (Value Addition Courses [VACs] under UGCF-2022)." 14 Sep. 2022. https://www.du.ac.in/uploads/new-web/26102022_VAC.pdf.

"When Saffron Sparks Debates: Exploring the Aftermath of Ram Mandir Inauguration in Educational Spaces." *DU Beat*, 30 Jan. 2024. https://dubeat.com/2024/01/30/when-saffron-sparks-debates-exploring-the-aftermath-of-ram-mandir-inauguration-in-educational-spaces/.

"Who Is an Urban Naxal, Asks Romila Thapar." *The Hindu*, 30 Sep. 2018. https://www.thehindu.com/news/national/who-is-an-urban-naxal-asks-romila-thapar/article25088465.ece.

Varma, Subodh. "Survey: Even Among Skilled Workers Joblessness is High." *The Times of India*, 20 Jul. 2015. https://timesofindia.indiatimes.com/india/survey-even-among-skilled-workers-joblessness-is-high/articleshow/48138599.cms.

Verma, Lalmani. "Harvard vs Hard Work: With GDP Data, PM Narendra Modi Snubs Note Ban Critics." *The Indian Express*, 2 Mar. 2017. https://indianexpress.com/elections/uttar-pradesh-assembly-elections-2017/harvard-vs-hard-work-with-gdp-data-pm-modi-snubs-noteban-critics-4550000/

Vijay, Sunidhi. "Ayodhya Ram Mandir: TISS, IITB Students Celebrate Inauguration." *The Free Press Journal*, 23 Jan. 2024. https://www.freepressjournal.in/education/ayodhya-ram-mandir-tiss-iitb-students-celebrate-inauguration.

Yamunan, Sruthisagar. "IIT-Madras Derecognises Student Group." *The Hindu*, 28 May 2015. https://www.thehindu.com/news/national/tamil-nadu/IIT-Madras-derecognises-student-group/article60327789.ece.

"9-Member Panel to Prepare Final Draft of National Education Policy." *Business Standard*, 26 Jun. 2017. https://www.business-standard.com/article/news-ians/9-member-panel-to-prepare-final-draft-of-national-education-policy-117062600537_1.html.

CONCLUSION

The Return to 'Publicness': A History for the University's Futures

What is Under Threat?

Let me end this book by plumbing a little deeper into the contemporary experience of the 'Indian university' against its policy instance. I have already noted how the post-independence shift in policy-thought – from *welfare* to the *market* to the *platform* – calls forth the gift of a totalitarian 'common' sense as the only protective bulwark against an uncertain (and therefore, uncanny) future. Interestingly, this common sense also plays up the radically uncommon histories and trajectories of movement along caste and religious lines, and enlists them within a 'common' minimum agenda of nationalist citizenship – felicitously euphemised in the NEP 2020 as a turn from the 'neoliberal' to the 'liberal' ends of university training. The means to this entire process of re-envisioning the priorities of higher education lies in trading in multidisciplinary derivatives for allocation of 'credit' – redeemable as future dividends on present investments. But, what is it about this social logic of the derivative that prevents us from seeing through these insidious operations of *risk management*? The answer, I contend in this conclusive trail to the book, may be found in a simultaneous evacuation of the twin horizons that delimit the *idea* of the 'Indian university'. The first is its claim to '*publicness*', which as a critical history has laid bare, was always fractured along the middle of the university's material negotiations with the truth of *caste* and *religion*. The second horizon, currently *also* under threat, is the very precipitate produced by the cleavages of the first: that is, a form of '*private life*' which it was the business of the university to produce and reproduce as historical privilege or professional entitlement. What we see today, in the platformised university's collaboration with Hindutva exercises in citizen-building, corresponds to the withering away of both these contradictory urges – towards proscribed 'publics' and disinterested 'private' reason – as internal to life at the Indian university. I will turn to Hannah Arendt, mentioned earlier in passing, to explain how this might have come to be. But, before that, let me point the reader to a recent vignette from 'multidisciplinary' curricular reform (again!) in the University of Delhi (DU) – also the most preferred experimental site for NEP-testing.

Happiness as National *Common Sense*

Soon after a celebrated announcement of DU's entry into the charmed circle of 'graded autonomy' as a 'Category I' (or, in the NEP's terminology, 'Tier 1') institution in February 2024,[1] the university management tried its hand at realising the meanings of such *autonomy*. The announcement was inspired by a set of "UGC Regulations" from nearly six years ago – then fiercely contested but now made *fait accompli* through incorporation into the NEP 2020 – which empowered these highest-*ranked* institutions to introduce any 'new course/programme/department/school/centre' at will and without any prior regulatory approvals ("Regulations 2018", Section 4, 8–9). The catch however was in that 'no demand for fund [could be] made from the government', which translated into all such potential curricular adventures being either cross-subsidised from existing resources or becoming completely self-financed appendages (ibid.). In much the same spirit, DU acted upon its 'gift' of autonomy just ahead of the International Working Women's Day on 8 March, by contracting five of its *top* affiliated women's colleges into introducing an elective 'multidisciplinary' course on the 'Science of Happiness'. Reportedly, this course was to be designed in collaboration with a US-origin NGO, Rekhi Foundation for Happiness ("Delhi

[1] See UGC's "Public Notice No. F. 76-1/2018 (CU)", dated 29.02.2024, https://www.ugc.gov.in/pdfnews/5411665_Public-Notice---Graded-Autonomy.pdf

University to Introduce Science of Happiness Course"), which claimed to be a 'firm believer' in 'empowering women' by 'setting up happiness centres in various universities'.[2] Started as a pilot project for women students enrolled in a few *chosen* colleges, the irony of how the historical memory of working women's class struggles was appropriated by a do-it-yourself 'happiness' menu is definitely not to be missed. Also, one cannot but ask: why are 'happiness centres' meant for women alone, as if they were both the source and the scourge of unhappiness, and should be better socialised into the responsibility for being or making happy? Isn't the woman student's training into happiness about forestalling the possibility of her becoming one of those disgruntled, 'killjoy', rights-demanding protestors who fought for the equality and dignity of work and pay across history? Or perhaps, isn't it also about marking off the college-going woman student against her right to sexual desire and agency, and a corresponding refusal to be quiet about structures of harassment and predatory behaviour within or outside academia? (Ahmed; Kannabiran; Chandra et al.; Falkof et al.) To this extent, centres for 'happiness studies' are the accurate antidote to and substitute for centres for 'women's studies' – and a calculated demobilisation of academia's #MeToo legacies. Finally, that 'happiness' is the only 'science' specifically earmarked for female subjects – as opposed to a gender-neutral value addition course (VAC) on the '*Art*' of 'Being Happy' already on offer in all colleges of the same university – is terribly significant. This is even one step ahead of the disciplinary postulation of something like 'home science' in early-twentieth-century India, when colonial modernity had opened educational opportunities for women and bred the dangers of breaching the boundaries between the home and the world (Hancock). Happiness, as a science, contains the promise of making the unequal spaces of both the *home* and the *world* underplay their horrors through behavioural recourse to women.

[2] See the Rekhi Foundation website here: http://rekhifoundation.com/about-rekhi-foundation

Being Happy, Becoming Public: An Impossible Detour

Randy Martin, whose theory of the 'social logic of the derivative' helped me bust the hollowness of NEP's enthusiasm for a 'multidisciplinary education', had a radically different take on interdisciplinarity. In an essay on "Derivative Logics for a Recharged Humanities", Martin argued for a resuscitation of the 'public' university through the derivative futurism of the 'studies' programmes. Within the austerity discourse in post-2008 global higher education, the public utility of humanities departments has been thoroughly questioned and the university's sponsorship of such fields of inquiry massively undermined through periodic fund cuts or punitive systems of audit. As a result, the institutional lives of humanist scholars have had to be increasingly justified through recourse to bureaucratic or *outcome-based* appraisals, such that the 'service' component in academic professions has swelled at the cost of intellectual/research 'expertise'. Martin suggested that this shift represents the ascendancy of administrative/managerial labour, which is precisely a legacy of the derivatives market and its reliance on 'portfolio management' *services*. Faced with a wholesale devaluation of peer-governed intellectual labour and the consequent drying up of public monies for the conduct of humanities research, Martin's provocation relates to a 'recharged humanities' that recognises the relationship between critical interdisciplinary 'studies' programmes and the administrative labour that goes into setting them up. To the author, while the 'studies' departments might be a way of engaging with post-professional and non-university 'publics' beyond the monastic ideal of disinterested research, the administrative 'services' they require at the level of planning and designing courses of study might help humanities faculty to negotiate with forms of unpaid and undervalued work within and outside the university. To Martin, this is a strategic parasitism of the 'social logic of the derivative' in the cause of renewing the *public* university.

> The administrative profile of the faculty portfolio, which weaves together the decision-making process around what gets taught and what knowledge is for, can also be engaged through affiliations

> with others to refigure what risks are worth taking and to what ends education should be reshaped. . . . In the order of university things, the humanities are threatened with relegation to the status of service, a common but undervalued realm that situates them as a cognate of administrative labor. If the sciences (natural and social) yield property and promise professions, what is the charge of the merely human? The humanities might disavow these resonances or energize themselves through a critical engagement with the derivative logics that join interdisciplinary initiatives and administrative labor navigating the shoals of what has proven expansive yet disruptive. (Martin 161–65)

I am not convinced by Martin's excitement about a 're-energized' humanities, taking off from 'derivative logics that join interdisciplinary initiatives and administrative labor.' It retains the assumption that 'the order of university things' is an enlightened *exception*, where despite the large-scale devaluation of *expertise* – in the face of 'risks' of an unknown and unknowable future – the faculty might still *stand for* 'what knowledge is for' and in fact even *know* 'to what ends education should be reshaped.' Such a hypothetical state of affairs also ignores the historical coincidence of a risk society (that itself fuels the derivatives market) with totalitarian common sense. That the fear of risk does not, necessarily or even liminally, produce 'critical engagement' but instead conjures the crutch of *common* sense – as the only hedge against the *loss of a world in common* – is something Martin does not attend to. The spawning of something like 'happiness' studies, as the NEP's 'multidisciplinary' analogue to Randy Martin's 'studies programmes', proves the case in point. This is the exact conjuncture at which the university loses touch with both the 'publicness' of a shared world and the self-assured safety of 'privately' acquired expertise/knowledge. Arendt might provide us with a clue here, to understand what becomes the grounds for such a *totalitarian takeover of the university in the age of the platform.* In her words, it calls for a detour into the human condition that makes for the emergence of 'happiness studies' as a university pursuit under the shadow of the NEP 2020.

Losing Touch with the World: Arendt in the Platform University

In the final chapter of *The Origins of Totalitarianism*, titled "Ideology and Terror", Arendt makes a striking formulation about the 'basic experience' that makes *total domination* possible. For her, the totalitarian government differs from prior (and other imminently possible) forms of the *excessive* exercise of power – namely, tyranny, dictatorship and despotism (460–61); but, it is not based on a mere rejection of positive laws, the '*consensus iuris*' (462). On the contrary, it makes questions of *legality* and *lawlessness* redundant by becoming the very embodiment of the Law of Nature or History. In this sense, the activities of living men and women are rendered immaterial to the working of total terror. To Arendt, this represents the scourge of totalitarian 'ideology' – bent on interpreting history as the *logical* progression of a singular *idea*, taken to its furthest limit and shorn of any reference to the reality of experience (468–74).

Arendt reserves her most clinching argument for the closing section of the chapter, where she contends that the 'ideal' condition of such rule is not the *loss of a world in common*, but *losing touch with the world* of men and objects altogether – that is, a 'materially and sensually given world [that] depends upon my being in contact with other men . . .' (475). By extension, the obverse of '*publicness*' – which is the 'basic experience [of] the living-together of men' such that they are capable of 'acting in concert' (474) – is not a form of 'private life' that is most often termed as 'isolation'. In fact, it is this private pursuit of isolated 'work' ('*poiesis*, the making of things' [475]) that defined the condition of the [Indian] university across the expanse of its history. Following Arendt's train of thought, the opposite of 'publicness' is '*loneliness*' – the very structural condition of possibility of the platform university. Within the latter, everyone is *free* to *bank* her own 'credit' in the form of derivatives, none of which has any relationship to the reality of a 'materially and sensually given world' – because it is all about hedging against some illegible (and unintelligible) future. The successive digitisation of the Indian university, accelerated by the memory of a pandemic, is only a symptom of the *loneliness of university life*. The Academic Bank of Credit (ABC) is yet another symptom, where despite the illusion of multiplicity mustered by the platform's 'network effects', every student is finally turned into a credit variable – unique but infinitely circulable. Arendt clarifies the susceptibility of 'loneliness' to totalitarian government thus:

> Totalitarian government, like all tyrannies, certainly could not exist without destroying the public realm of life, that is, without destroying, by isolating men, their political capacities. But *totalitarian domination as a form of government is new in that it is not content with this isolation and destroys private life as well. It bases itself on loneliness, on the experience of not belonging to the world at all*, which is among the most radical and desperate experiences of man. (475, emphasis mine)

The crisis of '*publicness*' that surrounds the public university, and which we have discerned through the chapters of this book as its immanent historical pathology, is not just about destroying its 'political capacities' – which is but the precondition for something else. The final blow comes in the shape of structures that accentuate what Arendt presciently names as 'organized loneliness' (478). Its purpose is to 'destroy private life as well' – the very edifice on which the historical intersections between caste/religious privilege and the right to intellectual labour has rested. The experience of the 'Indian university', trading in multidisciplinary derivatives to offset the irretrievable loss of an underlying asset of knowledge/expertise, may count as one of the 'most radical and desperate *experiences* of man'. This is because it issues from a corrosion of 'that elementary confidence in the world which is necessary to make *experiences* at all' (477).

Loneliness versus Private Intellectuality

Loneliness is the psychic-cognitive approximate of having lost that sense of a 'mutual guarantee' (Arendt 477) which it is the purpose of knowledge to generate, and of the derivative contract to countervail. Under conditions of absolute loneliness, Arendt warns us, men are pressed against each other till the space of 'acting-together' – as the basic principle of 'living-together' (in the university) – disappears. The post-COVID 'Indian university', with its policy insistence on curtailing physical infrastructures while inviting more enrolments through online credit transfers and suchlike, precisely aims at a *structural reproduction of loneliness*. It is a rudderless clutching at random 'particularit[ies] of sense data' (476), chosen from among a dizzying abundance of platformised offers, in the hope that such 'freedom' of choice will finally insure the 'meaning' of uncertain life-chances in the future. Arendt maintains that the accompanying conditions of 'uprootedness' and 'superfluousness' mark the aggravated nature of 'organized loneliness', until it becomes fodder for totalitarian domination (475). The multiple exit-and-entry options, the curricular patchwork of multidisciplinarity, the forced harnessing of a single course structure to differentiated degree-outcomes, a common university entrance test (CUET) pooling in students irrespective of the situated histories of institutions, and a hub-and-spoke model of merging widely divergent college demographies into concentrated 'complexes' – all features of university reform portended by the NEP 2020 – seem to converge around the intention of creating an 'uprooted' and 'superfluous' student subjectivity.

The political thinker in Arendt is careful to distinguish between 'loneliness' and 'solitude', the latter being a prerequisite for the 'dialogue of thought' (476). To that extent, both 'solitude' and 'isolation' have been constitutive of the monastic *ideal* of university-based practices of private intellectuality. They have been the institutional conditions of possibility for doing philosophy (*sophoi*) and making poetry (*poiesis*), respectively.

> Loneliness is not solitude. Solitude requires being alone whereas loneliness shows itself most sharply in company with others. . . . [T]he lonely man *(eremos)* finds himself surrounded by others with whom he cannot establish contact or to whose hostility he is exposed. . . . In solitude, in other words, I am "by myself," together with my self, and therefore two-in-one, whereas in loneliness I am actually one, deserted by all others. (476)

The private exercise of reason, even when done in isolation or in a state of solitude, never reduces the university professional to being-one; it is still a *dialogue with a world shared with others.* Hence, as I remarked earlier, *the bane of 'publicness' is not privacy; it is loneliness.* The work of loneliness consists in decimating the private life of the mind, by making both *thought* and *imagination* irrelevant to the university. All that remains is, Arendt cautions, 'ideology' – with its unending ability to explain history as a 'logical' deduction from one 'idea'. The "science of happiness" – or even, the "art of being happy" – represents but such culmination of ideology devolving into logicality.

The Bane of Publicness is Not Privacy!

To end: confronted as we are with the *platform university* of NEP-vintage, and passionately anxious about its futures, *what are we to do*? I believe we might embrace the risk of thinking a future together, without hedging against it. That is the work of a 'critical history', which this book is an attempt towards – not to re-evaluate pasts (distant and near) as enlightened critique, but to walk into the future from the resolute grounds of self-critique. That, I hold, is the only slow route of returning the 'Indian university' to its '*publicness*' – not as a detour back into its enchanted pasts of private entitlement (or Enlightenment?), but *as a site of the 'living-together of men' with whom we have nothing in common.* Not even common sense.

Such 'living-together' – extending an Arendtian move – consists in the ability to 'act in concert', despite the historical grounds of distrust and dissensus. That is the meaning of '*publicness*' that might truly *become* the 'Indian university', critically conscious of its own history.

References

Ahmed, Sara. *Complaint!* Duke University Press, 2021.

Arendt, Hannah. *The Origins of Totalitarianism.* Harcourt Brace and Company, 1973.

Chandra, Giti, Cynthia Enloe and Irma Erlingsdottir. "No Peace without Security: Shoring the Gains of the MeToo Movement." *Feminist Conversations on Peace*. Bristol University Press, 2022, pp. 76–90.

"Delhi University to introduce Science of Happiness course in women colleges." *The Indian Express*, 9 Mar. 2024. https://indianexpress.com/article/education/delhi-university-to-introduce-science-of-happiness-course-in-women-colleges-9202853/

Falkof, Nicky, Shilpa Phadke and Srila Roy, eds. *Intimacy and Injury: In the Wake of #MeToo in India and South Africa*. Manchester University Press, 2022.

Hancock, Mary. "Home Science and the Nationalization of Domesticity in Colonial India." *Modern Asian Studies*, vol. 35, no. 4, Oct. 2001, pp. 871–903. https://www.jstor.org/stable/313194

Kannabiran, Kalpana. "#WeToo: In The Footprints of Bhanwari Devi." *Outlook*, 3 Nov. 2018. https://www.outlookindia.com/national/know-gnawing-absences-in-metoo-let-travesty-of-bhanwari-devis-trial-be-a-reminder-news-300835

Martin, Randy. "Taking an Administrative Turn: Derivative Logics for a Recharged Humanities." *Representations*, vol. 116, Fall 2011, pp. 156–76.

"Rekhi Foundation for Happiness: About Us." http://rekhifoundation.com/about-rekhi-foundation.

University Grants Commission (UGC). "University Grants Commission [Categorisation of Universities (Only) for Grant of Graded Autonomy] Regulations." *The Gazette of India*, 12 Feb. 2018, Ministry of Human Resource Development.

______. "Public Notice No. F. 76-1/2018 (CU)," 29 Feb. 2024. https://www.ugc.gov.in/pdfnews/5411665_Public-Notice---Graded-Autonomy.pdf.

Index

C